# Jews in Nineteenth-Century Britain

# Jews in Nineteenth-Century Britain

*Charity, Community and Religion,
1830–1880*

Alysa Levene

BLOOMSBURY ACADEMIC
LONDON • NEW YORK • OXFORD • NEW DELHI • SYDNEY

BLOOMSBURY ACADEMIC
Bloomsbury Publishing Plc
50 Bedford Square, London, WC1B 3DP, UK
1385 Broadway, New York, NY 10018, USA
29 Earlsfort Terrace, Dublin 2, Ireland

BLOOMSBURY, BLOOMSBURY ACADEMIC and the Diana logo are trademarks of Bloomsbury Publishing Plc

First published in Great Britain 2020
This paperback edition published 2022

Copyright © Alysa Levene, 2020

Alysa Levene has asserted her right under the Copyright, Designs and Patents Act, 1988, to be identified as Author of this work.

Cover image: Entertaining in a Sukkah (1900, Postcard by Hermann Junker).
Picture courtesy of the Jewish Museum London

All rights reserved. No part of this publication may be reproduced or transmitted in any form or by any means, electronic or mechanical, including photocopying, recording, or any information storage or retrieval system, without prior permission in writing from the publishers.

Bloomsbury Publishing Plc does not have any control over, or responsibility for, any third-party websites referred to or in this book. All internet addresses given in this book were correct at the time of going to press. The author and publisher regret any inconvenience caused if addresses have changed or sites have ceased to exist, but can accept no responsibility for any such changes.

Every effort has been made to trace copyright holders and to obtain their permissions for the use of copyright material. The publisher apologizes for any errors or omissions and would be grateful if notified of any corrections that should be incorporated in future reprints or editions of this book.

A catalogue record for this book is available from the British Library.

Library of Congress Cataloging-in-Publication Data
Names: Levene, Alysa, 1976- author
Title: Jews in nineteenth-century Britain : charity, community and religion, 1830-1880 / Alysa Levene.
Description: New York : Bloomsbury Academic, 2020. | Includes bibliographical references and index. |
Identifiers: LCCN 2020019742 (print) | LCCN 2020019743 (ebook) | ISBN 9781350102187 (hardback) | ISBN 9781350102194 (ebook) | ISBN 9781350102200 (epub)
Subjects: LCSH: Jews–Great Britain–History–19th century. | Jews–Great Britain–Social conditions–19th century. | Jews–Great Britain–Ethnic identity | Great Britain–History–19th century. | Great Britain–Social conditions–19th century.
Classification: LCC DS135.E5 L43 2020 (print) | LCC DS135.E5 (ebook) | DDC 941/.004924009034–dc23
LC record available at https://lccn.loc.gov/2020019742
LC ebook record available at https://lccn.loc.gov/2020019743

| ISBN: | HB: | 978-1-3501-0218-7 |
|---|---|---|
| | PB: | 978-1-3502-0176-7 |
| | ePDF: | 978-1-3501-0219-4 |
| | eBook: | 978-1-3501-0220-0 |

Typeset by Integra Software Services Pvt. Ltd.

To find out more about our authors and books visit www.bloomsbury.com and sign up for our newsletters.

*For my family*

# Contents

| | |
|---|---|
| List of figures | viii |
| List of maps | ix |
| List of tables | x |
| Acknowledgements | xi |
| List of abbreviations | xii |

| | | |
|---|---|---|
| 1 | Introduction | 1 |

| | |
|---|---|
| Part I  Household and community among Jews in industrial Britain | 19 |

| | | |
|---|---|---|
| 2 | Households and family structures | 21 |
| 3 | Residence patterns and neighbourhoods | 45 |
| 4 | Occupations, poverty and wealth | 81 |

| | |
|---|---|
| Part II  Charity and communal networks | 107 |

| | | |
|---|---|---|
| 5 | Philanthropy, religion and community from 1840 to 1865 | 109 |
| 6 | Consolidation, reflection and discrimination: Jewish charity from 1865 to 1880 | 141 |

| | |
|---|---|
| Part III  Conclusion | 167 |

| | | |
|---|---|---|
| 7 | A community of British Jews? | 169 |

| | |
|---|---|
| Notes | 185 |
| Select bibliography | 233 |
| Index | 241 |

# Figures

5.1 Expenditure on the poor by the Manchester Old Hebrew Congregation, 1827/8–1848/9 — 123
5.2 Expenditure on poor relief per person, and as a proportion of total congregational outlay, Manchester Old Hebrew Congregation, 1827/8–1848/9 — 123
6.1 Numbers relieved by the Manchester Jewish Board of Guardians, 1868–76 — 154

# Maps

| | | |
|---|---|---|
| 3.1 | Jewish households in Liverpool, 1851 | 47 |
| 3.2 | Jewish households in Manchester, 1851 | 48 |
| 3.3 | Jewish households in Birmingham, 1851 | 49 |
| 3.4 | Outlying townships inhabited by Jews in Manchester, 1851 | 50 |
| 3.5 | Skill status of Jewish household heads and lodgers in Liverpool, 1851 | 58 |
| 3.6 | Skill status of Jewish household heads and lodgers in Manchester, 1851 | 59 |
| 3.7 | Skill status of Jewish household heads and lodgers in Birmingham, 1851 | 60 |
| 3.8 | Jewish household heads and lodgers born overseas, Liverpool, 1851 | 61 |
| 3.9 | Jewish household heads and lodgers born overseas, Manchester, 1851 | 62 |
| 3.10 | Jewish household heads and lodgers born overseas, Birmingham, 1851 | 63 |
| 3.11 | Kin links between Jewish households in Liverpool, 1851 | 70 |
| 3.12 | Kin links between Jewish households in Manchester, 1851 | 71 |
| 3.13 | Kin links between Jewish households in Birmingham, 1851 | 72 |

# Tables

| | | |
|---|---|---|
| 2.1 | Jews in seven British industrial towns, 1851 | 23 |
| 2.2 | Sex ratios among Jews in seven industrial towns, 1851 (%) | 24 |
| 2.3 | Average household sizes among Jews in seven industrial towns, 1851 | 25 |
| 2.4 | Household composition among Jews in seven industrial towns, 1851 (% of total) | 27 |
| 2.5 | Relatives found in 'composite' and 'extended' Jewish families, 1851 (% of all non-nuclear relatives) | 30 |
| 2.6 | Jewish lodgers as a proportion of the Jewish population in seven towns, 1851 | 37 |
| 3.1 | Occupational skill status of Jews in Liverpool, Manchester and Birmingham in 1851 (%) | 60 |
| 3.2 | Jewish households with family elsewhere in the town, 1851 | 70 |
| 4.1 | Occupational sectors in Manchester, Birmingham and Liverpool (all residents and Jews both sexes and all ages), 1851 (%) | 82 |
| 4.2 | Most common Jewish occupations: manufacture and trade (N in parentheses), 1851 | 85 |
| 4.3 | Occupations in the service sector, Jews and town populations (% of all individuals), 1851 | 88 |
| 4.4 | Most common occupations among all adults (20+ years), in Manchester, Birmingham and Liverpool, 1851 | 90 |
| 4.5 | Women (20+ years) with no stated occupation in Manchester, Birmingham and Liverpool, 1851 | 91 |
| 4.6 | Number of individuals described as leisured, professional and managerial in the AJDB, 1851 | 95 |

# Acknowledgements

I am happy to have the chance to say thank you to many people who have helped and encouraged me in the course of writing this book. Right at the start, Dr Angel-Luke O'Donnell photographed the records for the Liverpool congregation for me, and as the project grew, Tracey Bassett helped me to set up the 1851 database. Petra Laidlaw was generous with her time and encouragement in the use of the Anglo-Jewish Database (AJDB), and I am hugely grateful for the time David Green spent on the phone to me, helping me make sense of the history of urban spatial analysis. Oxford Brookes colleagues Joanne Begiato and Bill Gibson gave me insightful comments and ideas on the handling of the family and household, and the wider religious context. Joanne, Bill, Petra and David all read and commented on chapters, as did Dr Julie Marfany, who is also one of my oldest and most supportive friends in the history trade. Their comments are much appreciated, and any mistakes or misinterpretations that remain are entirely my own. Thanks to the staff at the Library of Birmingham, the Manchester Libraries, Information and Archives centre and the Liverpool Record Office for their help in accessing and tracking down archival material. The time spent carrying out the research and writing of this book was supported financially by the Oxford Brookes School of History, Philosophy and Culture, and the Oxford Centre for Methodism and Church History.

Permission to reproduce material in Chapter 2 was kindly given by the editors of the *Journal of Family History*, where it first appeared in volume 43, no. 3: 281–301 (2018). The maps in Chapter 4 are reproduced with permission from the David Rumsey Map Collection, www.davidrumsey.com. Permission to consult the records of the Birmingham Hebrew Benevolent Book and Clothing Society was received from the Archives and Collections department at the Birmingham Library.

Finally, I would like to thank my family, who first of all gave me the background to approach this subject, and whose insights, comments and help with Hebrew text I have enjoyed incorporating into the final work. Special thanks go to my mother Miriam, and my uncles, Danny and Ralph, as well as my grandfather Walter, who never knew, when he gave me his back catalogue of copies of the *Jewish Historical Studies*, just how useful they would turn out to be. And very last of all, for everything they do, always, Rich and Alex.

# Abbreviations

| | |
|---|---|
| AJDB | Anglo-Jewish Database |
| BAC | Birmingham Archive and Collections |
| BJHS | Birmingham Jewish History Society |
| COS | Charity Organisation Society |
| JC | *Jewish Chronicle* |
| LROLS | Liverpool Record Office and Local Studies |
| MLIA | Manchester Libraries, Information and Archives |
| MJBG | Manchester Jewish Board of Guardians |
| MO | Medical Officer |
| MOH | Medical Officer of Health |
| NHC | New Hebrew Congregation |
| OHC | Old Hebrew Congregation |

1

# Introduction

This book is a socio-economic history of the Jews in nineteenth-century industrial Britain. Its key concern is how far we can accurately use the word 'community' to describe this small minority in British society, bound together by the fellowship of shared religion and culture but in other ways very diverse. It examines how urban provincial Jews arranged themselves in households and neighbourhoods, how they responded to local work opportunities, and how they managed their own welfare needs, all amid the rush of social, economic and cultural change that accompanied industrialization. In doing so, it introduces a new perspective on the nature of community and religious life in a period of great social and economic transformation.

'Community' is a word that is easy to throw around and hard to pin down. In its broadest sense it refers to people with shared characteristics. If we drill down deeper into the literature we find that these bonds are usually positive in nature, offering traits like security, identity and solidarity.[1] For sociologists, 'community' refers to a form of social organization which is usually spatially bounded; for anthropologists shared culture is a more important feature; while political scientists look for political structures – often in contrast with national governance.[2] For historians, as Calhoun notes, the term is often used 'rather loosely' to refer to 'a geographically or administratively bounded population, or to a set or variety of social relations', often with a sense of nostalgic recall for a past time of shared identity and communal obligations.[3] While not overtly considering the theoretical boundaries of 'community', Wrightson and Levine refer to life in the early modern village of Terling, Essex in much these terms, as 'a constellation of institutions focusing [residents'] interaction, ... a network of ties between kin, friends, and neighbors' which together produce a 'special claim on their loyalties, a special place in their sense of personal identity'.[4] This is also, broadly speaking, the nature of the nineteenth-century working-class 'community', short on economic resources but rich on shared social and support networks evoked by scholars like Davin, though here the sense of shared and bounded space is also important.[5] Steve King's studies of eighteenth-century Yorkshire townships, meanwhile, point out that communities have less tangible borders too, such that while some are 'in', others are by definition 'out'.[6] These boundaries may be readily apparent to outsiders, in the form of shared nationality, religion or club membership. In other cases the borders are much fuzzier, allowing people to decide for themselves whether they – or others – belong or not. Communities are also very flexible in scale, ranging from a small, geographically bounded locale where everyone knows each other by name, to one of its most famous forms, the 'imagined' community coined by Benedict Anderson, where members might never meet, but know, nonetheless, that they share a common bond.[7] Furthermore, community allegiances can shift over time, and a person may be a member of several communities at once, either overlapping or completely distinct.[8]

Ties between community members are also variable in nature, ranging from horizontal ones among peers – as in Anderson's Preston, which we will explore in further detail below – or vertical, between those of different social status, as Wrightson and Levine emphasized as part of their analysis of Terling. In a religious community they are likely both, where shared faith is overlaid with a social hierarchy consisting of leadership, patronage and charity. Studies of the 'Jewish community' tend, while not engaging overtly with these issues, to assume that a key characteristic of a bounded community is leadership; hence 'community leaders', who shape and patrol its boundaries. On the other hand, religious bonds form a classic case of an 'imagined community', where common ties are transpatial.[9] One of the key concerns of this book is to examine how the transpatial community of British Jewry interacted with specific geographical settings.

Another feature of writing about 'community' in the early modern period is the impact of urbanization and the rise of the nation state. These were the conditions that made Anderson's imagined national community possible; they also produced the equally famous shift identified by Ferdinand Tönnies, from the interpersonal and emotional ties that made up the traditional *Gemeinschaft* community, to the formal ones of the modern *Gesellschaft*.[10] Social and economic historians have also identified a weakening of traditional community bonds with the mass urbanization that accompanied the Industrial Revolution: what Calhoun has called a change from 'the predictable and well-understood nexus of community life to the large-scale and uncertain affairs of political society'.[11] Geographic mobility, often for employment, thus (it was proposed) left people unsupported by traditional kin and community networks, living instead in more fragmented domestic units with less oversight of moral behaviour, and more dependent on the collectivity in the form of charities, the state Poor Law and official authorities.[12]

Many of these models of the impact of political and economic change on family and community life were quickly debunked. Comparative and long-range demographic studies, for instance, pointed out that nuclear families predated industrialization in Britain – and that elsewhere, extended family forms were not inconsistent with industry.[13] Michael Anderson's famous 1971 study of Preston – an industrial town in the north-west of England – was an early example. Drawing on demographic and social evidence and taking a sociological perspective, he highlighted the continued importance of family ties in an industrial town, albeit overlaid with a strong sense of instrumentality which he suggests arose partly from a breakdown in older systems of inheritance and network formation.[14] Nonetheless, family remained one of the key ports of call when people fell on hard times: as one survey has summarized, '[a]s the Industrial Revolution instigated new life-cycle risks and intensified existing ones, it seems likely that dense and functional family and kinship groups were one of the few effective defences which individuals could deploy'.[15]

Despite these qualifications, then, even the most recent studies acknowledge a *qualitative* change in social relations and personal behaviour which went hand in hand with both industrialization and urbanization. Emma Griffin has suggested, for example, that the reliable and comfortable wages afforded by industrial occupations had a liberating impact on decisions about marriage, work and living arrangements.[16] Furthermore, many of the most reassuring aspects of community (including religion) were portable, and chain migration meant that newcomers often joined family members, or people from the same place of origin, so establishing a new sense of shared fellowship.[17] The urban environment also brought new community identities based on religious affiliation, political and club membership, leisure activities or cultural groups. These could help to preserve familiar values and identities, or forge novel ones which provided an equivalent sense of belonging and support. It is probably, therefore, a mistake to see industrial conditions as sundering one type of community tie and replacing it with something inferior; we should instead interrogate the nature of community life in industrial settings anew, taking in emotional, linguistic, cultural *and* transactional market-based bonds.

One of the key aspects of Jewish 'community' ties is that they did indeed operate at several different levels. The first and least tangible were the 'imagined' bonds which went with shared religious, ethnic and social heritage. The evidence presented in this book suggests that in a very important and useful sense, Jews felt part of a shared Covenant with God, which brought common practices, a duty of care for one another and a sensitivity to their reputation as a body. However, at a more micro level there were many communities within British Jewry. For one thing, immigration meant that British Jewry included a very diverse set of people. From southern Spain to eastern Russia, the Jews living in Britain by the middle of the nineteenth century spoke a variety of languages, had different prior experiences of persecution and restriction (and thus urban life and choice of occupation and marriage), displayed different attitudes to their religion and to their host society, and varied from more or less destitute to fantastically wealthy. Some of these differences were more formal, particularly those between Ashkenazi Jews (from Eastern and Central Europe) and Sephardi Jews (from Southern Europe and northern Africa). These distinctions were principally cultural, based on different styles of worship and vernacular languages, but they were accompanied by very different reasons for settling in Britain.[18] There was also a strong core of Jews from both groups by the middle of the nineteenth century who had been British for generations and who were highly anglicized. These differences produced subcommunities within British Jewry as a whole, and also, no doubt, different priorities for life in Britain and attitudes to the utility, comfort or practice of religion. By the mid-nineteenth century, as we will see, new identities started to emerge with the growth of communities in the industrial towns.

Migration was a common feature of life in Britain generally, but it was heavily promoted by the opportunities presented by rapid urbanization.[19] Employment was one of the most common reasons for movement, but people also relocated for marriage, or simply to down-/upsize domestic arrangements in response to changed personal economic circumstances.[20] Jews, like their compatriots, moved for these reasons too, often over relatively short distances, and often to join friends and family. Any of these moves also brought potential isolation though: Steve King's work on migrants to the West Yorkshire township of Calverley suggests that incomers could suffer from long-lasting marginalization, to the extent of creating penalties in infant mortality and welfare.[21] However, Jews were far more likely than other Britons to have had the yet more dislocating experience of an international move, to escape persecution and restriction, or to seek economic betterment and business contacts. Petra Laidlaw has calculated that a fifth of the Jews in Britain in 1851 had made at least one long-distance international move in their lives so far.[22] This brought an added and outwardly obvious dimension of 'otherness' to large parts of the Jewish community, especially the newer waves from Poland and Russia, who looked and sounded notably 'foreign'. Even within their own religious community, they were treated with wariness because they were a potential threat to the respectable image of established British Jewry.[23]

Nineteenth-century British Jewry thus contained a notable proportion of new and often very 'othered' migrants, living in settings to which – as we will see over the course of this book – they were frequently poorly adapted because of their prior experiences of work and urban life. The way in which they were perceived in British society and popular culture by the period we are concerned with – the 1830s to the end of the 1870s – was ambivalent. While scholars point out that the introduction of an (ultimately unsuccessful) parliamentary bill to provide full civil liberties for British-born Jews in 1830 was not accompanied by the same sort of popular disturbance that accompanied the abortive 'Jew Bill' of 1753, Jews were still subject to the hangovers of long-held negative stereotypes about their religious and moral qualities, supported by a firm belief in their intrinsic separateness.[24] That said, they largely escaped the mass marginalization and prejudice which has been identified for that most studied of British minorities: the Irish (or, indeed, Jewish populations in parts of Continental Europe). They also benefited from the influence of Enlightenment-era tolerance – at least until the 'Eastern Crisis' of the mid-1870s, when Disraeli's support of the Muslim Turks over the Christian Bulgarians once again raised fears about malign Jewish influence within Britain.[25] In our period, the Jews were, however, a far smaller minority in British society than the Irish, and did not dominate neighbourhoods in the same way. They were not particularly political and nor were they singled out for their antisocial behaviour; in fact, Jews were often commented to be very family-oriented and abstemious when it came to drink.[26] Finally, their clerics were far less visible within the wider community (partly because they were much smaller in number), which was another way in which the Irish as a whole were 'othered'. Even when the huge upswing in Jewish immigration of the 1880s did start to attract greater opprobrium, critics were more likely than in earlier decades to cite the conditions under which the Jews had been forced to live in their countries of origin as an explanation for their supposed lack of hygiene and willingness to live and work in poor surroundings.[27] While both the Jews and the Irish thus remained targets for a bundle of fears and stereotypes of long standing, in the middle decades of the nineteenth century the Jews were living quietly enough that attitudes were, generally speaking, somewhere along a spectrum of accepting and apathetic. The poverty migration of the famine years, meanwhile, had turned the Catholic Irish – especially in towns like Liverpool where they settled in large numbers and dominated particular neighbourhoods – into a more evident and noisy threat.[28]

The nature of community ties and reactions to 'outsiders' in the industrial period is thus a central debate for this study. It also engages with a second important strand of research, which is the impact of industrialization, broadly defined, on religious practice. Scholars have suggested that new, competing forms of urban leisure, scientific discoveries which challenged the primacy of religion, and long hours of work, all combined to jolt people out of long-held patterns of church-going and religious feeling.[29] It certainly worried contemporaries, and especially Anglicans, who were sufficiently disturbed to commission a one-off Census of Worship in 1851 – the results of which did not allay their fears.[30] It showed that the manufacturing towns (already a focus for concerns about moral behaviour) had the lowest levels of church-going in the country: fewer than one in ten people went to a place of worship on census day in Birmingham, Liverpool, Manchester, Sheffield and Newcastle, and Anglican churches were the worst affected.[31] Many historians have criticized the emphasis placed on formal attendance in the religious decline narrative, and the underplaying of more personal and societally enshrined aspects of belief – what Callum Brown has called 'discursive Christianity' – which seem to have remained vibrant, if increasingly diverse.[32] Nonetheless, it seems undeniable that formal and state-based religious worship was coming under a barrage of alternative world views in this period, and that this was being translated into a more flexible and personal attitude to faith.

When it comes to the Jews, too, we know more about attendance and formal membership than we do either about the people who worshipped without paying regular membership to a synagogue (the poorer and more transient members of the community), or what they believed or did in their homes. The Census of Worship showed that Jews were no more rigorous about attending services than most other religions. In fact, Jews (who were counted on the Friday and Saturday of the census weekend – the Jewish Sabbath) filled a lower proportion of the accommodation they had available for worship than any other enumerated group bar the Quakers: only 24 per cent – although this clearly says as much about the relative size of their accommodation as it does about religious practice.[33] Nonetheless, only about a tenth of the Jewish population (around 3,000 people) had attended synagogue on the Sabbath in question, the rest of the accommodation presumably being filled only at the autumn High Holy Days (the Jewish New Year and Day of Atonement), when many synagogues required overflow facilities.[34] In Birmingham the congregation's secretary claimed that the turnout on Saturday afternoon was low because so many adult men were travelling for their work – a suggestion supported by the large numbers of hawkers and dealers in the Jewish population of the town.[35] Nonetheless, it underlines the characterization drawn by several historians of mid-century Jews as flexible, undogmatic and even ignorant in their religious practice: in the words of one leading scholar, 'what united most Jews was the synagogue they did not attend'.[36]

On the other hand, we know that there were also pockets of Jews who were deeply observant, especially in the middling ranks of society, or who (as today) prized highly certain aspects of their religion, such as keeping the Sabbath and High Holy Days, or the life-cycle rituals like circumcision and Jewish burial.[37] We will see that community records reveal significant numbers of people not wishing to work on Saturdays; the importance attached to provision for religious instruction and observance for those in state-operated institutions like workhouses and hospitals; and the perceived need for Jewish education as a way of preserving religious affiliation as well as of integrating newcomers. Giving money or time to Jewish charities was a way of gaining esteem within the community (and beyond it), while bodies such as Jewish friendly societies and Masonic lodges often barred people who did not meet minimum standards of observance. Conversely, given the weak and voluntaristic nature of internal control over Jewish life in Britain, there were arguably fewer consequences to lapses from the faith than there were in the Christian denominations (or Jewish communities abroad).[38] This means that people who did not practise or feel their Judaism actively shade out of sight in the records. It is also notoriously difficult to capture what people did and felt privately as distinct from the formal, outward observance which took place in synagogues or churches. However, synagogue and charity records do give us important insights into the ways that Judaism gave structure to people's lives and – more importantly for the current study – the extent to which this created and cemented communities.

These are particularly important themes for the current study, since Judaism is a religion with an unusual level of internal cohesion and exclusivity. Jews place great emphasis on endogamy and they do not seek to proselytize (in fact, conversion is difficult and protracted); religion is biological – it passes through the maternal line and can in almost no circumstances be completely renounced (even formal converts from the faith can be reabsorbed). Residential propinquity is necessary for public worship, which requires a minimum quorum (*minyan*) of ten adult men able to attend by foot,[39] and for creating a critical mass to attract provisioners licensed to deal in foodstuffs which conform to the dietary laws (*kashrut*).⁴⁰ Synagogue services are conducted in Hebrew or other vernaculars (English sermons started to be adopted during our period as a way to make Jewish worship less obviously 'other' to members of the established state religion, but even in modern-day Orthodox services, the only prayer read in English is the one for the Royal Family). Judaism is also traditionally defined as both religion and ethnic identity: it is possible to feel strongly Jewish, and to take part in aspects of that affiliation, without being formally observant – and vice versa.⁴¹ Furthermore, while Judaic rules are based on the Old Testament, they also have a certain 'living' quality as they are continually reinterpreted by scholars (hence the emphasis on learning among Orthodox Jews).⁴²

This bundle of features makes Judaism a revealing point of departure for a study of community forms and functions. The extent to which Jews blended their religiosity, the cultural and ethnic aspects of their religion and their desire to operate in wider society can tell us a lot about the power of ethnic or religious feeling, the attractiveness of opportunities beyond it, and the way that identity was framed. By the middle of the nineteenth century, British Jewry also had several formal bodies which shaped and represented it to the wider community. These consisted of the office of the chief rabbi, the court of the Beth Din and the Jewish Board of Deputies; all based in London, though with growing input from the provincial communities.⁴³ The influence of these institutions on British Jewry was variable. The highest profile was the Chief Rabbinate – an office held throughout the period covered by this book by the German scholar, Nathan Marcus Adler. He was a driving force behind the anglicization and Orthodox conformity of British Jewry at this time, and the terms of his role specifically required him to visit and direct provincial as well as metropolitan Jewry. Synagogue records reveal him frequently asserting his ideas on decorum and Orthodoxy (both invited and not), for example in the context of internal schism and local disputes – which were frequent.⁴⁴ One of his first actions on taking office was to commission a survey of the state of the congregations under his remit, and in 1847 he published a set of regulations that asserted his authority 'in all matters of ritual and practice'; authority that seems to have been generally (albeit sometimes reluctantly) accepted in the provincial communities studied here.⁴⁵ The Beth Din, in contrast, is rarely mentioned in the records utilized for this study, but the selection of representatives to the Jewish Board of Deputies (est. 1760) does crop up and as 'Anglo-Jewry's domestic political lobby', the latter was called on to co-ordinate campaigns for legal emancipation and the protection of the Jewish Sabbath for workmen.⁴⁶ The efforts of the Board have been described as sometimes half-hearted and their business rather a closed shop, but they did have an important role in representing British Jewry.⁴⁷

The Jewish press was also important in giving common identity and voice to British Jews, most famously the lively and sometimes outspoken *Jewish Chronicle* (*JC*). From 1847 this was published weekly and so could react much more rapidly to wider events than the Board of Deputies. Under the direction of several different editors it took a strong line on various topics of the day, from the growth of the Reform branch of Judaism (on which it was generally supportive), to the plight of the Jewish poor and the support of Jews overseas. It became something of a virtual community meeting point, with its extensive advertisements, personal announcements and charity subscription lists, and it reported frequently on developments in the provinces and overseas.⁴⁸ David Cesarani, the historian of the *JC*, has credited it with the creation of a Jewish public sphere, and with 'the evolution of a modern form of Jewish solidarity and ethnic identity'.⁴⁹ Its editorials and letters on the provincial communities offer another perspective on the themes developed in this study.

These bodies all arguably formed a common point of identity for British Jewry.⁵⁰ However, many historians have been more concerned with the question of assimilation or 'blending in' and how far that was taken as an acceptable – even desirable – trade-off of acculturation. By the middle of the nineteenth century, according to Lipman for example, 'Anglo-Jewry was ... a community of strong religious loyalty, but it was already one of some considerable degree of social assimilation.'⁵¹ This question is often handled rather simplistically, though, and with too much attention to the historical narratives and aspirations internalized by modern Jewry. Pointing this out, the American scholar Todd Endelman suggests that we must keep questions of secularization and 'blending in' separate. On the former, he notes that it would be surprising were Jews *not* susceptible to the same influences which promoted 'impiety and indifference' as Christians, especially given their concentration in towns like London and Amsterdam where these trends were writ large, and where the culture shock of exposure to new ideas would have been particularly striking.⁵² 'Blending in', meanwhile, lagged behind the loss of religious practice, implying that Jewish identity went deeper than religious observance.⁵³ We will return to these questions of acculturation and the shaping of British Jewry in the conclusion in Part III. In the meantime, however, we must try to draw some of these themes of religious observance, imagined community and urban industrial life together into a meaningful – and testable – definition of a Jewish social network.

## Social networks

The crux of this book is the extent to which British Jewry operated within an identifiable and useful community. There is obviously a limit to which we can answer this question with the information available. Nonetheless, we can frame the study appropriately by setting out a proper theoretical framework based on what we know about social networks. This is another term that has been easily adopted into everyday language, but which actually has quite a precise set of meanings. In its loosest sense, a social network refers simply to the interconnected web of interactions that most individuals negotiate on a daily or weekly basis, with friends, colleagues, neighbours, shopkeepers, local authorities and so on. However, within sociology, anthropology and the mathematical sciences it can have more specific and measurable attributes, for example based on the range, intensity, multiplexity and durability of interactions between individuals, firms or groups.[54] The key attribute of this type of social network for scholars is its focus on relationships between actors, and the reason that this is important is that it is relationships that facilitate (or impede) the transfer of material goods, information, esteem, and so on. As social network theory has grown, it has taken in new perspectives, from the ability of the network to provide opportunities and constraints on actors' actions, to the different ways that knowledge and goods can circulate.[55] Our focus here is principally on household and neighbourhood connectedness because of the type of information available, but alternative approaches can take in common and overlapping use of space, commercial transactions and information flow.[56] Essentially, social network theory has its basis in the idea of social capital: a social network arises when social capital between members is acknowledged and active. It cannot be created 'out of need alone'; it needs both resources of some sort, and a set of conduits around which it can flow.[57]

A local social network is thus most likely to develop where people have been resident for a long time, have kinship ties, where they belong to the same social class, and where there is a common local web of shops, places of employment and other facilities.[58] Anywhere with strong possibilities for social advancement is less likely to display this sort of community, since people will inevitably move on more rapidly – unless they have other reasons to remain affiliated to one another, such as common religious worship (it is worth registering here, then, that Rubinstein has characterized British Jewry as exhibiting high levels of social mobility[59]). When an area provides only residential facilities, the only ties likely to develop are those based on family and neighbourhood – although these are often categorized as among the deepest and most useful of social bonds.[60] Shared ethnic or cultural ties are often identified as important elements in a strong urban network, commonly referred to as 'ethnic urban villages'.[61] In this situation shared cultural backgrounds attract newcomers and provide them with a tight-knit community (potentially more closely knit than the one they left behind), which can in turn help with the acquisition of skills to launch them onwards.

One of the questions this book seeks to answer is whether this degree of homogeneity and fellow feeling can be perceived among Jews in provincial industrial cities in the 1850s, 1860s and 1870s. It takes note of the technical ways of measuring and describing a social network, but it also makes reference to a broader sense of community links which are embedded in shared identity and social capital, and reinforced by residential patterns. In all cases, it attempts to spotlight networks that were *functional* and *useful*, which contributed towards people's sense of identity and their ability to make ends meet. It looks, in essence, for evidence of Jews choosing to share their house-space with co-religionists, to common patterns of employment and residence, and for welfare facilities that protected poorer Jews and helped them to integrate into the local society. Naturally, this focus privileges positive evidence of networks and has the potential to overlook people who were either not well connected, or whose identity spanned different types of social networks. However, given the tenuousness of our grasp on the qualitative character of Jewish life at this time, this approach must be seen as a positive step forwards, and one which, as we will see, does allow us to see networks operating in many different ways, with varying aims and outcomes.

## Studying British Jewry

The current study thus aims to bring new perspectives to the history of British Jewry. While the historiography to date has been rich and detailed, it has tended to focus on several well-rehearsed themes connected to wider stories of acceptance and acculturation, and the growth of specific communities and institutions, especially in London. Detailed and comparative studies of different communities are still lacking, as are perspectives from social and economic history which spotlight life at a household level. Attention has been paid to the campaign for political emancipation (which came, finally, in 1858, almost thirty years after equivalent rights were given to Catholics[62]), but far less to the negotiations which shaped community life and framed its boundaries.

The growing provincial towns provide the perfect setting to probe these topics further, focusing as they do on the challenges of adaptation to a new socio-economic and cultural environment. The communities highlighted in this book – Manchester, Liverpool, Birmingham, Sheffield, Leeds, Glasgow and Hull – grew up with quite different forms and characteristics, but all went into a new and sustained phase of growth during the nineteenth century. Each community made their own decisions about their synagogues and ministers (under the direction of the Chief Rabbi); they formed their own relationships with the urban environment and living spaces; and they interacted with the wider cultural and political environment to differing degrees. We know most about the shape and direction of the Jewish community in Manchester, thanks to Bill Williams's seminal 1976 study, *The Making of Manchester Jewry*. However, his book has a distinct class perspective and it is time to test more thoroughly how Manchester compared to other communities in terms of a wider set of reference points concerning living arrangements, residence, occupation and welfare.

The trajectory of research on British Jewry echoes a path found in many other areas of historical enquiry, including the history of welfare and medicine. Thus, early work such as Cecil Roth's *A History of the Jews in England* and Vivian Lipman's *Social History of the Jews in England, 1850–1950*, which were published in the 1950s and 1960s respectively, tended to focus on elite individuals, families ('cousinhoods', to use a description coined by Chaim Bermant[63]) and communities, detailed but often somewhat hagiographic in tone, with minimal reference to wider social or economic trends and keen to tell a story of success and assimilation.[64] They are important reference points for identifying notable individuals and community schisms, but they are less useful for making sense of the status and behaviour of British Jewry within wider society.[65] Running in parallel, however, scholars like W. Rubinstein and Lloyd Gartner were starting to produce larger-scale studies of British Jewry, which took in relations with non-Jews, the history of political emancipation and the impact of mass Eastern European immigration from the 1880s.[66] These were useful in setting up a broader landscape for the history of British Jewry, but they tended to perpetuate similar 'stories' of success in a benign and liberal environment, especially compared to the more colourful and alarming histories of Jews in other European nations.[67]

A third wave of scholars, given impetus by Williams's 1976 work on Manchester Jewry, and influenced by the new emphasis on social history and 'history from below' in the field more broadly, started to bring a sense of wider contexts to bear on their topic. Williams was joined by scholars like Todd Endelman and

David Feldman, who had a much greater sense that they were writing social or political histories which focused on the Jewish community, but with an eye to what this could reveal about broader trends.[68] They were also much less inclined to trust earlier, hagiographic accounts of the Jewish community, and instead – most notably in Endelman's *Broadening Jewish History* – made room for analysis which emphasized division, criminality and poverty: that is, which allowed for the possibility that a shared religion did *not* necessarily produce a homogeneous or harmonious sense of a single community.[69] Others have taken a more overtly sociological perspective, most notably Kokosalakis's study of Liverpool Jewry, while local historians continue to produce a range of narrower single-town studies.[70]

The current book has its roots in this latter approach. However, it aims to move the field on further still, by drawing in a deeper sense of economic, social and demographic history, essentially drawing the history of the Jews further into the mainstream of modern British history. It does so from the household level up, retaining a sense of the community as a whole, and not merely the most notable or the most disadvantaged. These are areas in which Jewish history has yet to make much of a mark.[71] In 1994 Englander noted that Jewish family history was 'still in its infancy', made up of 'myths' 'in place of systematic knowledge on marriage, household structure, kinship relations and residence patterns'.[72] The publication of the impressive online Anglo-Jewish Database (AJDB), based on the 1851 census and explored in further detail below, opened up huge possibilities for investigating mid-century British Jews in just these terms (despite its name, the database includes Jews in Scotland, Wales and Ireland), but beyond the editor Petra Laidlaw's own work on marriage and occupations, these opportunities have not yet been taken up.[73] This is particularly surprising given that the database gives us the ideal opportunity to address the London bias in much of the work on British Jewry, and to join together isolated local studies to say something more meaningful about provincial Jewry at this time of economic change.

This book thus aims to fill several notable gaps in the treatment of British Jewry in the middle decades of the nineteenth century. By spotlighting the socio-economic experience of Jews living in some of the largest industrial and commercial towns in Britain it is able to take a far more fine-grained and comparative view of the composition of these communities.[74] Importantly, it also asks how far their imagined community translated into concrete and functional networks for support, worship and patronage. And finally, it examines whether migration to increasingly urbanized centres had an impact on family and household forms and whether there is evidence for a falling-off of religious feeling as Jews adapted to life as Britons in the most thoroughly modern of British cities.

## Sources and remit

The core source for this study is the 1851 decennial census (as distinct from the one-off Census of Worship of the same year, which was a simple head count). The English, Scottish and Welsh censuses did not record religious affiliation until 2001, but by intensive cross-referencing to local studies and records like naturalization papers, synagogue records and family histories, the AJDB has been able to capture an estimated 90 per cent of British Jewry in 1851, numbering 29,230 individuals.[75] The definition of a Jew for the purpose of drawing up the database was kept deliberately broad: 'anyone who was, or may be assumed to have been, Jewish by either birth, conversion or cultural affiliation, whether or not they retained that identity later in life'.[76] For the current purposes, people identified as Jewish and living in the seven selected towns in 1851 were extracted (over 3,500 in total, more than half of the total Jewish population of Britain living outside London at this time), and were each traced back to the census enumerators' books in order to reconstruct their households. This included capturing intra-household relationships, the incidence of shared housing and any non-Jews living in the home. In a separate exercise, all residents (Jews and non-Jews) on the most populous Jewish streets in each of the three largest communities (Manchester, Liverpool and Birmingham) were recorded for comparative purposes. It is worth noting that while the total number of Jews identified in the database is broadly in line with other estimates for the period at around 31,000–32,000, of whom around 22,500 were in London, those in Liverpool are notably lower.[77] It is unclear whether this represents incomplete coverage or a decline in the Jewish population of this town at this time. This will be borne in mind in the chapters which follow.

The seven towns were selected in order to capture the outward geographical movement of British Jewry into a variety of manufacturing and commercial cities. An additional consideration, given the growing significance of both immigration and transmigration in this period, was their location at or near the arrival and departure ports at Hull and Liverpool. We will see that this shaped the Jewish populations of all of the selected towns.[78] In other respects, the selected towns were very different. All had had a period of unprecedented growth in the decades before our study begins: between 1821 and 1831 the populations of Manchester, Leeds, Birmingham, Liverpool and Sheffield all grew by 40 per cent or more, Manchester topping a quarter of a million people by 1831, and Liverpool passing 375,000.[79] By the 1850s this was beginning to slow: the era of the 'shock' industrial city was ending and making way for a period of differentiated and emerging local character. Always characterized as a home of radical politics and class consciousness as well as the hub of a regional centre of cloth production and factory industry (a set of characteristics not unlike its Yorkshire rival, Leeds), Manchester was settling into a phase of respectability and local culture by 1851. Its successful Royal visit in that year perhaps confirms this new status.[80] Birmingham and Sheffield had longer histories of workshop-based manufacture and this was retained into the nineteenth century, but while the former attracted attention for the coherence of its approach to local governance, Sheffield remained a city of small and disparate communities.[81] Liverpool's wealth (like Hull's, though to a greater degree) was built on its docks: lacking in significant primary manufacturing, it remained largely a service industry with a heavy presence of migrants (most notably the Famine Irish of the 1840s) and maritime personnel – as well as the slums and public health problems which were to earn it the moniker 'black spot on the Mersey'.[82] Glasgow, meanwhile, as the primary manufacturing city in Scotland, housed a growing proportion of the Scottish population over the course of the century; from 5.1 per cent in 1801, this had reached 11.5 per cent: a larger percentage growth than that seen in London.[83]

Of the seven towns, Birmingham and Liverpool probably contained the longest-established Jewish communities. The Manchester congregation had taken up critical momentum only a few decades before this study begins, receiving its largest impetus from Jews moving from Liverpool and London, or migrating from Germany and Poland. By 1851 it had overtaken Birmingham to become the largest provincial community in the country. Together, these three cities will form the key focus of Chapters 3 to 6 because of their larger size and hence wider array of community documentation. The communities in Leeds, Glasgow and Sheffield remained small for much of our period, growing out of all proportion with later waves of immigration from Eastern Europe, while Hull Jewry expanded in line with the rise and fall of international migration.[84] By 1851 the seven communities varied in size from 1,107 individuals in Manchester to 104 in Glasgow and 112 in Sheffield. They will be introduced more thoroughly in the chapters which follow, and together form the basis of the demographic analysis reported in Chapter 2. Where possible, the smaller communities are also referenced in the context of wider charitable patterns in Chapters 5 and 6, and it is hoped that future work will allow a more detailed analysis of Jews in these cities.

The AJDB itself forms a key justification for the focus on the mid-nineteenth century. However, there are other reasons too. First, the period coincides with a phase of growth in the Jewish community, especially in the form of movement to the industrial towns, but precedes the mass immigration of the 1880s when numbers became both unmanageably large for comparative study and the subject of much greater attention in other work. Second, it falls at the end of the period of unprecedented growth in the industrial towns that was noted above, and which had radically altered their character and status. This opens up the possibility for a targeted study of how the Jewish population integrated into a new style of workforce and a new set of concerns about poverty and living standards. These concerns will be developed further in Chapter 4.

Third, there exists a very large amount of supplementary material generated by the various communities – and especially those reaching larger critical mass – which can be used to enrich the census information for the surrounding decades. These include synagogue minutes, charity records and articles in the Jewish press. Where possible these have been linked to the AJDB to build up a picture of community leaders, charity donors and recipients, allowing (thanks to the biographical detail in the AJDB) the perspective to be taken back to the 1830s and forwards to the end of the 1870s. This is a period of Jewish history often characterized, according to Williams, as one of tidying up 'loose ends', but otherwise constituting a 'plateau between two periods of substantial and fundamental change'.[85] This book confirms that Williams was right to be sceptical about this characterization, especially for the newer provincial communities where Jews were engaging in significant experiments in creating cohesion and identity, and in supporting – and moving on – growing numbers of poor.

The book is divided into two main parts. Chapters 2 to 4 focus on households, residence patterns, wealth and poverty. Chapter 2 explores the composition of Jewish households, and whether they shared their living space with others, Jewish or non-Jewish. Chapter 3 maps out where Jews settled within the spatial environment of the larger cities and whether this meant living close to community institutions and co-religionists. Chapter 4 traces the relative wealth and poverty of the Jews in the three largest communities via their occupations, skill levels and living standards. In doing so, it starts to pull out commonalities and differences between Jews in the larger towns. Together these chapters highlight evidence of community networks which seem to have brought positive and useful benefits.

The second part of the book (Chapters 5–6) deals with poverty, philanthropy and the shaping of the poor. This is a well-rehearsed topic, but previous studies of Jewish welfare have lacked a deep understanding of the wider context of poverty, charity and statutory relief, and the ways that these interacted with the economies of the industrial towns. Chapter 5 deals with the earlier part of the period, when Jewish charity took familiar philanthropic forms, but with what community leaders saw as a strong and distinctively Jewish ethos behind it. We can see several wider reference points about 'deservingness' and belonging at work, but heavily tempered by a sense of responsibility towards 'casual' and transient Jews. Chapter 6 turns to the 1860s and 1870s, when the Jewish community was challenged in new ways by rising immigration, but also moved into the forefront of attempts to triage and consolidate charity under the auspices of new local Jewish Boards of Guardians. The findings from the industrial towns acknowledge the much publicized theme of charity as a way to anglicize the immigrant poor and make them respectable, but finds that this is only part of the story. Wider trends in the economy and the charitable landscape also played their part, as did an increasingly desperate eye to the community balance sheet.

Finally, Chapter 7 offers an extended conclusion, readdressing what the evidence can add to our understanding of the ways that Jews experienced the industrial economy and the ways that they navigated what many of them saw as their key challenge: that of becoming both British and Jewish.

Part One

# Household and community among Jews in industrial Britain

2

# Households and family structures

This first part of the book starts off our investigation of Jewish social networks by focusing on some of the more measurable characteristics of provincial Jewry. It uses these to reflect on the nature of community ties and the part that shared religion played in people's decision-making about where to live and with whom, and the types of work that they did. This chapter deals with the household and family structures of the Jews in the seven selected towns. It is concerned to do several things. First, to examine how common it was for Jews to live with other Jews, which would suggest shared bonds and characteristics (as well, perhaps, as discrimination from non-Jews). The second aim is to test whether Jewish households conformed in size and shape to those around them; in other words, to examine whether they were using the household as a way to adapt to new surroundings, and if so, whether this was in any way distinctive. Part of this discussion will involve bearing in mind the much-debated issue of whether industrialization and migration disrupted 'traditional' family forms – particularly given the high proportion of international migrants among the Jews compared with the rest of the population (a point quantified below). And third, it will relate patterns of household structures to social network theories; specifically, the evidence for bonds and networks which facilitated information flow, or eased the transition for newcomers.

A key reference point for this approach is Michael Anderson's work on households in the north-western English town of Preston, which is also based on evidence from the 1851 census.[1] As noted in the Introduction, Anderson was one of the scholars whose work made a forceful contribution to the debunking of the idea that industrialization brought isolation for urban families. His Preston evidence showed that households were not uncommonly extended by kin beyond the immediate nuclear family, and that newcomers often retained strong links with family outside the town. However, he also suggested that these patterns often reflected a calculated and mutually beneficial relationship based on shared costs or childcare. Thus, families took in orphaned children or widowed grandparents who could make a financial contribution or help around the home (often freeing up other adults to earn), while grown siblings could offer childcare or rent money. More recently Naomi Tadmor and others have pushed this idea of fluidity in household forms further, signalling the range of forms one family might take over the course of the life cycle, and making such apparently strict classifications as 'nuclear' and 'extended' rather unhelpful.[2] This chapter keeps both theories very much in view, finding that Jewish households were frequently 'extended' by kin and (especially) non-kin. However, there is little evidence for the calculated instrumentality put forward by Anderson: in this respect the Jews did not follow the patterns shown by their neighbours, possibly because of the high proportion of international migrants they contained, and also because they had a very different relationship with the industrial workforce and its high wages. Religion and shared places of origin thus take a much more prominent place in the factors governing Jewish household forms than the impact of industrialization per se. The shape of their households, meanwhile, suggests that labels like 'nuclear' and 'extended' are indeed insufficient to capture the norm of shared and flexible domestic arrangements.

## Jews in the 1851 census

As outlined in the Introduction, the data for this study are an enriched version of the information contained in the AJDB for Jews in the selected towns, which has been supplemented by additional data on intra-household relationships from the census enumerators' books. This meant that all members of the household could be identified, including any servants, lodgers, visitors or landlords (both Jewish and non-Jews, the latter of whom were naturally not included in the AJDB).[3] The numbers involved can be seen in Table 2.1, and comprise 12.3 per cent of the total population in the AJDB (56.2 per cent of the non-London population). The remainder of the non-metropolitan population was principally in older centres like Plymouth, Portsmouth and Bristol.

It is clear from Table 2.1 that the sampled communities varied greatly in size, from only a little over 100 individuals and twenty-seven to thirty-four households in Glasgow, Sheffield and Leeds – where the highest levels of Jewish immigration were to come later – to 800 and above in Liverpool, Manchester and Birmingham, consisting of 159–279 households. Hull also had quite a sizeable Jewish community, reflecting its importance as a key entry point to Britain from Eastern and Central Europe. The number of Jewish households there suggests that people were not simply passing through, however. Some were attracted, no

*Households and Family Structures*  23

Table 2.1 Jews in seven British industrial towns, 1851

|  | Liverpool | Birmingham | Leeds | Glasgow | Hull | Manchester | Sheffield | Total |
|---|---|---|---|---|---|---|---|---|
| N individuals | 848 | 906 | 128 | 104 | 320 | 1,106 | 112 | 3,524 |
| N households | 159 | 223 | 34 | 27 | 99 | 279 | 34 | 855 |

Source: AJDB/census database

doubt, by the possibilities a port town offered for hawking and selling – common Jewish occupations for new arrivals – as well as those in trade and currency exchange for the better off. Others likely simply ran out of money and settled where they disembarked. Certainly, immigration formed an important part of the story of mid-century Jewish settlement in the industrial towns: 39 per cent of Jews in the sample had been born overseas compared with 20 to 30 per cent in the AJDB as a whole depending on age group, and many others had moved from elsewhere in Britain to cities like Manchester, Birmingham and Leeds.[4] In Leeds, Glasgow and Hull only a quarter or less of the Jewish populations started life in the town and only a fraction more in the much larger community in Manchester. Birmingham and Sheffield stood somewhere in between these two positions, but in Liverpool, surprisingly (given its reputation as a 'melting pot' city and an embarkation point for transmigrants), overseas birth was somewhat less common: almost half of the identified Jewish population there had been born in the town and less than a quarter overseas (the remainder originated from elsewhere in Britain).[5] Whatever their origin, we should beware of assuming that the foreign-born were newly arrived at the time that we encounter them in 1851, and it should not divert us from the fact that the majority of Jews were British-born. Nonetheless, it is true that most Jews in the current sample were relatively new to the industrial and manufacturing cities. Furthermore, most migrants would at some stage have required assistance in getting a job, finding a home and generally getting acquainted with a new linguistic and cultural environment; exactly the sort of social network functions we are concerned to examine.

The impact of migration is reflected in sex ratios, which were skewed towards young working-age men (see Table 2.2).[6] Interestingly, this was least true in Liverpool, again suggesting that the community had a larger proportion of settled families there by 1851, and that onward migration was either in a temporary lull or enabled people not suited to the employment market to move on rapidly.[7] In Manchester and Birmingham too, the skew towards men was not as large as

**Table 2.2** Sex ratios among Jews in seven industrial towns, 1851 (%)

| Sex | Liverpool | Birmingham | Leeds | Glasgow | Hull | Manchester | Sheffield |
|---|---|---|---|---|---|---|---|
| Female | 49.4 | 46.6 | 32.8 | 39.4 | 40.6 | 43.7 | 37.5 |
| Male | 50.7 | 53.4 | 67.2 | 60.6 | 59.4 | 56.3 | 62.5 |

Source: AJDB/census database

in the other towns, perhaps as these communities also settled into patterns of more secure development. In the remaining towns, though, there was a notable over-representation of men, among whom those born overseas were very visible. The skew also rose with age: 73 per cent of immigrants in their twenties were male across the dataset, reaching 85 per cent by the forties, although the extra information in the AJDB shows that many of the latter had immigrated in their twenties or thirties rather than more recently. A small number of these older immigrants were single in 1851 but on the whole they had married – and many had married British-born women (quite possibly enhancing their integration into the community in the process; a point Laidlaw stresses in her study of marriage patterns[8]). Only just over a third of the younger foreign-born men were married in 1851 and most had arrived in the country alone. It was likely these individuals were responsible for the skew in the sex ratio in the smaller communities, reflecting the importance of economic push factors for immigration.[9]

## Jewish households

How, then, did the Jewish residents of the seven towns arrange themselves into households, and was this distinctive compared to those around them? We may start by looking briefly at the average size of Jewish households on census night (Table 2.3). These figures include visitors, servants and lodgers, both Jewish and non-Jewish, hence the use of the term 'household' rather than 'family'.[10] The early studies of English households carried out by Peter Laslett pointed to a long-lasting mean average of 4.75 people (though he was keen to stress that there was considerably more variance than this when it came to individual experiences).[11] Bearing this in mind, the Jewish establishments seem quite large, with means falling between 5.5 (Sheffield) and 7.0 (Liverpool).[12] The modal (most common) averages are closer to the British 'norm', however, falling between 3 and 6, with households in Leeds, Hull and Sheffield at the lower

Table 2.3 Average household sizes among Jews in seven industrial towns, 1851

|         | Liverpool | Birmingham | Leeds | Glasgow | Hull | Manchester | Sheffield |
|---------|-----------|------------|-------|---------|------|------------|-----------|
| Mean    | 7.0       | 6.3        | 6.8   | 6.7     | 5.9  | 6.8        | 5.5       |
| Mode    | 5         | 6          | 3, 5  | 6       | 4, 6 | 6          | 4         |
| Maximum | 17        | 27         | 24    | 14      | 18   | 29         | 12        |
| N       | 147       | 198        | 30    | 24      | 89   | 238        | 26        |

Source: AJDB/census database

end, and the larger communities in Liverpool, Birmingham and Manchester at the upper. Glasgow also had a high modal average, but as will be discussed further below, this maps on to a high incidence of Jewish lodging houses. In both Liverpool and Sheffield, too, however, notable quantities of people lived in households of nine or ten, and in Birmingham seven households numbered seventeen or more. The largest single household, of twenty-nine people, lived in Manchester. We will return to these households later. In both Birmingham and Sheffield, meanwhile, over 10 per cent of households consisted of only two individuals.

Averages can only tell us so much, and to understand more we must commit to some form of classification. The difficulty lies in the choice of categories, so that they strike a balance between utility for comparative purposes, and meaningfulness in terms of past understandings of household and family. For example, critics have stressed that the use of impermeable classes in earlier classifications perpetuates simplistic assumptions about location and change over time.[13] The scheme used here is based on the classic taxonomy devised by Peter Laslett and Richard Wall, but with several important modifications in order to address some of these concerns.[14] Laslett and Wall's scheme comprised broad classes: singles, nuclear units, extended and multiple households. Any of these classes could be extended by servants, but this was not bedded in to the classification. In the current case, a specific measure has been introduced to capture whether servants or other non-kin were present, and the term 'composite' has been used in placed of the traditional 'extended' label. This is in recognition of the fact that 'nuclear' families could in fact be much more expansive (or 'extended') than was acknowledged in earlier work on demography and household structure. The analysis that follows will demonstrate how these different emphases allow us to be more subtle in our interpretation of household patterns.

'Nuclearity' may be a problematic concept when applied too rigidly, but it remains a useful starting point. As illustrated in Table 2.4, the Jewish households in the seven sampled towns shared the British tendency towards this household form: a fifth or more consisted only of parent/s and child/ren (category 2ai). In Leeds this reached a quarter of the total. This was, however, much lower than their non-Jewish neighbours on a few selected streets where Jews were most prominent, where two-thirds of households consisted simply of parents and children.[15] Things become more interesting and more complex still if we expand the view to include nuclear families plus all non-relatives (servants, visitors, lodgers). This produces a higher total of 56.7 per cent of households in Manchester to 71.3 per cent in Liverpool, with a mean average of 62.4; a little under figures for British communities, which usually show in excess of 70 per cent of households in nuclear form.[16] On the whole, then, Jewish households consisted of a small and nuclear core, but they often also included people who might not be related to them. Whether we can regard this as a more flexible and expansive notion of nuclearity as Tadmor suggests is open to debate, but it certainly shows that while the Jews did not very often live with other kin beyond parents and children, this did not necessarily mean that living spaces were not shared with other people. In Hull, in contrast, there was a relatively large proportion of co-resident individuals who were not related to each other at all; a pattern to which we will return in the context of lodging. In all cases it was rare for Jews to live alone (the higher proportion in Sheffield is based on only two individuals). The small proportions of lone parents with children suggests that the death rate among adults of child-rearing age was low – or alternatively that there was a rapid rate of remarriage. Again, this will be picked up again in the context of welfare.

This tendency towards nuclearity, broadly speaking, has been observed in the small number of other studies of the Jewish population, too. According to Schurer, the immigrant Jews of the East End of London in the late nineteenth century were 'more given to a tight nuclear family structure than their neighbours'.[17] Laidlaw also found a preponderance of nuclear families, sometimes living with close kin, in the AJDB as a whole.[18] However, the high incidence of non-kin in Jewish households has not been highlighted previously.

If nuclearity should be seen as something rather more fluid than was traditionally the case in past classifications, then this has an impact too on what can be regarded as an 'extended' household. In Laslett's scheme a household becomes extended when it contains family members beyond the nuclear core, yet if we follow Tadmor, then we should see this in many cases as simply a life-cycle expansion and contraction of the core family.[19] If we stick with the narrower

**Table 2.4** Household composition among Jews in seven industrial towns, 1851 (% of total)

| | Liverpool | Birmingham | Leeds | Glasgow | Hull | Manchester | Sheffield |
|---|---|---|---|---|---|---|---|
| **Singles (1)** | 2.5 | 1.4 | 3.0 | 3.7 | 1.0 | 0.7 | 5.9 |
| **Nuclear** | | | | | | | |
| 2ai (Couple with children) | 8.2 | 9.6 | 21.2 | 14.8 | 17.4 | 6.1 | 8.8 |
| 2aii (Couple without children) | 1.3 | 6.4 | 3.0 | 3.7 | 5.1 | 1.1 | 2.9 |
| 2b (Father with children) | 0.6 | 0.5 | 0.0 | 0.0 | 0.0 | 0.4 | 0.0 |
| 2c (Mother with children) | 0.6 | 3.6 | 3.0 | 3.7 | 1.0 | 1.1 | 0.0 |
| *Nuclear, total* | *10.7* | *20.0* | *27.3* | *22.2* | *23.5* | *8.6* | *11.8* |
| **Extended** | | | | | | | |
| 3a (Nuclear family with other kin) | 2.5 | 1.8 | 0.0 | 3.7 | 1.0 | 3.3 | 0.0 |
| 3b (Two or more related nuclear families only) | 0.0 | 0.9 | 0.0 | 0.0 | 1.0 | 0.0 | 0.0 |
| 3c (Two or more related nuclear families plus other kin) | 0.0 | 0.0 | 0.0 | 0.0 | 0.0 | 0.0 | 0.0 |
| 3d (Two or more related persons, not family nuclei) | 1.3 | 0.9 | 0.0 | 0.0 | 0.0 | 0.0 | 0.0 |
| *Extended, total* | *3.8* | *3.6* | *0.0* | *3.7* | *2.0* | *3.3* | *0.0* |

| | Liverpool | Birmingham | Leeds | Glasgow | Hull | Manchester | Sheffield |
|---|---|---|---|---|---|---|---|
| **Composite** | | | | | | | |
| 4a (Single nuclear family, plus kin and non-kin) | 14.5 | 15.0 | 15.2 | 11.1 | 14.1 | 14.4 | 2.9 |
| 4b (Single nuclear family plus non-kin) | 54.1 | 43.6 | 39.4 | 40.7 | 34.3 | 48.0 | 47.1 |
| 4c (Two or more related nuclear families, plus kin and non-kin) | 0.6 | 0.5 | 0.0 | 0.0 | 1.0 | 0.0 | 0.0 |
| 4d (Two or more related nuclear families, plus non-kin) | 1.3 | 0.5 | 0.0 | 0.0 | 2.0 | 0.0 | 2.9 |
| 4e (Two or more non-related nuclear families, with or without others) | 1.3 | 1.8 | 0.0 | 0.0 | 2.0 | 1.8 | 0.0 |
| 4f (Two or more related persons but not a nuclear family, plus non-kin) | 1.9 | 1.4 | 0.0 | 0.0 | 2.0 | 1.1 | 0.0 |
| 4g (Non related persons only) | 2.5 | 5.0 | 6.1 | 7.4 | 9.1 | 7.6 | 5.9 |
| *Composite, total* | *76.2* | *67.7* | *60.6* | *59.3* | *64.6* | *72.9* | *58.8* |
| **Other/unknown** (5) | *6.9* | *8.6* | *9.1* | *11.1* | *9.2* | *14.1* | *23.5* |
| **N households** | 159 | 220 | 33 | 27 | 99 | 277 | 34 |

Source: AJDB/census database

definition of extension first, for comparative purposes, the Jewish households do conform to the traditional impression: 'extended' households were not particularly common at all across the entire dataset (a maximum of 3.8 per cent, which was found in Liverpool). If, however, we expand the remit to other forms of extension – namely, households with *non-kin* alongside 'extended kin' (that is, taking in some of the 'composite' classes in Table 2.4), we reach totals varying from 25.2 per cent of all households in Liverpool, to an outlying 5.9 per cent in Sheffield. The most general experience was from 15 to 25 per cent. This is notably higher than the figure found for non-industrial communities in 1851 (analysis by Laslett showed that between 11 and 17 per cent of households were extended), although it is broadly in line with the urban samples examined by Anderson and Armstrong, both of which revealed an upper end of 20 to 23 per cent.[20] The Jewish population thus show a tendency to live in extended *households* in urban settings, but ones most likely containing non-kin as well as members of the wider family. In the traditional British case, this would generally have meant servants; we will see that in the current context things were a little different, with lodgers and fellow immigrants featuring prominently too. The prevalence of extension did not necessarily mean that Jewish households were particularly large – although there were some in this situation – they did not, for example, tend to include large numbers of children.[21] The likelihood of Jews living with wider family or non-kin, though, further rejects the suggestion that urbanization bred smaller families or weaker family and community ties.[22] However, the range of people found in these households strongly supports the utility of the term 'composite', rather than the narrower 'extended'.

Let us remain focused first on the other live-in family members in these households. Although one did not need to be co-resident to provide assistance, the presence of wider kin in the home is often taken as a measure of functional support (demographic conditions permitting; high adult mortality in middle life, for example, will remove many potential sources of aid from grandparents).[23] This is particularly pertinent in the current setting, as kin were often a vital aid for new arrivals to adjust to the conditions of urban industrial life, and we know that overseas migrants were more common in the provincial towns than in the AJDB as a whole. The data on co-residence therefore hints at the extent to which families provided deep and functional solidarity and support. This was especially important given that alternative sources of support in the form of the Poor Law, or non-Jewish charities, would likely be unable to cater for the important Jewish demands for special foods and modes of worship (see Chapters 5 and 6).

Table 2.5 shows the number of times 'extended' relatives types appeared in Jewish households in the four largest communities in the study (there were not enough households in each of these groups in Leeds, Sheffield and Glasgow to permit meaningful analysis). Some households contained more than one type of relative, and all relationships are to the household head.

It is evident that Jewish households contained a wide range of relatives by blood and marriage, consisting both of vertical ties (a generation above and below the head), and lateral ones (brothers and sisters and their offspring). Overall, the most common co-resident relatives were nieces, followed by nephews and sisters. This is very similar to the pattern Anderson found for Preston, although nieces and nephews are more prominent in the Jewish

**Table 2.5** Relatives found in 'composite' and 'extended' Jewish families, 1851 (% of all non-nuclear relatives)

|  | Liverpool | Birmingham | Hull | Manchester | Total |
| --- | --- | --- | --- | --- | --- |
| Aunt | 6.3 | 3.5 | 0.0 | 0.0 | 3.1 |
| Brother | 3.1 | 8.8 | 17.7 | 1.8 | 5.7 |
| Brother-in-law | 7.8 | 7.0 | 0.0 | 3.6 | 5.7 |
| Cousin | 10.9 | 1.8 | 0.0 | 1.8 | 4.6 |
| Daughter-in-law | 1.6 | 1.8 | 0.0 | 1.8 | 1.6 |
| Father | 0.0 | 5.3 | 0.0 | 0.0 | 1.6 |
| Father-in-law | 3.1 | 0.0 | 5.9 | 7.1 | 4.1 |
| Granddaughter | 6.3 | 3.5 | 11.8 | 3.6 | 5.2 |
| Grandmother | 1.6 | 0.0 | 0.0 | 3.6 | 1.6 |
| Grandson | 4.7 | 0.0 | 0.0 | 5.4 | 3.1 |
| Grown-up daughter | 4.7 | 1.8 | 11.8 | 5.4 | 4.6 |
| Mother | 4.7 | 10.5 | 0.0 | 5.4 | 6.2 |
| Mother-in-law | 4.7 | 3.5 | 0.0 | 10.7 | 5.7 |
| Nephew | 9.4 | 15.8 | 11.8 | 3.6 | 9.8 |
| Niece | 14.1 | 12.3 | 29.4 | 10.7 | 13.9 |
| 'Relative' | 1.6 | 0.0 | 0.0 | 23.2 | 7.2 |
| Sister | 12.5 | 7.0 | 5.9 | 7.1 | 8.6 |
| Sister-in-law | 3.1 | 14.0 | 0.0 | 5.4 | 6.7 |
| Son-in-law | 0.0 | 3.5 | 5.9 | 0.0 | 1.0 |
| **Total** | **64** | **57** | **17** | **56** | **194** |

Source: AJDB/census database

sample. Grandchildren, on the other hand (with or without parents), were notably less common in the Jewish dataset than they were in Preston, where they formed 24 per cent of all extended co-resident relatives.[24] This could partly be a function of the relatively recent beginnings of the Jewish communities in these towns, which had not yet had time to produce three-generation families. In other cases it probably related to adult mortality or a need for help with childcare; certainly there were Jewish nieces and nephews who were resident without their own parents. In Liverpool, for example, two out of ten nieces had their mothers with them and one had a father, two were without parents but with a brother, and five were without any members of their own nuclear family. Most were aged ten or under and only two were over eighteen. In Birmingham too, the majority of co-resident nieces were without parents and most were under fourteen. Several of the younger girls were recorded as scholars on the census form but there were exceptions, such as fourteen-year-old London-born Julia Olsher, who was described as a shop assistant (possibly working with her relatives, who were both listed as confectioners). Elizabeth Davis, aged twenty-one, meanwhile, was listed as a 'companion', presumably to her aunt and uncle, who headed a busy household on census night consisting of their small daughter, a lodger, and their business partner and his wife. Elizabeth was to marry a few years after the census, whereupon she emigrated to America where her husband worked as a Jewish minister. Other evidence captured in the ADJB places her husband in Liverpool in 1851. Few of these nieces have information on their own parents recorded in the AJDB, although we know that Elizabeth's father was widowed and living in Birmingham too. It seems likely that she had left his house to take up a useful, albeit possibly unpaid, position in the house of a close family member. All bar one of the nieces with information on birthplace were British. Finally, it is worth noting that more of the nieces were on the maternal side of the household; that is, related by blood to the head's wife. This is in line with Anderson's finding for Preston, that aid was more often given matrilineally.[25]

The presence of nieces, nephews and grandchildren does not entirely conform to the framework of 'calculative reciprocity' devised by Anderson to explain patterns of co-residence in Preston. Some of the lone children he found in his sample were, he suggested, illegitimate, others were orphaned or left by parents who had remarried or migrated elsewhere. Some had left the family home to relieve overcrowding (sometimes partially supported by the Poor Law), or to help relatives as an alternative to paid labour.[26] Few of these suggestions seem to apply so straightforwardly in the Jewish case. The census data suggest that illegitimacy was fairly rare among nineteenth-century Jewry, and few seem to have entered into the sort of relationship with the Poor Law that Anderson identifies for Preston (although more work needs to be done in this area; Chapter 5 gives some examples of the ways that Jewish charities supported fragmented families).[27] Children did not often live with elderly grandparents and so potentially provide aid to them, and most were too young to contribute much to the household (many, we have seen, were described as scholars). Moreover, many were with a parent, which in Anderson's terms was a less financially rewarding extension of the nuclear family in terms of costs and benefits, although it may have freed up an adult to earn money.

These patterns suggest that Jewish families acted in less instrumental ways than other parts of the industrial population when it came to household formation, perhaps because they participated little in the manufacturing sector with its relatively high wages, perhaps also because of their underlying demographic structure compared with non-Jews. We may also be seeing evidence of one of Tadmor's other criticisms of work on households: the tendency to see instrumentalism and affection as binary opposites.[28] Perhaps Jews moved in together because it was an accepted part of family duty or cultural expectation rather than because it was an economically rational choice; perhaps rational choices operated in different ways in a population with such high levels of migration.

The elderly provide a revealing test case. While Ottaway has shown that the older generation (especially women) did quite often move in with their grown children in the eighteenth century, both she and Thane stress that this represented aid flowing from the older person to their children. In other cases, the elderly remained in their own homes.[29] Ruggles's study of American households from the mid-nineteenth century onwards pushes this further, revealing that it was often the older generation who held the cards, with the younger reliant on them for inheritance and marriage prospects.[30] Further, when the two generations did co-reside (which was common: only 11 per cent of his sample lived alone or with their spouse), the poor and sick (the traditional recipients of houseroom) were *less* likely to live with their grown children, which he speculates is because they had less to offer.[31] It is worth noting that his model relates specifically to agricultural communities, and that he sees the transition to waged labour – the conditions we see in the AJDB population – as disrupting older patterns. Nonetheless, it is an instructive suggestion that co-resident relationships between the generations may be complex and mutually interdependent.

The older generation of Jews was not very likely to move in with their grown children, though mothers were more frequent co-residents than fathers (a not uncommon pattern in other samples too). The elderly were more prominent (relatively speaking) among families in Birmingham than elsewhere, most described as widowed, although in a couple of cases they were apparently married, albeit with no sign of their husband.[32] In two cases widowed mothers in their forties were living with widowed daughters who were in their twenties, a very definite suggestion of mutually functional support. The remaining co-resident (grand)mothers ranged in age from fifty to seventy-seven, with four out of nine in total over the age of sixty. Elderly co-resident fathers were rarer, but there are a few examples which are also suggestive of mutual aid, either financial or emotional. Baer Kantrovitz, aged sixty-six, for example, a retired Hebrew minister in Manchester, was living with his son Jacob, Reader to the Old Hebrew Congregation, together with a Jewish lodger and a servant in 1851.[33] Widowed 85-year-old Simeon Cohen, meanwhile, also lived in Manchester, with his widowed daughter, Amelia Franks, his widowed grandson (and household head) Abraham Franks, aged forty-five, and six grown siblings of Abraham's, ranging in age from twelve to twenty-seven.[34] There are many reasons to think that this household was serving mutually beneficial roles for its otherwise lone or dependent members.

Compared with other studies, urban Jews were not particularly likely to share accommodation with elderly parents.[35] This is partly for demographic reasons: as Ruggles observed, there were, numerically speaking, relatively few elderly compared to the pool of sons and daughters, and this was probably even more true of the provincial Jewish populations, with their relatively large proportions of working-age migrants.[36] Another factor is employment: most of the older generation were recorded with an occupation and were living as heads of their own households. In Jewish Manchester, Birmingham and Liverpool between 40 and 47 per cent of the over-sixties were household heads (and others were spouses of heads). Fully two-thirds had an occupation listed in Birmingham, over half in Manchester and just over a third in Liverpool. In fact the two oldest people in the Manchester sample were both heads of their households, while all but one of the elderly household heads in Birmingham had an occupation given (occasionally these indicated that they were retired). Many of them had (or had had) fairly high-status jobs too: agents, merchants, warehousemen and clothiers, all of which may have been better suited to work in older age than jobs in more mechanized parts of the economy.[37] Moreover – per Ruggles – these people were frequently affording houseroom to relatives themselves. It may be splitting hairs to suggest that this was so very different from moving in with a son or daughter; the title of household head may in some cases have been simply a mark of respect. Nonetheless, it is notable that so many of the older generation were pooling resources with their sons or daughters. However, it is equally notable that so many seem to have remained independent, at least in terms of housing arrangements.

The evidence for urban Jews thus suggests quite strongly that the binaries of nuclear/extended and instrumental/affection are not a useful way to think about household patterns. While the majority of Jews did live with nuclear family in the strictest sense of the word, it was very common also to accommodate servants, lodgers, visitors and a variety of other relatives. Rather than Anderson's scenario of a kinship system 'weak on trust' and 'strong on calculativeness', though, this looks like a combination of mutual assistance, cultural expectations and compassion for family members in need.[38] The findings do, however, agree with Anderson's assessment that very few people lived entirely separately from kin; only 1 to 4 per cent of Jews lived alone in 1851 in all the towns except Sheffield.[39] We will test in the next chapter how often these people also lacked kin nearby. Whatever the potential disruption of urban life, then, it seems not to have weakened kinship ties among Jews. We turn next to see how far it affected co-residence with non-kin: in particular, lodgers and servants.

## Lodgers and servants

By widening the net to include non-kin we gain another perspective on the nature of ties within the Jewish community. For example, a high incidence of Jewish lodgers and servants will support the suggestion that the community was strong on functional aid and information systems which assisted adaptation and integration, and that this in turn promoted Jewish identity. The alternative would reveal different networks and priorities at work, or other constraints in supply or demand. Since ties like these are one of the principal ways that 'imagined' bonds became real, these considerations are one of our first major insights into whether we can justifiably talk about a Jewish 'community'.

Lodging has not received the attention that other aspects of demography at the household level have – Laslett's early studies overlooked the importance of lodgers, who were regarded as 'inmates' of the 'houseful' (the total living space) but not members of the household or family, while the census enumerators in 1851 were inclined to record lodgers as separate households.[40] However, a growing number of studies have pointed to lodging in private dwellings as a vital means for lone individuals, particularly migrants, to integrate into a new setting; acting, in fact, as a sort of pseudo family.[41] Modell and Hareven, for example, found in their study of several nineteenth-century American towns that lodgers frequently found houseroom with people from the same location or same occupation as themselves – thus building on common bonds and sharing vital knowledge about jobs. Furthermore, they discovered that young lodgers often literally took the place of a recently departed grown son, enabling host families to maximize their income using the space in their home.[42] Meek has recently found a similar situation for late nineteenth-century Scotland, pointing to Russian Jewish immigrants as an example of a tightly bound community when it came to lodging.[43] This has not yet been tested for earlier decades.

The enriched AJDB identifies lodgers who were Jews and the households where they lived. Any non-Jewish lodgers in the Jewish households were also recorded. It is immediately clear that lodgers were particularly likely to be foreign-born and were thus classic candidates for people in need of networks to help them bed into their new setting: 77 per cent were international migrants compared with 39 per cent of the whole Jewish population of the seven towns (86 per cent if we exclude Glasgow, which was an outlier with only a fifth of its lodgers born overseas). The most common place of birth in all towns apart from Glasgow was Poland (most notably in Leeds), followed by Germany, while Russian Jews were a notable presence in Liverpool, but not elsewhere. Liverpool and Glasgow also had an elevated presence of London-born lodgers, perhaps representing the outward spread of certain trades from the capital. Many of the foreign-born lodgers hailed from urban locations and so did not have quite the culture shock of a previously rural dweller, but in other places Jews were specifically barred from living in towns and had limitations on the trades they could follow.[44] Either way, new migrants needed to find somewhere to live on arriving in their new town, and lodging in Jewish households was a good way to combine shared cultural roots, language and religious requirements like accessing kosher food, with practical considerations like the ability to meet potential marriage and business partners and to find jobs which could accommodate the Jewish Sabbath and festivals. The incidence and spatial patterns of lodgers thus has something very significant to tell us about the ways that newcomers were integrated into the community and how actively beneficial those ties of Judaism were.

Lodgers were found in 10 to 20 per cent of Jewish households in the three largest communities (8.8 in Liverpool, 11.0 in Birmingham and 20.8 in

Manchester). This is slightly lower than Meek found for Jews in Glasgow's Govan area between 1861 and 1911, and also than studies of non-Jews in several other towns, where levels reached 20 to 25 per cent. This probably reflects the slightly earlier period of settlement in the current study than Meek's, the larger number of potential host households in towns like Liverpool and Manchester compared with Glasgow, and the wider range of reasons for taking up lodgings in the wider population.[45] The Jewish lodgers in the current sample were concentrated in households with no other kin present, suggesting that families were unlikely to have the room both for extended kin and for paying boarders, although they likely brought different costs and benefits for the family. A lodger brought cash into the household, but was far less likely to offer domestic services like childcare or to make a long-term investment (emotional or financial) in the household. Rather than the 'empty-nesters' identified by Modell and Hareven, however, the heads who took in lodgers tended to have young children at home and were themselves slightly younger than the average.[46] Both characteristics suggest that taking in lodgers was something one did at a slightly earlier stage of the life course. (The heads who employed servants, in contrast, were a few years older than the mean, and they also had larger numbers of children than the average. This is perhaps unsurprising given that children brought more work and the potential for specific nursing staff. It also, however, suggests a certain level of wealth, which may be another – intuitively likely – way in which some of the servant-keeping households can be distinguished from those hosting lodgers.)

The picture is quite different if we examine the frequency of lodging from a population point of view, rather than a household one, however (Table 2.6). Here we find that while only around 5 per cent of Jews were in lodgings in Liverpool and Glasgow, this reached over 15 per cent in Hull (where there were many people living in houses where they were not related to anyone else) and fully a third of the whole community in Leeds. This suggests that lodgers were concentrated in individual households in different ways. Over 85 per cent of all lodgers were men in all the towns except Glasgow, where only five Jewish lodgers have been identified.

The lodgers in the database were also relatively young: an average across all seven towns of 28.8 years (minimum 24 in Sheffield, maximum 35 in Glasgow). However, this is skewed somewhat by a small proportion of lodgers in Liverpool, Birmingham, Leeds and Manchester who were under the age of ten. Some were children boarding along with their parents; a few others in Manchester were scholars at a small boarding establishment. At the other end of the age range there were a few elderly lodgers, possibly (in contrast with the examples given

**Table 2.6** Jewish lodgers as a proportion of the Jewish population in seven towns, 1851

|  | Liverpool | Birmingham | Leeds | Glasgow | Hull | Manchester | Sheffield | Total |
|---|---|---|---|---|---|---|---|---|
| N Jewish lodgers | 34 | 84 | 42 | 5 | 51 | 154 | 10 | 380 |
| Proportion of the Jewish population who were lodgers (%) | 4.0 | 9.3 | 32.8 | 4.8 | 15.9 | 13.9 | 8.9 | 10.8 |

Source: AJDB/census database

above) lodging because they lacked kin willing to take them in: three in both Manchester and Birmingham were over seventy, half of whom had an occupation listed. All were single or widowed. In Sheffield, Glasgow and Hull, meanwhile, there were no lodgers over the age of fifty-five. If we remove the outliers at either end of the age spectrum from the analysis, the average age rises slightly to 29.1 years: firmly in the age range of young working life and also the age range at which immigrants were most prominent.

Lodgers most often found themselves in households with no other paying members, again suggesting that this was a way for a family to make a little extra money in their existing space. It also by extension meant that a large number were single: more than 80 per cent of the lodgers in all the larger towns.[47] In Liverpool, and most particularly in Manchester, however, a sizeable number of lodgers were one of two or more. Some of these were couples or even families, like Jacob and Mary Bloom, who were lodging in 1851 with their two-year-old daughter in the home of Sarah and King Shinefeld and two other lodgers in Fernie Street, Manchester; or Abraham and Marley Morris who lodged with their three children with Simon and Rosa Morris and *their* three children in Verdon Street, also Manchester – both streets that, as we will see in Chapter 3, were in poorer (and increasingly, Jewish) areas of town. Two other lodgers with different surnames completed the household. The foreign (German) birthplaces and young ages of all of the Morris children suggest that both families – quite possibly relations given their shared surname – had immigrated to Britain only a handful of years before 1851. This may well, therefore, have been a case of the classic 'chain' migration, where migrants followed family members and friends to places where they had already established themselves – and in the process temporarily creating a composite or extended household.[48] It certainly supports the idea that lodging was a vital way to start putting down roots in a new place.

No further information is available in the AJDB on either of the two lodging families to indicate whether they were still in Manchester in 1861, or whether they had moved on.

The data also show the same marked tendency to occupational and national clustering among lodgers which is a feature of several other studies for this period. Altogether forty-four household heads had three or more lodgers in Manchester and so can be called upon to test this further. The largest were headed by the Portuges and Levi families respectively, neither of which were identified as lodging houses on the census form, although they certainly look like them. Aaron Portuges, a 29-year-old hawker of jewellery and another resident of Verdon Street, shared his house with his 22-year-old wife, Risel, their three young daughters and seven lodgers, all Jewish, one of whom was also a hawker of jewellery. Four of the lodgers had the surname Cohen: a common Jewish name, and not necessarily an indicator of kinship, although one pair was a widowed mother with her ten-year-old daughter. Three of the lodgers were cap makers. This potentially complex household was therefore bound together internally by at least one tie of kinship and several of occupation. Moreover, all of the household members were born in Poland except for one lodger, who was another hawker of jewellery. Every member thus had at least one tie in common with at least some of the others.

The Levi household was similar: Abraham and Minna Levi were slightly older than Abraham and Risel Portuges (fifty-three and forty), and the elder of their five children were in their late teens, although the younger three were aged eight, six and two. They also kept a servant and had seven lodgers living with them, all Jewish, and including three named Rosenthall, who look like a couple and the husband's brother. There are, again, further ties of fellowship in common: Abraham Levi was a tailor, as were two of the lodgers, and all the members of the household were born in Poland including the two youngest children – making them (like the Morrises) likely to have been recent immigrants.

Even the smaller establishments had internal ties. Samuel and Charlotte Hadida of Manchester, for example, were Sephardi Jews – unusual for provincial Jewry although more common in Manchester than elsewhere.[49] Samuel was born in Gibraltar and his three lodgers hailed from Istanbul and Morocco, also Sephardi areas (one of the lodgers was affiliated to the Sephardi Bevis Marks Synagogue in London). Furthermore, Samuel and two of his lodgers were merchants. The common cultural bonds of the Sephardi tradition and its common geographical origins make the bonds here unlikely to be coincidental, and may well point to a 'community within a community' within

Manchester Jewry.[50] More traditional ties can be seen within the household of King Shinefeld, whom we met earlier: four of five lodgers were hawkers of pencils, although their landlord and his son were both shoemakers. Here the national backgrounds were more mixed: Hungary, Poland and Belgium. In total, however, shared nationality between lodgers and the household head was more common than shared occupation in all three towns.[51]

There were also Jewish establishments that were specifically described as lodging houses in the census: eight in Manchester, for example, all except one run by women. This supports the suggestion made by others that keeping a lodging house was an acceptable – perhaps vital – occupation for women, and particularly women with no husband present.[52] It was not connected with a particular stage of the life cycle: the female lodging house keepers ranged in age from Ann Levy, at twenty-eight, who kept a house of eleven lodgers and no live-in servants or relatives, to 54-year-old Sarah Abrams, living with her daughter, a servant and just one lodger. Ann's certainly looks like the more successful business operation, especially since she had no dependents; widowed Fanny Selig, in contrast, was supporting her mother and five children on the income of her two lodgers. Only one of Ann Levy's lodgers was Jewish and there are few obvious common bonds within her household; the same was true of Sarah Abrams. We must assume that their lodgers found their landladies via other means: a more generalized grapevine, advertisements or other intermediaries; adverts were certainly placed in the *Jewish Chronicle* for vacancies in people's homes. However, in most of the houses examined here, shared religion was clearly a factor, even if we can only speculate on its nature or importance. A key attraction may have been the ability to observe *kashrut* (or at least the avoidance of truly taboo foodstuffs like pork and bacon) if landladies were providing food, or even just cooking the food provided by their lodgers. In other cases, shared language could have been an attraction, or simply the knowledge that there was a common understanding of inherited culture or national backgrounds.

Not all Jewish lodgers sought out co-religionists, however, whether by choice or necessity. In Liverpool ten out of thirteen households containing Jewish lodgers were also Jewish, but in Hull the figure was only eleven of thirty-two and in Leeds, two of thirteen. Yet a little unpacking reveals evidence of Jewish networks in many of these cases too. In Leeds, for example, only four out of the forty-two Jewish lodgers lodged with household heads who were also Jewish, but they were very likely to live with other Jewish lodgers. In fact, many of them lodged in just two establishments, both in John's Square in Leeds, which housed a total of nineteen Jewish lodgers. Ten, all hawkers bar one who was a glazier (both unskilled and impoverished trades), lived at number seven, with a non-Jewish family. A further nine resided at number eight with William and Mary Rea, their three grandchildren, a servant and three other non-Jewish lodgers. The size of both establishments suggests that they were lodging houses – the Reas were described as housekeepers which could denote this too. Their Jewish lodgers were, again, all hawkers, apart from one who was a watchmaker. We cannot assume, therefore, that shared religious practice and identity were unimportant for these people. The concentration of so many Jewish hawkers in two houses in close proximity in Leeds (a population with few Jewish families to lodge with) does point to there being a focus for Jewish rituals or fellowship in this town, as well, perhaps, as a good base for sourcing the sorts of items they sold. It also strongly suggests that information about lodging places was shared between co-religionists. Laidlaw notes a similar concentration of gangs of itinerant Jewish workers in lodgings in Birmingham, Merthyr Tydfil and Newcastle too.[53]

The foreign birth of so many of the Jewish lodgers inevitably directs our attention to boarding as a way of integrating into a new setting, often for single people, but quite frequently for families in various forms too. Certainly it outweighs use of lodging by locally born newlyweds, or non-immigrants lacking in kin, as Anderson found in Preston – or its instrumental use as an alternative to the negative demands of living with family (with the possible exception of some of the elderly cases noted above). This may account for the lower proportions of Jewish households that contained lodgers compared with other studies I have cited. Jewish households were also more likely to contain only one lodger and Jews were less often found in large lodging houses than the population at large; a reflection of their low density in the population, but also, perhaps, a reluctance to use non-Jewish establishments.[54] Yet we can still see the same functions of the lodging relationship at work: living with another family or in a lodging house was a vital way to adapt, save money, find work, and put down roots. In this static snapshot it is impossible to comment on how rapidly the Jewish lodgers moved on to their own homes – if, indeed, they did so. Some limited information in the AJDB from earlier decades suggests that not all of the Jewish lodgers were recent arrivals and that some were already in Britain in the 1830s. Establishing oneself did not necessarily mean the end of lodging; it may well have been a longer-term choice for unmarried immigrants, again pointing to its utility as a mode of modern living. Nor can we do more than speculate on how useful shared religion was as a means of finding a home. Certainly it must have brought certain advantages for so many single males, and especially those from overseas, to have utilized it in this way. An alternative, of course, is that Jews were not welcome as lodgers in non-Jewish households. This is more difficult to test, although generally speaking, British anti-Semitism is characterized as being low-lying in this period.[55] Still, certain commonly accepted stereotypes of Jews as unclean, deviant, or breakers of the Christian Sabbath may have affected the willingness of non-Jews to take them into their homes.

The experience of servant keeping, on the other hand, is quite different and the evidence shows that Jews very often employed people who did not share their religion. Employing live-in staff was common: 71 per cent of all Jewish household heads in Liverpool had at least one servant or employee in their home, 55 per cent in Birmingham and 68 per cent in Manchester.[56] This is notably higher than figures for non-Jews in other industrial and urban locations at this time, pointing potentially to greater affluence in the current sample.[57] It is also affected by the inclusion of a few households that contained a large number of business employees, as will be shown.

Most of the Jewish households contained only one employee, although a handful kept large staffs of domestic servants. The largest was that of Salis Schwabe of Crumpsall House in Manchester, which contained twenty servants including a companion, a Jewish cook, a lady's maid, a clerk, nurse, kitchen maid, laundry maid, butler, footman, groom and four footmen to look after Schwabe, his wife, six young children and a niece. Schwabe was not a practising Jew; indeed by 1851 he was a thoroughly integrated Unitarian and Liberal, yet it is interesting to note that he still chose to keep a (German) Jewish cook. Ironically, given that the household presumably did not keep kosher, she was one of only two Jewish cooks in the dataset.[58] Live-in servants were rarely Jewish, although where they appear, they did tend to work for fellow Jews.[59] There were eleven such employees in the Liverpool community, seven in Birmingham and Hull and eighteen in Manchester, mainly working in clothing firms such as Benjamin Hyams's in Manchester, and his partner James Cohen Pirani in Birmingham.[60] The Cohen Piranis lived alongside their employees on Union Street, only three of whom were Jewish out of a total of twenty-three. Given its size it might be more appropriate to class this household as a business-cum-lodging house. Hyam, meanwhile, employed twenty-four co-resident workers, thirteen of whom were Jewish, eleven of them men, and working mainly in managerial and clerical roles rather than domestic service: two managers, six salesmen, a cashier, a clerk and a collector. He did not, however, live alongside them, preferring his well-serviced residence at Park Hill in Salford.

Although the Jewish employees worked preferentially for Jews, most employers were clearly willing to have non-Jews in their households. This might have been because they were not concerned to keep their households exclusively Jewish despite the potential for transgressing Jewish laws, particularly in the preparation of food. A second possibility is that it was a way of demonstrating acculturation.[61] A third was simply that it was hard to find Jewish servants. We have seen that Jewish cooks were very rare; not one of the women employed in childcare capacities (including one wet nurse) was Jewish either, and only one household had a Jewish governess.

In contrast to the Jewish lodgers, Jewish employees of all types were frequently British-born, although not necessarily from the town where they were living in 1851. Only in the port towns was foreign birth more common among employees, and in all cases only a handful of Jewish employees worked *and lived with* non-Jewish employers. For most of these people, then, their employment and domestic arrangements can be seen as part of a functional Jewish network, either where Jews were preferentially employed over non-Jews, or where Jews were more likely to receive notice of employment opportunities via their communal networks than non-Jews. On the other hand, it is also clear that non-Jews were willing not only to work for, but to live with, Jews; in itself a not insignificant indication of tolerance and acculturation.

We may return, then, to the question posed at the start of the chapter: what can Jewish households tell us about the nature of community and the impact of rapid economic change on social networks? First, the current dataset confirms that there is no evidence to support the old theory that exposure to industrialization – or equally potently in this case, migration – brought about shrinking family sizes and a lessening of kinship ties. Jews had a strong tendency to live with close kin, and quite frequently to extend their families to accommodate other relatives too, particularly young nieces and nephews. We will see in Part II that this resonated particularly strongly with Jewish ideas about charity; in the words of one scholar on Jewish ethics, '[d]ominant in the life of the practising Jew will be commitment to family … and to community in terms of respecting, honouring and offering charitable and welfare support'.[62]

What the evidence suggests perhaps even more strongly, though – and in keeping with recent writing on the eighteenth century – is that Jewish families were fluid in form and in ways which defy brittle classifications, particularly when it came to non-kin. On the related question of the supposed instrumentality brought about by industrial conditions, the Jews also offer a more tempered view. There is little evidence that they entered into calculated relationships, taking in small children and truncated family units who might not be best placed to contribute to the household. The elderly did sometimes move in with their grown children, perhaps contributing childcare or economic resources in the way that Anderson suggested, but they even more frequently remained in their own homes, possibly pooling resources or offering aid to other family members by sharing their own houseroom. It is not enough to characterize these household arrangements as *either* instrumental *or* affectionate; there was clearly a combination of factors at work, which are not easily boiled down to economic rationality.

Motivations are notoriously hard to read into demographic sources, especially when they capture only one point in time, but patterns of lodging and servant keeping offer an even more revealing insight into intra-communal ties among provincial Jews. The evidence suggests very strongly that Jews chose to lodge with co-religionists and that their shared religious faith (and the commonalities that it brought in terms of national origins, shared culture and language) must have played a big part in their choices about where to live. Although not all lodgers were recent arrivals, the young, male, single and foreign-born were particularly well represented. The same was not true for employees, where a very small number of Jewish domestics forced families to look outside the faith, even for cooks. However, there is evidence of businesses employing relatively large numbers of Jews and housing them too. It seems, then, that migration – domestic and especially international – is a key to understanding the ways that many Jewish households worked in this period rather than the industrial setting per se. There are also strong hints that the stage of development in individual communities also played a part, with Liverpool, Manchester and Birmingham containing notably higher proportions of complete families than Leeds or Glasgow.

In terms of social networks, then, the household information has given us our first hints about the connectedness of the Jewish communities. The evidence of clustering among lodgers and Jewish hosts is a strong indicator that the community did function as a conduit of knowledge, especially for migrants, which is one of the characteristics of a network. A second feature is the co-residence of family members, which could again be a way to reinforce cultural specificity and keep people less well endowed with money or social capital off welfare services. These two types of ties do not necessarily indicate similar levels of connectedness though. Bonds between family members are likely to be long-standing and held together by behavioural norms and expectations such that the cost of defaulting is high. Those observed here are also often about goods: houseroom, pooling of finances, food and so on. Ties that permit knowledge exchange, on the other hand, are often based on weaker ties; otherwise everyone receives the same information, which obviously becomes less helpful when landladies or employers have limited opportunities available. They are also more about a monetary exchange relationship than those between co-residing kin.[63] In the current case, however, they were often foregrounded in shared culture, place of origin, or occupation, which brings them into closer alignment with family bonds in terms of shared social capital, durability and depth. The household evidence, therefore, points to a set of links among Jews in these urban settings (both kin and non-kin), which aided integration and community cohesion; possibly also group intimacy and the formation of common expectations as to behaviour. A corollary of this, however, could be that they reinforced community cohesion to the point of holding back integration into wider British culture. We will return to this in the final chapter.

It is worth ending the chapter by noting that although the Jews were not remarkable in displaying this sort of preference to live with people with whom they shared characteristics, the unusual blend of moral, religious and cultural bonds which makes up the Jewish religion may have been a particularly strong force for inclusivity. Anderson's original model for a well-functioning network included ties of shared ideology or culture, as these offer greater assurances that obligations between members would be repaid. In his words, mutual religion or language 'seem to have increased the extent to which, in a strange town, immigrants … felt dependent on, and were glad to be integrated into, a community of this kind'.[64] In the next chapter we will examine how far this translated into residential propinquity: another measure of community and access to functional and emotional aid.

3

# Residence patterns and neighbourhoods

In this chapter we turn to the spatial location of Jewish households in the three largest Jewish communities highlighted in this book: Manchester, Liverpool and Birmingham. We have already seen evidence for networks of support and information flow at the household level which underline the idea of a functioning social network. Now, we pay specific attention to patterns of residence: the extent of clustering in particular parts of town; the importance of economic, social and cultural factors in decisions about where to live; and proximity to close kin. In social network terminology this moves us towards an appraisal of the *intensity, density* and *reachability* of the community; that is, the strength of the links between households, the completeness of the network relative to all the Jews in the town, and the ease with which information or goods could flow around it.[1] Numbers are too small to allow detailed quantitative analysis, but by mapping and interpreting residential patterns we can reach a much more accurate appraisal of the nature of Jewish community ties both from an individual and a group perspective.

Let us begin our exploration with two families, both called Samuel, and both living in Liverpool in 1851. First is 69-year-old widow Flora. Described as a 'gentlewoman' in the census, she lived on salubrious Rodney Street with two unmarried daughters, Rose and Maria, and two servants. All three women were British-born and both daughters were donors to the Liverpool Hebrew Philanthropic Society. Their affluence, leisure and British-Jewish pedigree contrast sharply with the second family, who were living about two miles away on Carlton Street in Scotland Ward near the crowded Liverpool dockside. This household consisted of Polish-born Israel, his wife Catherine and their seven children aged between eighteen and four. These two Samuel households appear to span the range of Jewish households in the town, both economically and geographically. In fact, between them they highlight that explaining residence patterns is not straightforward, and that families did not always fit into neat categories based on their skill status, the economic profile of their neighbourhood, or their proximity to other Jews.

Flora Samuel's family was much as it seems: well established and leisured – both the Samuel clan into which she married and the Yates into which she had been born were scions of the Liverpool Jewish community. But Israel and Catherine Samuel were not quite the poor, newly arrived 'greenhorns' that their birthplace and residence in one of Liverpool's poorer districts would suggest. For one thing, their seven children had all been born in Liverpool, and since the eldest of them was eighteen, the family had clearly been in Britain for some time. Second, while none of the children had occupations recorded in 1851 (itself a suggestion that the family was not struggling to make ends meet; three of the younger children –all boys – were described as scholars), Israel himself was a grocer and provisioner, a semi-skilled non-manual occupation, and he employed a servant and a clerk who lived with the family in their home.[2] These details make the household harder to classify than it seems at first glance. Perhaps the docks were simply a sensible place for a provisioner to live, close to the goods being unloaded and to a market of sailors and migrants. Perhaps, having been in Liverpool for a long time, the family felt they had more in common, socially, economically or culturally, with the other dockside dwellers, especially if they had little formal contact with their religion. Perhaps Israel's business was not doing terribly well and the family could not afford to live elsewhere; or the business was too well established to risk moving his home. Furthermore, since the main synagogue in Seel Street was only about a half hour's walk away, their choice of residence did not preclude them from taking part in the religious community. At this distance in time, it is very difficult to untangle all the possible reasons that this family lived where they did. However, by mapping out household locations across the community we can reach a better level of understanding of motivations and priorities.

To this end, the Jewish households in Liverpool, Manchester and Birmingham were plotted onto a set of contemporary maps in order to visualize their spread over the town. The maps were originally drawn for an 1851 atlas and they offer a particularly clear layout of the city streets and landmarks (including hospitals and workhouses).[3] Where streets were not named on the map and do not correspond to modern streets, the census enumerator's description of the area was used to pinpoint the location as accurately as possible relative to nearby roads, and the same method was used to place individual houses on long streets. Since neither the sequence of house numbers nor the order of streets as they are presented in the census are an exact guide to location, the points marked on the map may not reflect the precise situation of individual houses, but they are as close as possible.[4] This means that we cannot be certain about exact distances between households, but the exercise does allow us to see the general pattern of Jewish residence, and moreover, in a way that facilitates comparison between towns.[5]

## Mapping Jewish households

Maps 3.1–3.3 show the location of the households headed by Jews or containing Jewish lodgers in the three towns. In the first instance this reveals the basic pattern of Jewish residence, about which our knowledge has been fairly impressionistic for this point in time. It also introduces a second theme, which is a major topic of interest in urban spatial analysis: the degree to which minorities were clustered and/or segregated in certain parts of town.[6] Attractive job prospects and

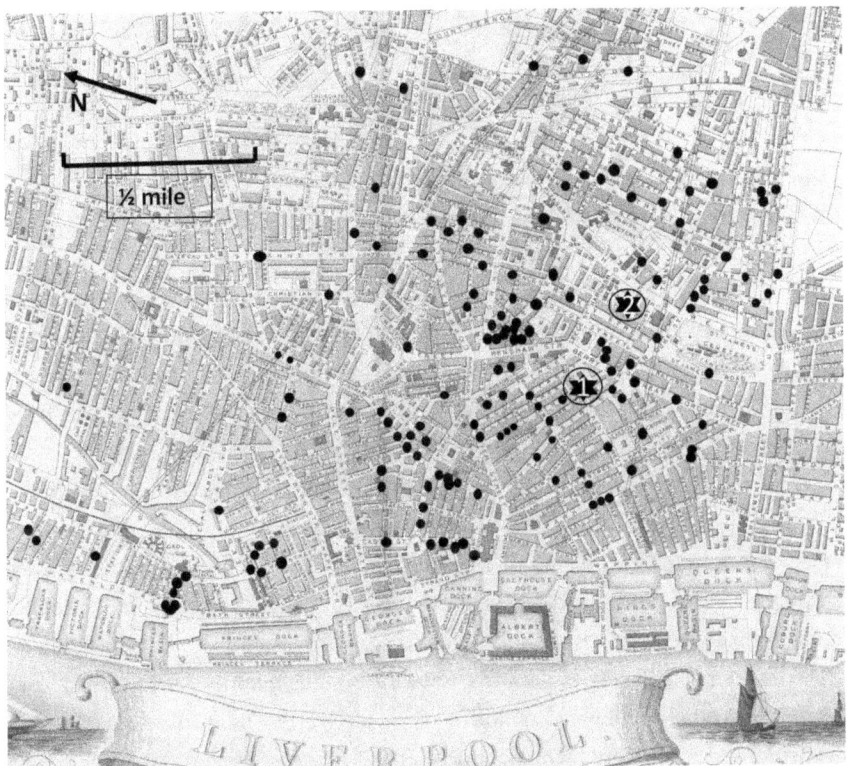

**Map 3.1** Jewish households in Liverpool, 1851.

Source: AJDB/Census database. Map from *The Illustrated Atlas, and Modern History of the World Geographical, Political, Commercial & Statistical*, ed. R. Montgomery Martin, Esq. (London and New York: J. and F. Tallis, 1851), available and used with permission from David Rumsey Collections Online (www.davidrumsey.com). Key: 1: Synagogue of the Old Hebrew Congregation; 2: Synagogue of the New Hebrew Congregation.

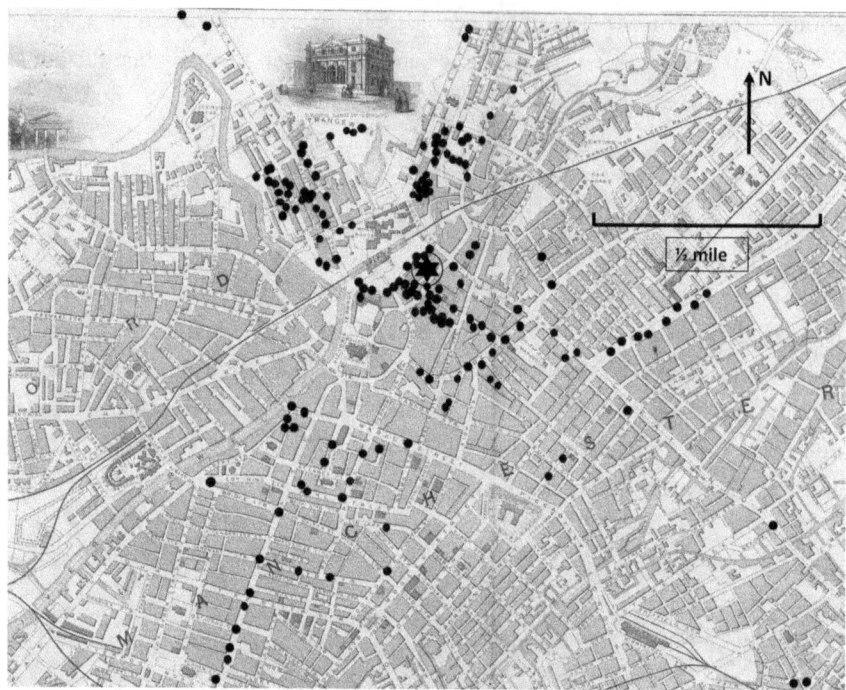

**Map 3.2** Jewish households in Manchester, 1851.
Source: AJDB/Census database. Map from *The Illustrated Atlas, and Modern History of the World*.

good transport networks meant that all three towns housed large numbers of immigrants in 1851: over 40 per cent of the total population (almost 60 per cent in Birmingham). Only a very small proportion of these had come from overseas (0.5 to 1.5 per cent), but of these, Jews formed the majority.[7] Many of our focal group were therefore 'minorities' on several different counts.

Even at a first glance the maps reveal both similarities and differences in the way that Jewish households were distributed in the three towns. In Liverpool and Birmingham, Jews were quite dispersed across the central area of the town (though the difference in scales means that Birmingham Jewry covered a smaller geographical area). In Liverpool the main spread ranged from the dockside on the river Mersey – where Israel and Catherine Samuel lived – to more prosperous Mount Pleasant and beyond, including Brownlow Hill where some ten or eleven Jewish households were located, and where a synagogue serving the OHC (Old Hebrew Congregation) in Princes Road was erected in 1874. In Manchester, there is evidence of several clusters, one around the Halliwell Street area near Victoria station and the workhouse, and others in Strangeways and Red Bank where Bury New Road and York Street fork at the northern edge of the map. There

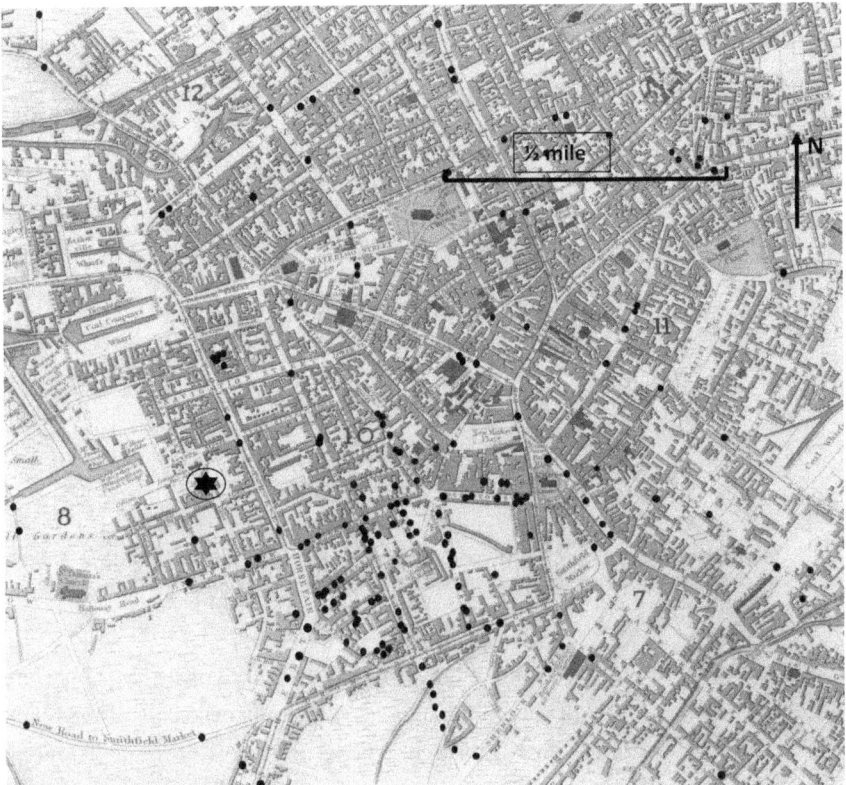

**Map 3.3** Jewish households in Birmingham, 1851.
Source: AJDB/Census database. Map from *The Illustrated Atlas, and Modern History of the World*.

were further clusters beyond the central area, as will be discussed below, and depicted on Map 3.4: to the north in Cheetham Hill, where there were twenty-four Jewish households, to the north-east and east in Salford and Broughton, where ten households were located, and to the south-east in Chorlton-upon-Medlock (twenty-one households).[8] This pattern of dispersal beyond the core urban centre in Manchester suggests immediately that a notable proportion of the community lived on the periphery of the commercial and industrial parts of the city; we will see that these tended to be the wealthier households.

In Birmingham, meanwhile, the community had started life congregated in the low-lying area of the Froggery, which was replaced by New Street station in 1845.[9] By 1851 we can see much more of a spread, albeit over a fairly small area, and tending towards the south-west quadrant of the map, clustered between Exeter Row/Smallbrook Street and Bromsgrove Street, to the west of the Bull Ring and Smithfield market zone (an important area for commerce and civic

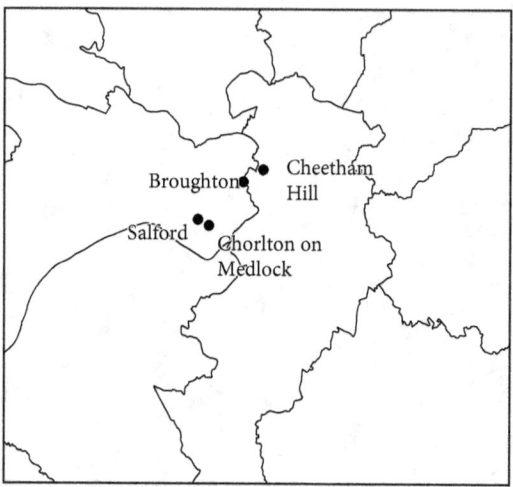

**Map 3.4** Outlying townships inhabited by Jews in Manchester, 1851.

Source: Modified from www.wikimedia.org, available under Creative Commons Attribution-Share Alike 3.0 Unported license (https://creativecommons.org/licenses/by-sa/3.0/deed.en).

administration, though also known for drunkenness and fighting[10]). There were other Jewish households scattered in an arc over the northern side of the town. The initial impression of Jewish residence patterns is thus of a fair degree of spread in Birmingham and even more so in Liverpool, where the core area of Jewish settlement was larger, and a much greater suggestion of clustering in Manchester, but focused on several separate areas, including several well outside the urban core.[11] There are also hints at social differentiation between richer and poorer Jews in satellite areas like Cheetham (Manchester) and Mount Pleasant (Liverpool) in particular. A more detailed discussion of each of the three towns allows us to drill down further into these patterns.

## Liverpool

The population of Liverpool had a greater ethnic mix than any British city bar London. This explains the attention its migrant populations have attracted from historians and geographers.[12] Studies have focused particularly on the Irish, who were by far the largest of the immigrant groups in the city at this time, and who had a notable centre of gravity around the north-central part of town and the deprived north dock area.[13] There was a small number of Jewish households in this part of town too: a total of eight lived in the notorious Scotland and Vauxhall wards behind Clarence, Trafalgar and Victoria docks, both of which were targets for concern about public health and immorality in the decades after mid-century. Another small cluster of Jews was located around the adjoining Exchange and St Paul's wards. We will see that many of these were headed by Jews born overseas and following unskilled and semi-skilled trades; both indicators of lower social status and a lower level of social integration. However, these households were heavily outweighed by those further inland, and several households were located in the most salubrious wards of Rodney and Abercromby – like that of Flora Samuel whom we met at the start of the chapter. Five Jewish families lived on Canning Street, described in one history of Liverpool Jewry as 'Liverpool's then equivalent of Millionaire's Row'.[14] Indeed, the largest house on the street – number 27 – was inhabited by the Jewish Ralph Henry Samuel, who had recently returned from Rio de Janeiro as a widower with eight young children. He was away from home on census night, but the house contained his mother, three siblings, five of his children and four members of domestic staff (three other daughters were at boarding school in Hackney). Ralph rapidly took up a place within the community's elite (aided, no doubt, by his membership of the Samuel clan): he was elected to the Select Committee of the Old Hebrew Congregation in 1853 and was a subscriber to the Liverpool Hebrew Philanthropic Society. Another Samuel household, married couple Henry and Fanny (whose mother was a Yates), lived nearby at number 50.

The Jewish community in Liverpool was tiny compared with the Irish. There is thus less of a critical mass to observe when it comes to living patterns. It was also considerably more diverse in terms of languages and nationalities, but like the mass of immigrant Irish it shared a common culture and religion. There are therefore factors weighing both for and against the likelihood that Jewish households would show similar residential patterns to other minorities. Having said that, the distance between Mount Pleasant, at the far side of the area of Jewish settlement, and Salthouse Dock on the coast is still only just over a mile – an easy walk – so even here the central core of the Jewish community was hardly dispersed over a very large area.

The largest cluster of Jews in Liverpool lay in the main commercial centre of the town. Almost 40 per cent of all Jewish households (sixty-one in total) were located in the Mount Pleasant sub-registration district, followed by St George (twenty-six households), immediately to the south of Dale Street, and Islington, behind them to the east (nineteen households). In fact, most of these were clustered along a relatively narrow east–west corridor; there is little dispersal towards newer suburbs of Toxteth to the south, for example, or to Everton (where many of the better-off Welsh lived) and Kirkdale to the north and east, although some lived in the Edge Hill/West Derby area which borders Everton.[15]

Most of the Jewish families in Liverpool thus lived within a mile-wide circle, which included the synagogue in Seel Street just to the east of Hanover Street (marked with '1' on Map 3.1). Fourteen or fifteen families lived in the streets immediately around Seel Street and four lived on Seel Street itself. It is likely that the synagogue was sited where there was a large concentration of Jews, although once established it could have been a focal point for later settlement.[16] At any rate, it is clear that the more affluent families had started to move outwards even by 1851, and it is no coincidence that the synagogue was relocated to the more northern Princes Park area in Toxteth in 1874, in a grand new building. The breakaway New Hebrew Congregation (established in 1839), meanwhile, settled in Hardman Street (marked '2' in Map 3.1), which lay behind Rodney Street, very close to the cluster of households around Mount Pleasant.[17] It in turn moved round the corner to Hope Place in 1857. The Jewish Deane Road Cemetery, which opened in 1837, and where many of the mid-century community notables are buried, lay well outside the main area of settlement, in West Derby. In terms of Jewish-owned shops, there was a notable concentration of people described as victuallers, grocers and provisioners near the docks, and in the core of Jewish households around the Hanover Street area. We cannot be sure which, if any, of them served the Jewish community specifically, but it is likely that like the synagogue, shopkeepers who spoke Yiddish or dealt kindly with fellow Jews set up shop to cater for existing groups of customers rather than acting as a magnet for settlement.

## Manchester

In Manchester the most notable cluster of Jewish households lay in an inverted triangle from a point just south and east of Halliwell Street, where the synagogue of the 'Old' congregation was situated (so named after a breakaway 'New' congregation was formed in 1844; they were reunited in 1851), up to Strangeways and Red Bank. In total fifty-five to sixty Jewish households were located around the lower point. Smaller clusters lived along the main arterial roads of Oldham Road and Deansgate to the east and south respectively. In Red Bank there was a very obvious cluster on Fernie Street (six households) and Verdon Street (ten, including Back Verdon Street). Both roads were cut into the side of a sandstone ridge and bordered an area of factories and warehouses. The houses there were notorious for their cramped space and over subsequent decades Red Bank increasingly took on the characteristics of a slum.[18] In total just under half of all of the Jewish households were located in the central Market Street sub-registration district (46.3 per cent or 113 households), and a further sixty were in Cheetham, which included both Strangeways and the more salubrious Cheetham Hill just to the north, whence many tradesmen were on the move, leaving lock-up shop premises behind in the centre.[19] It is striking, though, that the entire concentration of Jewish households in 1851 lay several streets above Oxford Road, which was identified in a spatial study of the later nineteenth-century city as the main line of 'integration' or access in the town.[20] This suggests immediately that Jews did not utilize the city space in the same way as the rest of the town, but instead that there was some advantage to clustering together in a slightly less central location.

The Red Bank area was clearly already an area of settlement for less-well-off Jews in 1851 and its population was to triple over the rest of the decade.[21] However, it was at this stage still (in Williams's words) a 'peripheral slum district' as opposed to the Jewish 'colony' of poorly off and poorly skilled workers it was to become in the 1860s and 1870s, when immigration from Eastern Europe caused its Jewish population to grow almost exponentially. By 1871 it housed over a third of Manchester's Jews and by 1881 Jews made up 40 per cent of inhabitants of the area.[22] In 1851 this cultural 'pull' factor was still in an early stage and was likely formed by affordable rental levels, or proximity to jobs. Certainly, Williams believes that prior to the 1860s Red Bank lacked sufficient density of Jewish households to have its own distinct social and religious life as it was to do later; its members worshipped at Halliwell Street, where they aspired to become seat holders.[23] Nonetheless, we should not dismiss the suggestion that certain streets were known as hospitable or convenient for Jews: it is the very local neighbourhood to which individuals look for their sense of security and belonging, after all, and the dense presence of Jews on a few neighbouring streets could have created a feeling of identity and refuge.

The more distant clusters in Broughton, Chorlton and Cheetham Hill, to the south and north of the area on Map 3.2, meanwhile, had started to emerge from the end of the 1820s, when the growing Jewish middle class began an exodus from the smoky, tumultuous and crowded city centre. By 1851 there were no Jewish families left living on Mosley Street, which in 1832 had still housed some of the wealthy in the town centre; instead they had moved out to the newly built York Street, which turned into Cheetham Hill Road (some of them renting properties from fellow Jew Joseph Braham), or further afield still, where some of the very wealthiest Jews lived.[24] Choice of residence for these wealthier people was a means of staking out one's social status, and perhaps also one's social integration.

As a community, Manchester Jewry looks rather less coherent overall than their near neighbours in Liverpool, especially if we consider the distance from Cheetham on one side to Chorlton on the other (approximately three miles). On the other hand, the central cluster had strong focal points on several key streets, meaning that a greater proportion of Jews had fellow Jews as near neighbours. If this was a factor in building support networks then parts of the Manchester community at least may have had more social capital to draw on than those in Liverpool. On the other hand, by this stage, most of their wealthier members were living in relative isolation from the central district. The synagogue of the (by now reunited) congregation opened on Cheetham Hill Road in 1858; the later Manchester Jewish Board of Guardians was also located there, in keeping with the northward movement of the socially mobile immigrants who founded it. The Reform Synagogue (est. 1858), meanwhile, was located a little south of the Old Congregation, where Cheetham Hill Road met Park Place, and the Sephardim built a splendid synagogue of their own in 1873–4 also on Cheetham Hill Road.[25] Ongoing migration from the centre formed the impetus for a South Manchester synagogue in 1872, meeting initially in Chorlton Town Hall, and later in Sidney Street.[26] In contrast to Liverpool, there is almost no evidence of Jewish provisioners in Manchester at this time, according to the occupational labels in the census (in all three towns, kosher meat was available from non-Jewish butchers who had been licensed by the synagogues). A new Jewish burial ground was purchased in 1843 at Prestwich, to the north of the town, while the Hebrew National School, completed in 1851, was at the top of the slope down to Red Bank, between Lord Street and Cheetham Hill Road, conveniently situated to attract children of all social classes.[27]

## Birmingham

Birmingham Jewry lived in a relatively restricted geographical area, but with more of a scattered pattern than the other towns. Nonetheless, a concentration can be discerned moving outwards from the central market areas and 43 per cent of households were located in the central St Martins sub-registration district, near Smithfield Market. There were again several clusters on large roads: ten families on Hurst Street and another eight on Lower Hurst Street or their associated courts; eight on Smallbrook Street; and eleven on Pershore Street, often only a few houses apart from one another (all in the lower left quadrant of Map 3.3, where sixty to seventy Jewish households were located in total). The synagogue, described by a contemporary as 'a very nice, neat and commodious building', was located on Severn Street (marked with a star), off the central conduit of Suffolk Street and away from the central concentration of Jewish households, but only half a mile from Hurst Street (an earlier synagogue, built in 1791, had been on Hurst Street itself).[28] It was enlarged in 1823 but was replaced by the grand Singers Hill Synagogue, in 1856, which lay slightly further yet to the west.[29] By the time the new synagogue was founded, the cluster focused around Hurst Street had grown outwards to the west, and was identified with working-class immigrant Jews living in an apparently self-contained enclave. These residents felt quite separate from the more anglicized Jews who worshipped at Singer's Hill (or, as the former called it, the *Englische schule* – *shul* being the Yiddish word for a synagogue).[30] Further afield, only three households had addresses in more salubrious Edgbaston in 1851 (which was at this stage a small, exclusive and landowner-controlled community), although small numbers lived around Aston and working-class Duddeston to the north (six households), and in the artisanal Jewellery Quarter, near St Pauls Square, around two miles from the Bull Ring market. By 1871 nearly 100 families were located in Edgbaston.[31]

Work by Birmingham Jewish local historians suggests that Jews did not live in areas further to the east because it was too far from the congregation's main facilities: most of the children who attended the Jewish school in Lower Hurst Street in the 1860s lived within half a mile of the institution, for example.[32] This suggests that the individual households further north and east from the main cluster were less attached to the formal aspects of Jewish life. Although they do not form as concentrated a cluster as we saw in Mount Pleasant in Liverpool, or Cheetham in Manchester, they were again not necessarily completely isolated from co-religionists, however. There was a small group of five households around Howard Place, for example, and the handful stretched out along the more affluent Great Charles Street and Snow Hill were probably not much more than half a mile's walk from one another. Others lived around St Phillip's Church, which was also a better-off area, and along Waterloo Road. The more central part of town meanwhile, where the majority of Jewish households lived, offered a more mixed range of properties, with retail premises side by side with residential housing, and the well-off often living alongside poorer households because of their business connections with the central area. While some of the older parts of town were neglected and run down, and back-to-back court housing was ubiquitous for poorer families, the streets were generally 'wide and well ventilated' in the words of an official sanitary report in 1842, while the water supply was ample.[33]

## Explaining residence patterns

At this stage we need to start thinking about models to explain Jewish patterns of residence. Motivations can of course only be guessed at from this distance in time, but other studies have suggested fruitful ways of capturing some of the most important variables. Two of these are key for our purposes. The first is economic: how far could people choose where they lived and how far were they constrained by affordability (which might also relate to how recently they had arrived and their stage in the life cycle)? The second is more social and cultural in nature, and concerns proximity to fellow Jews, emerging communal facilities like the synagogue and schools, and/or family, which could suggest a strong sense of fellow-feeling and community. Both mechanisms could result in clusters of Jews in particular areas, either from choice or from constraint. Such encapsulation could preserve them from prejudice and ease the maintenance of internal rules and endogamous marriage, while not necessarily precluding the shared use of public space with people outside their own group.[34] On the other hand, it could also reinforce a perception of difference from the outside which can in turn further ethnic animosity and exclusivity.

Pooley introduced several interesting lines of enquiry in this area in his study of Liverpool minorities in 1871. In particular, he showed that Irish, Scots and Welsh migrants lived in quite distinct parts of town, and proposed that this was for different reasons. The Irish, he suggested, clustered together because of socio-economic homogeneity – a 'ghetto'-like situation where poor economic prospects prevented upward social or residential mobility. The Welsh, meanwhile, were economically more diverse, but remained in residential proximity because of a strong sense of cultural cohesion, while the Scots fell midway between the two other groups, with a similar socio-economic spread to the Welsh, but cultural affiliations which were more like the Irish.[35] It is worth noting also that by 1871 the smaller numbers of foreign-born (among whom Jews were the largest group) showed the greatest degree of segregation of all minority groups, suggesting that the patterns we see in 1851 were further reinforced over the following twenty years.[36] We have already had hints that the Jewish population was more mixed than the Irish when it came to occupations, although with their heavy concentration in retail and direct dealing they were not completely representative of the population around them. On the other hand, their cultural institutions were exclusive and specific – like both the Irish and Welsh. We must therefore do some more digging to find out which of the several available models fits best with their residential behaviour.

## Economic factors

Economic considerations are often heavily tangled up with more personal factors, but the bottom line is that at the lower end of the social scale people likely had little choice over where to live: they clustered in areas with low rents. However, areas populated by fellow countrymen, co-religionists or those with other traits in common are likely to have a particular draw, as we suggested above in the case of Manchester's Red Bank. Prejudice against tenants of certain backgrounds would also serve to shape the population in a given area. At higher socio-economic levels, income is likely to bring greater choice over where to live, and people can choose to prioritize locations which are convenient for work, for worship, to be near friends and family, or to make a statement about their sense of identity.[37] Since people tend to select neighbourhoods with which they have some sense of affinity, it is unsurprising that we find a strong level of cultural cohesion in many cases, even if the primary reason for living there is economic. The better off may also choose to live alongside others of their own background if that is a way of improving their quality of life, privileging cultural factors above the strictly economic.[38] Since frequent contact breeds further social capital and emphasizes commonalities, this is a good way of establishing a social network in one's neighbourhood.

Mid-century Jews were extremely diverse in terms of socio-economic status, national background and religious feeling. Nonetheless, we have already seen that their household arrangements suggested a strong sense of cultural or economic cohesion. However, even a brief glance at their residential arrangements at a street or neighbourhood level points to heterogeneity. While many did live near fellow Jews, others lived in a more scattered pattern such that their day-to-day contacts were likely to be predominately with non-Jews. It is thus likely that decisions about where to live had a range of motivations for different families. Furthermore, even on the most 'Jewish' of streets, Jews in no way dominated the population as they were to do, for example, in parts of Red Bank by the 1880s (when they comprised 95 per cent of households on certain streets[39]).

In 1851 Jews made up a still notable 23 per cent of residents on Manchester's Verdon Street, for example (and 13 per cent of households), but only 7 per cent on Liverpool's Paradise Street, and 11 per cent on Birmingham's Pershore Street (7 and 13 per cent of households respectively).[40]

In the absence of data on incomes we must use proxy measures to capture economic status: first, a broad measure of occupation (skill status – explained further in Chapter 4), shown in Maps 3.5–3.7,[41] followed by birth overseas (Maps 3.8–3.10). The latter is not strictly a measure of wealth, but potentially one

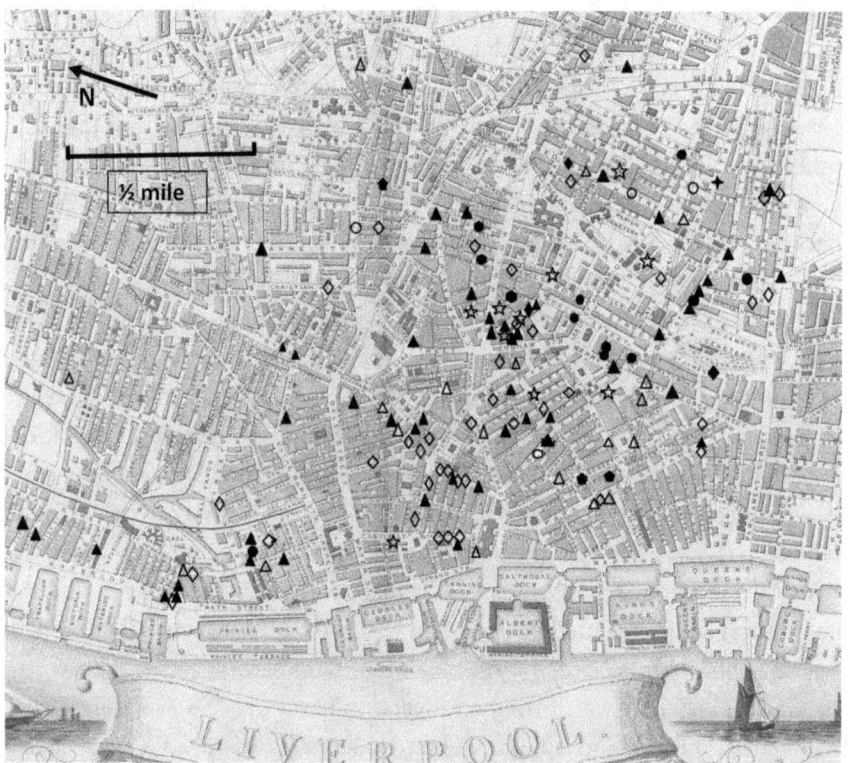

**Map 3.5** Skill status of Jewish household heads and lodgers in Liverpool, 1851.
Source: AJDB/Census database. Map from *The Illustrated Atlas, and Modern History of the World*.

| | | | |
|---|---|---|---|
| ● | Leisured | ○ | Managerial |
| ★ | Professional | △ | Semi-skilled manual |
| ▲ | Semi-skilled non-manual | ◇ | Skilled manual |
| ◆ | Skilled non-manual | ⬢ | Unskilled |
| ✢ | Misc/unknown | | |

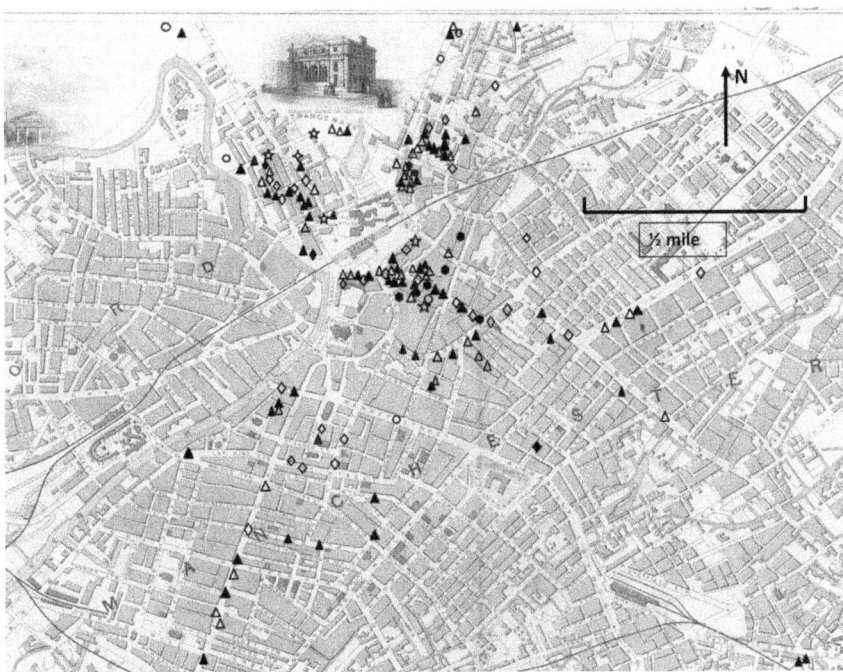

**Map 3.6** Skill status of Jewish household heads and lodgers in Manchester, 1851.
Source: AJDB/Census database. Map from *The Illustrated Atlas, and Modern History of the World*.

of integration and knowledge of employment networks. In fact, as we will see, it does often correlate with lower skill status occupations.[42] The occupational skill categories are relatively unnuanced, especially for the bulk of the population, who fall into one of four classes: skilled or semi-skilled manual, and skilled or semi-skilled non-manual jobs. Given the predominance of jobs in retail, however, skill status is a better way of differentiating between types of occupation than sector, and moreover, allows comparison between towns.[43] We would broadly expect the skilled classes to have higher incomes or status than the semi-skilled, although the hierarchy between manual and non-manual occupations was probably less clear-cut, as some of the examples below indicate. An alternative measure of economic status – servant keeping – is less helpful since this was quite common across the Jewish community. However, some observations will be made on this in the context of the discussion below.

Table 3.1 sets out the distribution of skill levels among Jews in the three towns, and these are mapped in Maps 3.5–3.7. The maps suggest that there were no clear-cut patterns of residence based on skill status in any of the three towns. However, if we focus on specific areas we can see some trends. In the

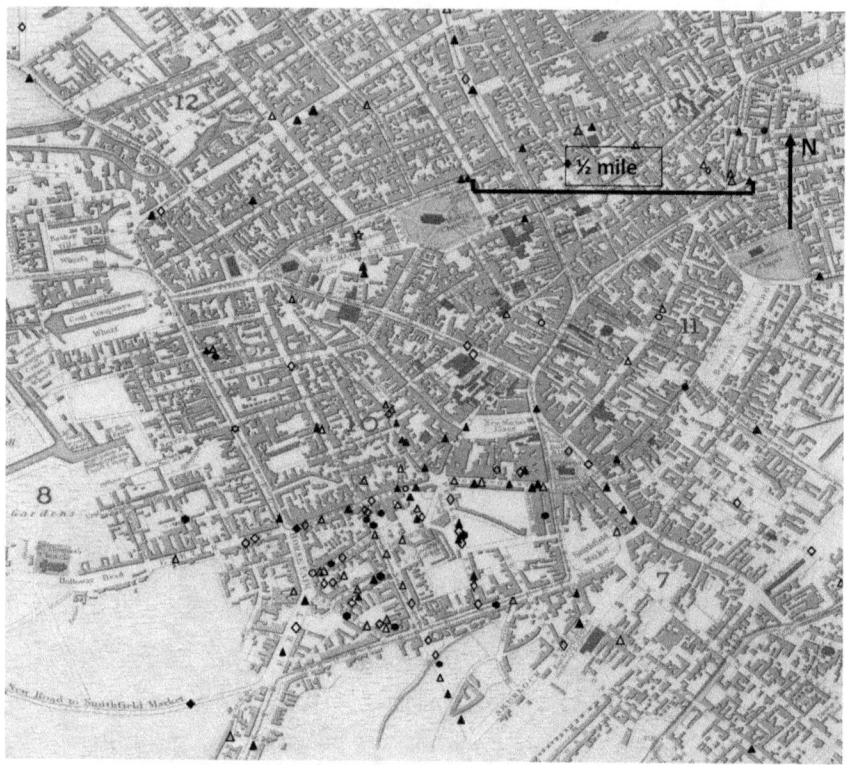

**Map 3.7** Skill status of Jewish household heads and lodgers in Birmingham, 1851.
Source: AJDB/Census database. Map from *The Illustrated Atlas, and Modern History of the World.*

**Table 3.1** Occupational skill status of Jews in Liverpool, Manchester and Birmingham in 1851 (%)

| Skill status | Liverpool | Manchester | Birmingham |
|---|---|---|---|
| Inactive | 0.0 | 0.0 | 0.2 |
| Indeterminate | 1.1 | 0.3 | 0.8 |
| Leisured | 4.6 | 0.3 | 0.8 |
| Managerial | 2.5 | 3.1 | 1.0 |
| Professional | 7.6 | 3.9 | 1.2 |
| Semi-skilled manual | 14.4 | 28.3 | 27.3 |
| Semi-skilled non-manual | 36.2 | 39.0 | 32.1 |
| Skilled manual | 21.3 | 12.6 | 21.6 |
| Skilled non-manual | 3.0 | 3.1 | 2.8 |
| Unskilled | 9.4 | 9.4 | 12.1 |
| N | 437 | 587 | 495 |

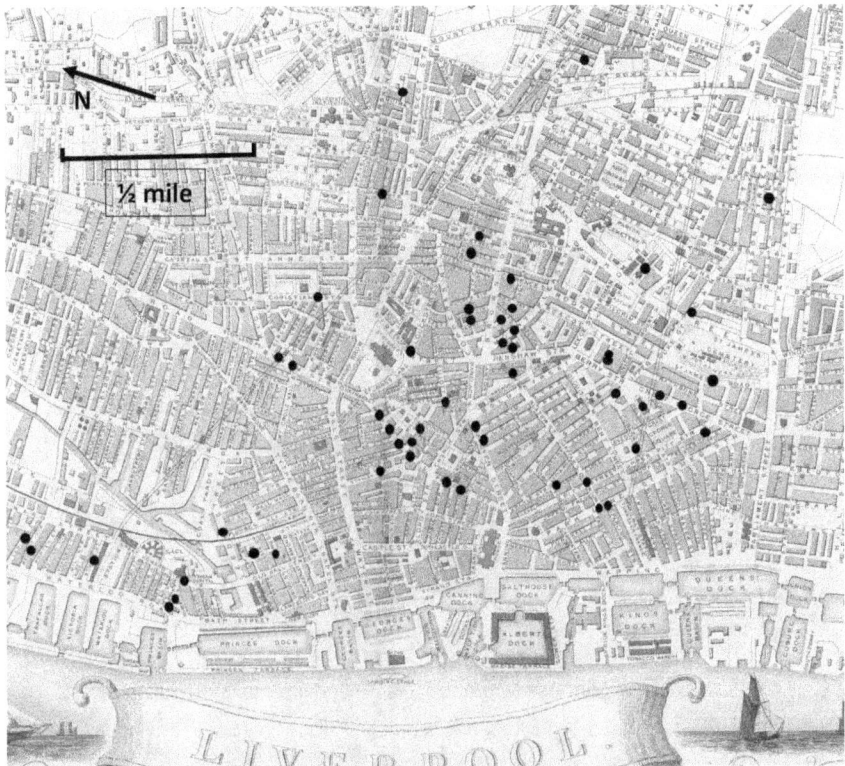

**Map 3.8** Jewish household heads and lodgers born overseas, Liverpool, 1851.
Source: AJDB/Census database. Map from *The Illustrated Atlas, and Modern History of the World*.

busy dock area of Liverpool, for instance, semi-skilled non-manual workers were in particular evidence, principally dealers, travelling salesmen and grocers. Almost all of these earners were household heads rather than lodgers – heads tended towards more skilled categories than lodgers, perhaps as their prospects stabilized (heads in Liverpool also had a higher average age of almost forty-two, compared with just under twenty-seven for lodgers).[44] The skilled manual workers, meanwhile, were more heavily concentrated in the central area of Jewish settlement, including the corridor between Hanover Street and Dale Street where more of the town's shops and businesses were located. This is reflected in the occupations in this category: thirty out of thirty-seven were in manufacturing jobs, principally jewellers, watchmakers, cabinetmakers and the like. There were very few households with unskilled heads in the dataset, and the professional, managerial and leisured heads were scattered with little evidence of any geographic concentration – bar, perhaps, a slight preference for the areas furthest from the docks.

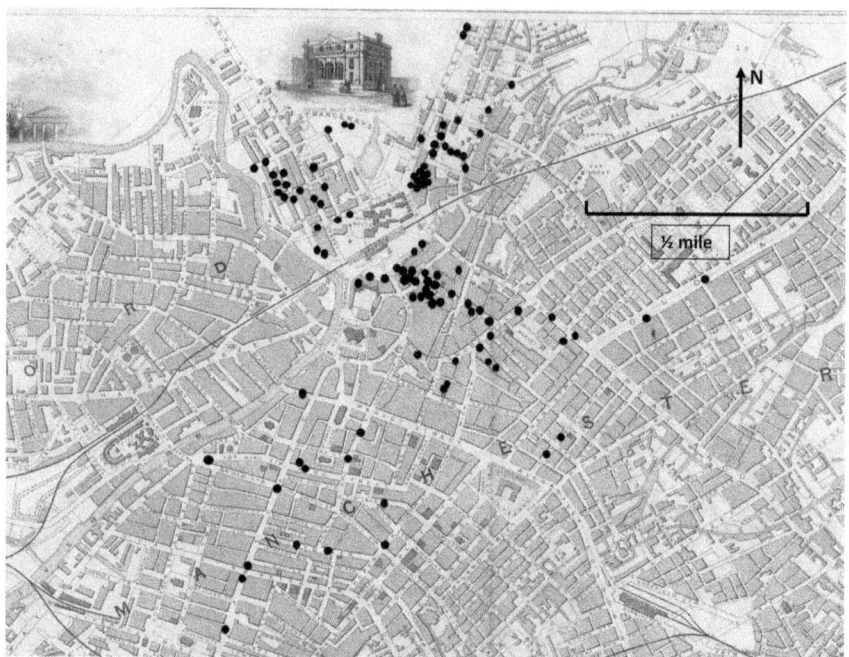

**Map 3.9** Jewish household heads and lodgers born overseas, Manchester, 1851.
Source: AJDB/Census database. Map from *The Illustrated Atlas, and Modern History of the World*.

In Manchester there were again few unskilled Jewish workers, but there is some evidence that they clustered immediately south of the workhouse and railway station; there was also a small handful of professional and managerial households in this area, perhaps still living near businesses. Vaughan and Penn highlighted proximity to work as a key reason behind patterns of Jewish settlement in Manchester and Leeds in the 1880s so this would make sense; Williams also notes that by the 1860s and 1870s houses in Red Bank lent themselves to shared used as workshops.[45] Jews in Red Bank had a leaning towards semi-skilled occupations, with manual jobs more common than non-manual ones. These consisted mainly of cap making and glazing, the former of which could be done as piecework with tasks shared among family members.[46] These were not occupations found exclusively in this area though: an equal number of cap makers lived in the Halliwell Street area. The small number of semi-skilled non-manual workers on Verdon Street and Fernie Street were dealers and travellers, but these occupations were similarly shared with residents in the area to the south of Red Bank.[47] At this stage, then, occupational skill levels were not notably different in Red Bank than in other parts of town favoured by

**Map 3.10** Jewish household heads and lodgers born overseas, Birmingham, 1851.
Source: AJDB/Census database. Map from *The Illustrated Atlas, and Modern History of the World*.

Jews, although they were perhaps more homogeneous. The Market Street area, in contrast, had a higher proportion of heads in skilled non-manual professions, but also in unskilled jobs. The outlying areas did show some differentiation: while 78 per cent of the Jewish heads living in Chorlton worked in semi-skilled non-manual occupation, the figure was 67 per cent in Salford and Broughton and only 55 per cent in the northern part of Cheetham, suggesting a sliding scale of upskilling. While patterns are not absolutely clear-cut, therefore, there is some evidence for economic differentiation across the Jewish parts of town.

Birmingham had the most even split of household heads across the three largest skill categories, with 22 per cent classed as skilled manual, 27 per cent in semi-skilled manual occupations and 32 per cent in semi-skilled non-manual jobs. This is reflected on Map 3.7, which shows a mixture of symbols in the central area. The proportion of people in unskilled occupations was a little higher in Birmingham than elsewhere (12 per cent compared with 9 per cent in both Liverpool and Manchester) and these people do seem to have been concentrated around Hurst Street, which was an area with a lot of court housing. The large majority of people in the unskilled category were the usual dealers and hawkers – in line with the preponderance of small goods manufacture in the town generally. Further afield, in the broad arc to the north of the main area of settlement, there was some tendency towards semi-skilled rather than skilled jobs.

By subdividing the Birmingham population into sub-registration districts we can again see a little more nuance. The two most populous areas for Jewish households were St Thomas and St Martin, which adjoined near Hurst Street (Hurst Street itself lay in the St Thomas district, but Inge Street, which bisects Hurst, was partly located in both). Smallbrook Street, which caps Hurst Street to the north, was in St Martins. Further to the west St Thomas housed gardens and wharves (as well as the Jewish burial ground), giving it quite a mixed topographical character. St Martin contained approximately twice the number of Jewish households as St Thomas (seventy-three and thirty-five). The two districts had very similar proportions of Jewish heads in unskilled and skilled manual jobs (the latter focusing on boot and shoemaking, but also covering cabinetmaking, jewellery making and other skilled trades). However, St Martin had a much higher proportion of Jewish heads in semi-skilled non-manual trades (the largest being pawnbroking and travelling sales), while St Thomas was over-represented in semi-skilled manual jobs (tailors, slipper makers, clothiers). This suggests both that occupation was indeed a strong factor dictating the choice of place to live, with people joining neighbours doing similar jobs or following their example, and that there was some division within the Jewish population between manual and non-manual trades. The only two leisured households in the two districts lived in St Martins, while the only professional (a dentist) and the two individuals of managerial status (managers of a warehouse and a clothing business respectively) were located in St Thomas's.

The residential patterns of household heads born overseas (Maps 3.8–3.10) offer some further insights. In Liverpool, foreign-born heads or lodgers were, as has already been noted, less common than in the other towns, but there is still evidence of geographic differentiation across the urban area.[48] This is in the predicted direction: a greater proportion in the areas closer to the docks and in certain parts of the central commercial area, and far fewer in the areas towards Mount Pleasant and the peripheral parts of the central district. This suggests that much of the wealthy core of the Jewish population had been born in England and thus had longer experience of British – and highly likely urban – life. Immigration was too common an experience within the Jewish population in the provinces to expect this to neatly explain everything about residential patterns. However, in Liverpool the British-born do seem to have behaved a bit differently when it came to residence than the foreign-born. Servant keeping, however, was relatively well represented across the board, in marked contrast with the poor Liverpool Irish, for whom a low incidence of servant keeping correlated with multiple house occupancy, poor housing and use of court dwellings (all markers of low socio-economic status).[49]

Things were quite different in Manchester, where almost half of the Jewish population had been born abroad: 45.3 per cent of the total compared with 31.1 in Birmingham and 23.0 in Liverpool. Overseas birth was particularly common among Jewish heads on Fernie Street and Verdon Street – but also on Hanover Street and Shudehill in the more central station area, so this was not simply a story of a single immigrant-heavy cluster. One of the most striking things about the patterns of residence in Manchester compared with Liverpool, however, was the high proportion of foreign-born heads in the more 'salubrious' outer areas: 72 per cent. As Williams's study of Manchester has shown, many foreigners who had arrived in the town in the 1830s and 1840s went on to become well established and affluent.[50] In Manchester, then, foreign birth did not necessarily go hand in hand with low socio-economic status, although it might be a function of its more recent period of Jewish settlement compared with Liverpool. Rates of servant keeping uphold this, with a higher proportion of households employing domestic staff in the Cheetham sub-registration district (72 per cent) than in the Market Street area (51 per cent). It is notable that Red Bank had higher rates of servant keeping than Market Street, suggesting that in 1851 at least, this area was better off in some respects than those closer to the commercial centre.

In Birmingham, overseas birth was heavily focused in the area bordering St Martin and St Thomas. In fact, the Jews living in the court-heavy area around Hurst Street and Inge Street were almost all born overseas, this time in keeping with the thesis that newer arrivals are more likely to live in areas of cheaper housing. In the current case we can say with some confidence that this also brought proximity to fellow Jews, to the extent that when the heritage preservation charity the National Trust recreated some of the dwellings in one court on the corner of Inge Street and Hurst Street, they selected a Jewish household of Eastern European origin as one of those representative of life in the 1850s.[51] Information on children's ages and birthplaces on these streets suggests that the families were often fairly recent arrivals in Britain in 1851. Servant keeping was not high here; the households employing domestic staff were concentrated on Smallbrook Street, Edgbaston Street and Pershore Street.

What, then, do these patterns suggest about economic choice and constraint in determining where Jews lived? First, they do suggest very strongly that birth overseas was a good predictor of residence in what we can loosely identify as lower-class housing, at least in Birmingham and Liverpool. Foreign birth does not necessarily correlate with recent arrival in Britain – indeed, often it did not – but this only underlines even more firmly the commonalities that those born overseas had with those of a similar background. We know that some immigrants did very well after their arrival in Britain, and this is reflected in settlement patterns in Manchester in particular. Those still in the poorer areas ten or more years after their arrival had either failed to make this step to greater economic security (which is out of line with the suggestion that Jews were generally upwardly mobile in this period), or they were choosing to remain in areas where they felt at home in some other sense. Religion and culture likely formed an important aspect of this sense of identity, especially given that Jews did not always share the occupational characteristics of their neighbours. By grouping themselves in this way, Jews also conformed to the predicted pattern of dispersal of minorities, clustering in identifiable 'wedges' moving outwards from the central business district. Groups of lower socio-economic status tend not to move far beyond the narrow 'V' of the wedge, while greater prosperity – and arguably greater assimilation – bring a dispersal outwards, towards the edge of the outward arc.[52] However, while the Jews did tend to move away from the town centre as they became more prosperous, they were at this stage dispersed in several small clusters around the suburbs.

Choice worked in other ways, too. Migration studies have shown that the working classes were often very mobile, but that they tended to remain in the same area.[53] In the middle ranks – the professional and intermediate occupations – people are the least likely to move, presumably because the advantages of remaining near their businesses or practices outweighed the social benefits of trading up. These factors would explain some of the patterns in the Jewish dataset, whereby the more affluent had moved further from the centre, at least in Liverpool and Manchester, while others in the more intermediate skill categories had remained in the centre, particularly in Manchester and Birmingham. This, naturally, had an impact on the stability of the local community, although this could be compensated for if movers had another reason to remain associated with the community they had left behind – such as joint membership of a religious or welfare network. These would inevitably start to fragment as new synagogues were built in the new areas of settlement, however. Wealth, therefore, certainly had a big impact when it came to choice of residence, but we should not discount the affinity that people could develop for parts of town where they felt most at home; hence the tendency identified by Vaughan and Penn for lower-class Jews to congregate in Red Bank, which was spatially cut off from the main town facilities, but which afforded insulation from the growing levels of prejudice outside.[54]

## Cultural and family factors

Pooley's study of Liverpool migrants in 1871 also highlighted the importance of what he called cultural explanations for residential patterns. He focused on the most measurable of these: the incidence of intermarriage with other groups, the composition of migrant-headed households, the strength of religious organizations and attitudes to the migrant group from the outside.[55] The Welsh exhibited the strongest cultural bonds and least degree of intermixing with others which, he suggested, is 'evidence of cultural insularity and ... a positive action to preserve a Welsh identity in an alien environment'.[56] Furthermore, the Welsh attracted little negative attention from outside, which could be another way of cementing an ethnic identity. The migrant Scots had a lesser incidence of all of these cultural markers, perhaps because of the lack of a widely used separate language or a specific church, and they were also internally more divided on geographical and economic lines. This, Pooley suggested, may have led to more assimilation with the host population, as did their frequent prior experience of urban life. The Irish, in contrast, despite their commonly understood internal cultural coherence, had no widespread common language or exclusive churches. Cultural affiliation was instead spread via informal centres like public houses, which are harder to build into a model of networks and internal ties. The strong sense of community within the working-class Irish population might also have been the result of the antipathy from the host population; it certainly had an impact on patterns of settlement.[57]

In many respects the Jewish population show the greatest similarity with the Welsh in Pooley's study. Jews rarely married outside the faith in this period, they tended to take in Jewish lodgers or to lodge alongside fellow Jews, and their places of worship were highly distinctive and exclusive.[58] We know that not all Jews attended synagogue and that relatively small numbers did leave the faith.[59] However, overall, it seems that most either remained affiliated to a synagogue, or (judging by the demand placed on the synagogues at the High Holy Days) at least culturally attached to some aspects of worship.[60] Meanwhile, centralized bodies like the Office of the Chief Rabbi and the Board of Deputies meant that there were focal points for British Jewry, while the emergence of the *Jewish Chronicle* gave it a public voice. As subsequent chapters will show, there was also a burgeoning number of Jewish educational and charitable associations to support the poor and ensure that the young grew up with a good knowledge of their heritage and position as British Jews. These gave cultural focus for the elite too, via committee work and fundraising events. Distinctive Jewish cultural organizations were less conspicuous in the provincial towns at this stage, largely because the more culturally inclined chose to integrate with secular societies (membership of which could be a useful way to assimilate into more mixed circles). However, much informal association took place within the small groups known as *chevroth*, which were generally composed of immigrants originating from the same place, and which offered religious and social support functions.

In terms of cultural prejudice, mid-century provincial Jewry was again more akin to the Welsh than the Irish. Although some of the immigrant Jews did appear very different from the native-born British (or native-born Jews) in terms of dress and language, as was suggested in Chapter 1, they do not in the 1850s seem to have elicited enough negative attention to be classed as a threatening 'other'. There was a set of cultural attributes in circulation which made a negative stereotype of the Jew easy to recognize – but this was at least partially balanced by an appreciation of their economic utility. Furthermore, in terms of civic status, immigrant Jews could earn a parish settlement (which entitled them to poor relief) as any new arrival could; those with sufficient resources were taxed for local rates and they could and did hold local office as mayors and councillors. There is therefore considerable reason to think that the Jewish population as a whole did form what Pooley calls an 'ethnic community', with strong internal ties rather than those imposed from without.

The rest of this section takes a slightly different approach to the investigation of social and cultural influences on residential patterns, by mapping kin relationships between households. Proximity of family is often overlooked in historical studies of community, partly because it is very onerous and time-consuming to trace, especially down the maternal line when names change on marriage, and also where populations were large. Exceptions, such as those by Michael Anderson for mid-nineteenth-century Preston, Barry Reay for rural Kent, or Wrightson and Levine for Terling, tend to reveal high levels of kin-connectedness between households.[61] The exercise is made more possible for the provincial Jewish communities because they were so self-contained in nature, and also because the AJDB contains some parental names of adults. Proximity of family is important because, as Katherine Lynch has pointed out, it is 'the most important single determinant of kin solidarity'; that is, access to useful and reliable networks.[62] It is also a particularly useful approach for a population with a large proportion of migrants, because of the role of family in chain migration. Having kin nearby could be a vital way to acclimatize and gain knowledge of a new environment, and could also be a key explanatory factor in people's choice of where to live – especially if they lacked other support networks.

Tracking kin relationships beyond the household requires significantly more intensive work than mapping relationships within it. It necessitates partial family reconstitution in order to identify parents, siblings, aunts, uncles and cousins, and then to trace them to their own households where possible. Jews, naturally, do not feature in parish registers; many marriages (vital for giving the wife's maiden name and the names of her parents) took place abroad, or prior to the start of civil registration in 1837, and with such a high proportion of the population born overseas we cannot utilize birth registration for information on parents' names either. We must rely, therefore, almost exclusively on the detail provided by the contributors to the AJDB. Fortunately, many of these were engaged in community-level micro studies and had a deep underlying familiarity with the connections between local families. Others consulted documents like naturalization papers and synagogue marriage registers, which do provide parents' names. Nonetheless, in most cases, it was only possible to track parents and grown siblings; occasionally this could be extended laterally to uncles and aunts if the common parent was captured in the AJDB with details of all of their offspring. As a result, the following results on kinship ties beyond the household – while highly suggestive for patterns of connectedness – should be regarded as a minimum level. They also omit links where families were sharing a house (those revealed in the previous chapter) which comprised 21 to 26 per cent of all households.

Maps 3.11–3.13 present these household links graphically in the form of a map-based sociogram. This is a form of presentation borrowed from sociology, which depicts the connections between different 'nodes' (individuals or households in the current case) in a network. It is an effectively simple way to illustrate relationships, and in its most advanced form can depict flows of information, influence and friendship, as well as the centrality of particular nodes and the completeness of the network.[63] Most of these are beyond the current evidence. However, since family provide the most reliable contacts in terms of support, we are almost certainly capturing some of the most valuable links in the network.

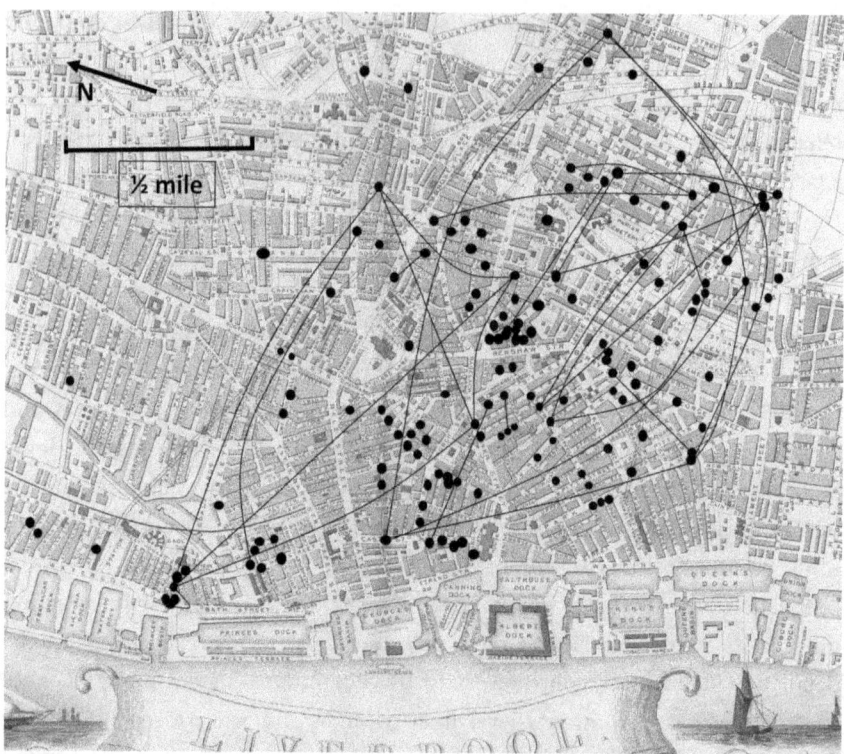

**Map 3.11** Kin links between Jewish households in Liverpool, 1851.

Source: AJDB/Census database. Map from *The Illustrated Atlas, and Modern History of the World.*

**Table 3.2** Jewish households with family elsewhere in the town, 1851

|  | Liverpool | Manchester | Birmingham |
| --- | --- | --- | --- |
| N households with family elsewhere in the town | 36 | 28 | 48 |
| Total number of households | 159 | 278 | 222 |
| % with family ties | 22.6 | 10.1 | 21.6 |

Source: AJDB/census database

As Table 3.2 shows, between 10 and 23 per cent of Jewish households were definitely related to at least one other household in the town.[64] This is much lower than Reay found for his rural Kent parishes for a similar period (where 60 per cent of households were related to other households), and also for Wrightson and Levine's study of the Essex village of Terling for an earlier century (39 to 53 per cent), where the authors characterize household links as 'loose'.[65] In Preston,

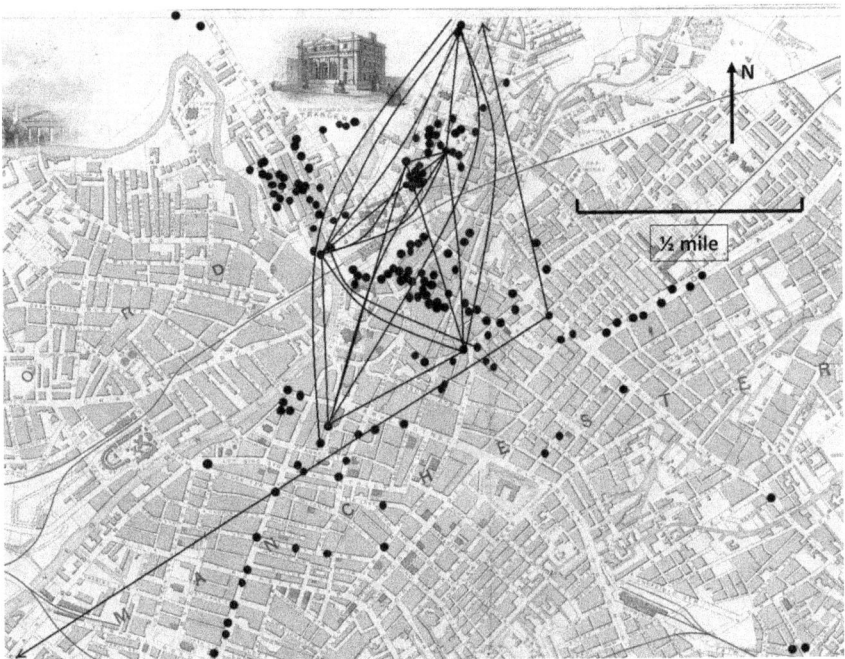

**Map 3.12** Kin links between Jewish households in Manchester, 1851.
Source: AJDB/Census database. Map from *The Illustrated Atlas, and Modern History of the World*.

Anderson traced only eighty cases out of 1,700 where households were definitely linked by kinship, but he speculates that 'many, perhaps even a majority, of people did deliberately live near one or more kinsmen and many others probably tried to'.[66] Links in Manchester were particularly uncommon, partly because the proportion of migrants was notably high here, and partly because the settled Jewish community was of more recent origin than those in Liverpool and Birmingham (several Manchester families had kin in Liverpool, whence many of its founding members had come). Manchester also had the highest rates of co-residence with kin of all three towns, suggesting that family connections may have worked in different ways here. If we add in all the households containing wider kin, then 30 to 40 per cent could have had family in the town. In reality it was likely to lie somewhere between the two extremes since some families with co-resident kin were probably also connected to other households, as will be illustrated below.

Maps 3.11 to 3.13 show all of the links that could be traced and mapped; some could not be pinned down precisely because an address was not provided in the AJDB or it could not be located; or because (in Manchester)

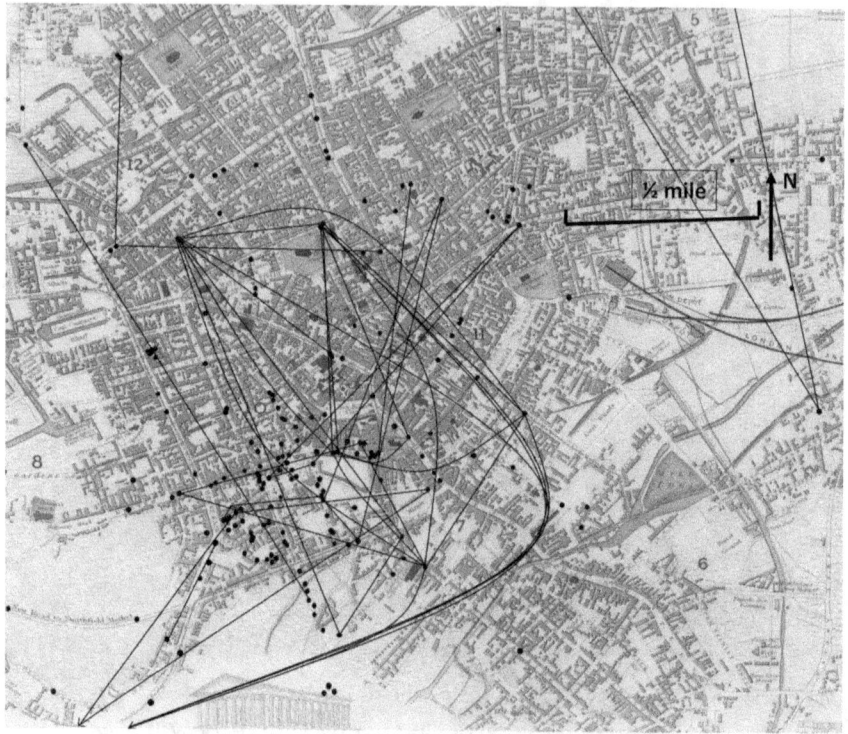

**Map 3.13** Kin links between Jewish households in Birmingham, 1851.

Source: AJDB/Census database. Map from *The Illustrated Atlas, and Modern History of the World*. Note: the scale of this map has been adjusted to show the direction of the households at a greater distance from the centre.

one or more addresses lay beyond the area of the map (these areas are shown in Map 3.4). It is readily apparent, however, that in most cases such ties linked pairs of households (twenty households in Liverpool, eighteen in Manchester and twelve in Birmingham). These tended to be either pairs of grown siblings with their own families, or grown children with parents and sibling/s living together in another home. In Manchester it was somewhat less likely that older parents were also living in the town, either because they had died, or because they were elsewhere.

All three towns also housed family networks that spanned three or more households. In Liverpool there were ten sets of families linked across three addresses; most of them were sibling sets, like Charles Mozley (senior warden at the OHC), who lived with his wife and children at 123 Mount Pleasant and had brothers nearby at Sandon Terrace and Abercrombie Square. A further three families had other types of relatives in the town, including cousins and a nephew. The three-household networks in Birmingham were somewhat more likely to involve the elder generation than was the case in Liverpool – three of nine sets. This suggests that they had been in the town for a long time, with the grown children moving out to form their own households.

As the kin networks become more complex and extensive they inevitably spotlight the longest-resident families – who, in turn, were often the community elite. Thus, five of the seven families spread across four homes in Liverpool were from the wealthy Samuel clan, whose association with the town had begun with the arrival of brothers Louis and Moses in the early years of the century, when Moses was still a child.[67] Louis and his wife Henrietta were living in London at the time of the census, as were four of their six living children. The remaining two, Edwin Louis and Elizabeth, were both in Liverpool: Edwin in his own house on Castle Street with his sister and niece who were visiting from London, and Elizabeth (age eight) living with her aunt, Kate Yates, and her family on Huskisson Street.[68] Their uncle Moses, meanwhile, was recorded in Southport in 1851, although he may have been visiting his eldest daughter there since his addresses in both 1841 and 1861 were in Liverpool. His other four children (all born in Liverpool in the 1820s) were all living in the town in 1851 with their families. This was a well-established British-Jewish family of high status in the community, who took up many of the offices in the synagogue and communal charities. Their households also neatly illustrate some of the fluidity inherent within the nuclear family which was set out in Chapter 2.

The four siblings from the Mayer family present a similar story in Manchester: Nathan, Saul, Fanny and Rachael, who were all married with children. The three eldest were born in Poland and arrived in Britain with their father in the 1820s; Rachael was born after they had settled in Staffordshire. Saul and Fanny lived close to one another on Swan Street in 1851, while Rachael was off Deansgate, a little to the south, and Nathan was in Cheetham Hill. We might imagine that Saul and Fanny, living a few houses apart, were likely to have been intimate parts of each other's lives, especially given that between them they had eight children under the age of nine by the end of 1851. There are other reasons, too, to think that this family spent time together: Fanny's husband, Louis Beaver, and two of her brothers were among the group of 'sharp, ambitious, competitive, self-made men of the city centre and the Old Town' who were instrumental in registering grievances with the Old Congregation in the 1840s.[69] Saul and Nathan Mayer were among the founders of the (Reform) Manchester Congregation of British Jews a few years after the census was taken, and Nathan was on the committee of the Manchester Jewish Board of Guardians in 1869.[70]

The two clans with the largest number of links had connections in several directions. The Manchester Sampsons, for instance, were spread over six addresses: parents and four children (living on St Chad's Place, off York Street, at the base of Cheetham Hill Road); two grown sons with their own families (both on or just off York Street); and another two living separately as lodgers. One of the married sons (Samuel, who was to go on to be president of the Old Hebrew Congregation in the 1870s) had a sister-in-law living with her Liverpool-born husband and their children on St Ann's Square in the market district. The most remarkable family in terms of inter-household connections, however, was that of the Birmingham Aarons, who were spread over nine addresses. While they did not have quite the status of the Manchester Sampsons or the Liverpool Samuelses, the Aarons were similarly enmeshed in many of the community committees and networks, and other branches of the family had professional status as doctors.[71] In all three cases, then, the management of the more formal aspects of the Jewish network did frequently go with long residence; the adult Aaronses had all been born in Birmingham (including the matriarch, Maria, who was aged seventy in 1851). Four of the adult heads of households shared the occupation of pawnbroker.

Maria's own household was a classically fluid family. She lived at 18–19 Edgbaston Street, in the heart of the Jewish area of settlement, with her 32-year-old son Isaac, an unmarried sister-in-law, a three-year-old granddaughter, Sarah, whose parents lived elsewhere in the town, and a non-Jewish servant. Seven other grown children were spread across five households in the town. Four lived with their spouses and children – including young Sarah's parents and five other children under twelve, who had evidently only fairly recently resettled in Birmingham (the youngest child, age two, had been born, like most of Sarah's siblings, on the south coast). Two other sons and a daughter lived together on Colmore Row, about half a mile to the north. Two of the households also had connections via the other side of the family. The adult son of Nathan Cohen Spiers's first marriage (his second wife was Sophia (née Aaron)) lived alone elsewhere in Birmingham, and their live-in shop assistant, Ellen Jacob (possibly a relative of Nathan's), also had parents and a sister at other addresses, as well as siblings in London, Shropshire and Sheffield. Morris Aaron's wife, Abigail (who had been born into another Aaron family in the town), meanwhile, had close kin in two other Birmingham households: her father and several siblings in one house also on Edgbaston Street, and a sister on Exeter Row.

Communal records, which we will explore in greater detail in later chapters, again offer some hard proof that this large family occupied a central place within the organized Jewish community in the town.[72] Maria's son John Aaron (always described as 'junior' in the records, to distinguish him from his sister-in-law Juliana's father, who had the same name and was also active in the community) was elected President of the Hebrew Philanthropic Society in 1851; he was also involved in later years with the Jewish school and donated eighteen cloth caps to it in 1866. His elder brother Morris sat on the committee of the synagogue in 1851; his sister Sophia's husband was on several communal committees in the 1840s and 1850s, was elected treasurer of the congregation in 1851 and stood security for at least one loan application to the Hebrew Philanthropic Society; and his sister Clara's husband was president of the Philanthropic Society in 1836, and president of the congregation in 1847. The snapshot that we see of this family in 1851 represents them at the centre of a communal network which is reflected in their size and interconnectedness as well as their extracurricular activities.

The maps also allow us to examine how close by the members of these kin networks were to one another. Given that proximity is an important influence on how useful and well used such connections were, this is an important consideration. A few linked households were very close indeed: widowed Rosina Nathan and her four grown children at number 50 Bold Street in Liverpool, for example, were less than two hundred yards from their son and brother, Mosely, and his young family at 42 Seel Street.[73] Lewis and Frances Woolf at 8 Russell Terrace were a similarly short distance away from Frances's sister at 96 Faulkner Street (she also had a brother in Liverpool, at 19 Slater Street, just under a mile away). On the dockside, Samuel and Esther Barnet and their four children at 12 Waterloo Road were only a street or two away from relatives at number 5 Greenock Street. Others had a slightly longer walk, although almost none of the linked households were more than a mile apart from one another. The most scattered was the Samuel nexus described above, who were all between a mile and a mile and a half apart, probably reflecting the greater degree of choice available to those with more financial capital (still, it is interesting that their choices took them in different directions). None of these distances would have taken more than half an hour to travel on foot, so they did not preclude regular contact, but may have ruled out regular informal visits such as characterize a close neighbourhood. This family probably had less urgent need of the sort of material aid cited for working-class neighbourhoods, though, and they were also more likely to have carriages for longer distances. Moreover, other evidence suggests that the men likely met regularly over synagogue business given how often their names appear on committees. The Birmingham Aarons were not particularly close to each other either, geographically speaking, with several households in further-flung Aston and Edgbaston. However, several others were closer to half a mile apart, and, again, regular contact was maintained via their committee work. There were other families who lived in much closer proximity: two linked households at numbers 2 and 12 Thorpe Street, for example, and another cluster on Digbeth, Colmore Row and Edgbaston Street.

The maps make it clear that some families were well connected with other households in the same town, and in many cases proximity would have made ad hoc help like lending, borrowing and childcare very feasible. In some of the more elite examples we can also see that regular contact was kept up via the network of community business. Some of these household heads were probably central to the networks utilized by the community more widely, acting as gatekeepers of resources and knowledge, and – as charity subscribers – also perhaps providing a link between richer and poorer households.[74] There is a limit to how far we can push the evidence to support the idea of a wider social network; we would need more information on other connections and interactions to do that, female as well as male.[75] It would also be instructive to understand more about the connections between Jewish and non-Jewish houses in the same neighbourhood, although this would be even more difficult to capture.[76] But the evidence has still revealed an aspect of intra-community relationship which has not been studied for this period before, or in such a comparative way. It has also pointed to similarities and differences between the three towns, not only in degrees of connectedness, but also in patterns of dispersal which suggest links with social status and length of time in the town.

We should not lose sight of the fact that the majority of Jewish households did not have identifiable links with any others in the same town (81 per cent in Manchester, although some of these had relatives living with them). This is partly because of the paucity of evidence on parents' names in the AJDB, but it also reflects the high proportion of migrants, who were less likely to have extended family with them. It would be wonderful to know how this affected their experience of urban life and whether it was a hindrance to getting by, or getting on. On the other hand, we should also not overstate the degree of isolation from family experienced by those with no other kin in the town. The linkage exercise revealed that many had relatives elsewhere in Britain: in London or other provincial towns. Four of the Liverpool families had relatives in Birmingham and six in Manchester, for example, while others had family connections in a range of smaller towns like Portsmouth, Plymouth and Canterbury.[77] Nor should the census snapshot be allowed to convey a sense that lives in the town were static. Liverpool jeweller Joseph Joseph and his wife Phoebe, for example, had been born, respectively, in Falmouth and Plymouth, and were aged fifty and thirty-eight in 1851 when they were found at 19 Slater Street in Liverpool. The birthplaces of their nine children (whose ages ranged from twenty-one to infancy – the last was actually born just after the census) maps out an itinerant life: Bristol, Frome, Bristol, New York and Liverpool. Both had siblings living elsewhere in the country too: Newcastle upon Tyne, Penzance and Plymouth. The family of fellow Liverpudlians, oil and pickle dealer Joseph Charles Lyons and his wife Esther, meanwhile, had been taking a tour around industrial towns by the time they settled in Liverpool for the births of their three youngest children: the elder four were born in Liverpool, Hull and Manchester respectively. It is easy to see how families like these could become isolated from regular contact with kin, but it is not to say that they did not have people to turn to.

## Conclusions

We opened the chapter with two Liverpool families, both named Samuel. They lived in very different parts of town and had very different backgrounds. Neither had close relatives in the town, as far as can be traced, but both lived near to other Jewish households, and to the Seel Street synagogue, albeit approaching from opposite directions. What, then, has this chapter suggested about the social networks of these and the other families living in mid-century Liverpool, Manchester and Birmingham?

The first point to note is that there is strong evidence in all three locations of discernible clusters of Jews in one or more parts of town. In most cases this had a socio-economic element too, with the better-off and better-established Jews living separately from the poorer families. Even in Birmingham, where such clustering was initially least evident, this becomes apparent when we dig down into the sub-registration districts and place them alongside measures of affluence. However, the population density of the Jews at this time, and their mixed socio-economic status, meant that there is little sense that this approached the (voluntary) Jewish 'ghetto' discussed in later decades in the context of London, Manchester and Leeds. We will return to this as part of a discussion of housing conditions in the next chapter.

In terms of underlying reasons for residential patterns, the evidence points both to economic and cultural factors at work. Occupational skill status and overseas birth both show discernible patterns, but they also highlight some distinctive points in different towns. In Manchester, for example, where much of the community elite was foreign-born, the distinction based on overseas birth was much less clear-cut than elsewhere. In Birmingham in particular, there is evidence of considerable intermingling of socio-economic groups at a neighbourhood level, while Jewish families in the poor Red Bank area frequently employed servants. Economic factors can explain a lot, but there are limits. Social and cultural factors are harder to quantify from this distance, but the clustering seen in the maps suggests strongly that there was some advantage to living near to other Jews, whether for religious reasons (Williams characterizes Manchester's Jewish Red Bank as held together by religious observance, for instance[78]) or the reassurance that came from contact with people of similar cultures, or because an ethnic social network had promoted recommendations for those areas. One aspect of belonging to a community is that one wishes to emulate others and live close to people with whom one has characteristics in common, after all. This would also promote the patterns seen here, and which were further built on in later decades.

The most novel way of measuring social ties used here was the mapping of family connections between households. This showed that – in the context of a population with many migrants – many families did have kin in the same town and that some of these were close neighbours. Others lived further away but clearly met regularly in the course of their social, business and religious lives. Williams cites evidence of regular socializing within the Jewish elite in Manchester, and also of the 'warmth and informality' of the immigrant households in Red Bank by 1860, which adds some more colour to this impression.[79] We know little about how Jews found places to live (at least one Jewish landowner rented houses to fellow Jews in Manchester[80]), but advertisements for vacant rooms placed in the *Jewish Chronicle* suggest that a range of formal and informal networks were in play.

One of the key characteristics of a social network is that it facilitates the spread of information and goods. Here, we can only go so far with family ties, but the snippets of information added from synagogue and charity records start to illustrate how much deeper these went, giving these connected individuals a multiplex role within the network, as members both of established families, and by extension also of the community hierarchy. Such ties thus served not only to cement people's identity as part of a network, but also helped the network to function more effectively. Membership of one type of system (religion and family) could bring membership of others (power and status). Further down the social scale, where communal influence was further from reach (partly because of the deliberately closed nature of the elites in most of the provincial towns), we would need to look to economic ties to replace this multiplexity, or the sharing of neighbourhood spaces.

At this stage in the history of provincial Jewry, population density meant that Jews were still highly likely to live alongside non-Jews. They did not necessarily share the same demographic characteristics as their non-Jewish neighbours: they tended to have larger families, employed servants more frequently and more often shared their houses with lodgers. Nonetheless, in their social and daily lives they were likely to encounter non-Jews frequently, share common spaces, frequent the same shops and social institutions, and hear their language, accents and dialect on a regular basis. If kin and religious ties did provide an anchor for many of these people – as their residential patterns both at a household and a neighbourhood level suggest – they must also have had to operate in a more mixed cultural environment. It is thus possible that their housing arrangements – often close to other Jews or actually alongside them, and near to synagogues, Jewish schools and charity headquarters – allowed them to function at this dual level, reinforcing their cultural identity in its broadest sense, while also permitting some level of integration into the wider society. Vaughan draws a similar conclusion for London's East End in the 1890s, which she relates to use of the city's space and access routes. Thus, residential patterns can reinforce 'imagined' or 'transpatial' community identities as well as local, spatially anchored ones.[81] This could balance out the tendency for an exclusive social network to shape its members' interests to the exclusion of other influences.

So far we have been dealing with measures of community integration; the existence of a common cultural and interconnected set of links between individuals which could sum to something approaching a network. In the next chapter we will turn to another measure of community cohesion: the occupational profile of the provincial Jews. This was another way in which Jews could present a distinctive profile to outsiders, especially if they occupied their own niche within the occupational profile of the town. On the other hand, it also presented opportunities to blend in, to diversify their frame of reference and enhance the outward-looking aspect of their identity.

4

# Occupations, poverty and wealth

We have had many hints so far that the Jewish communities in the manufacturing towns were not as poor as other minority groups like the Irish, but also that they did not take part in the full range of occupations on offer in the industrial sector. On the other hand we have also had suggestions of considerable wealth at the top end of society. In this chapter we move this perspective on further by focusing on the economic characteristics of the three larger communities considered in this book. In particular, the chapter is concerned with two key questions. The first is how far the Jews mirrored local employment patterns as opposed to retaining a distinctive occupational profile of their own. The second is how this mapped on to housing conditions and personal wealth or poverty. The two questions together allow us to spotlight another way to understand community cohesion and the place of the community in the wider industrial setting. They also lay the foundation for the consideration of communal resources and risks of poverty in subsequent chapters.

## Jews and the industrial economy

Other studies have suggested that British Jews remained focused in non-industrial occupations in this period (such as dealing and non-industrial manufacture), or alternatively – at the other end of the social scale – that they were concentrated in banking and financial sectors.[1] Local studies, meanwhile, have tended not to relate Jewish patterns of employment to wider trends.[2] The current approach allows us to compare Jewish occupations directly with those around them by using a common occupational classification, and also to examine them in the context of the opportunities offered in the 'shock' cities of the mid-nineteenth century. To this end, the occupations of Jews in Manchester, Birmingham and Liverpool were coded according to the scheme developed by Tony Wrigley for the 'Occupational Structure of Britain c.1379–1911' project.[3] This is a refinement of the much-utilized Booth–Armstrong classification, which is based on division into primary (agriculture and mining), secondary (manufacturing) and tertiary (dealing, retail and services) sectors of the economy. The data are supplemented with an additional taxonomy designed by Petra Laidlaw specifically for the AJDB.[4] This was created to address the fact that British Jewry do not conform to the balance of occupations seen in England and Wales more generally: for example, they had little participation in the primary sector but were over-represented in trades and services. The

Table 4.1 Occupational sectors in Manchester, Birmingham and Liverpool (all residents and Jews both sexes and all ages), 1851 (%)

|  | Liverpool | | Manchester | | Birmingham | |
| --- | --- | --- | --- | --- | --- | --- |
|  | All | Jews | All | Jews | All | Jews |
| Primary | 0.8 | 0.0 | 0.8 | 0.0 | 0.8 | 0.0 |
| Secondary | 17.1 | 13.0 | 33.1 | 15.2 | 31.7 | 18.3 |
| Tertiary | 24.4 | 22.5 | 16.5 | 14.8 | 15.2 | 21.2 |
| Unspecified | 3.4 | 0.1 | 1.8 | 0.4 | 1.7 | 0.2 |
| No occupation | 54.3 | 64.1 | 47.9 | 69.6 | 50.6 | 60.3 |
| Total | 100 | 100 | 100 | 100 | 100 | 100 |
| N | 375,955 | 843 | 401,321 | 1,295 | 232,841 | 906 |
| **Primary, secondary and tertiary sectors only** | | | | | | |
| Primary | 2.0 | 0.0 | 1.5 | 0.0 | 1.6 | 0.0 |
| Secondary | 40.4 | 37.1 | 66.8 | 50.6 | 66.4 | 46.4 |
| Tertiary | 57.6 | 62.9 | 32.7 | 49.4 | 31.9 | 53.6 |
| N | 159,120 | 302 | 201,885 | 389 | 111,062 | 358 |
| **Tertiary sector only** | | | | | | |
| Dealing and selling | 14.3 | 55.8 | 17.6 | 62.5 | 16.4 | 80.2 |
| Services | 85.7 | 44.2 | 82.4 | 37.5 | 83.7 | 19.8 |
| N | 91,691 | 190 | 66,103 | 288 | 35,462 | 192 |

Source: AJDB/census database; 'Occupational structure of Britain' database.[5]

combination of the two schemes is particularly helpful for our current purposes as it allows for the most robust comparison of the Jewish urban population with those around them, while grafting on a measure of what this meant in terms of localized skill level.

Table 4.1 presents an overview of the occupational structure of the Jewish communities in the three provincial towns, alongside the full populations of the towns. It confirms immediately that Jews did not participate in the primary sector, even compared to the small size of this area of the job market in the industrial towns more generally. This is in keeping with the types of skills and experience that Jewish immigrants brought with them, but it is even more magnified in these three towns than it is for the AJDB as a whole, where Laidlaw's scheme places twenty-seven individuals in the primary sector, mainly from the London area.[6] A second factor of note is the larger proportion of Jews with no occupation given: around a half compared with approximately a third of the populations around them. As we will see below, this was connected with the much lower proportion of Jewish women and children described as employed in the census.

Jews also differed from their townsmen and women in their much lesser engagement with the manufacturing sector, especially in Manchester. This is important as it signals a lesser integration into the newer modes of industrial work, which was such a characteristic feature of the local occupational network in these towns. It may also relate to the areas of town where Jews lived: in Manchester, for example, they were not clustered in the areas of densest industrial development, but instead in the commercial areas. Since work is thought to be one of the keenest explanatory variables when it comes to residence, this could be an early pointer to their existing skills and preferences. In dealing, selling and services, however (the tertiary sector), Jews were proportionately more on a par with those around them, and exceeded them in Birmingham.

If we focus solely on the primary, secondary and tertiary sectors (the middle panel of Table 4.1), to avoid the distorting impact of those with no occupation, we can see the underlying patterns a little more clearly. Now it becomes particularly obvious that the Jews in Manchester and Birmingham had an inverted representation across the secondary and tertiary sectors compared with their fellow townspeople. In both of these towns, two-thirds of all residents working in these sectors were in manufacturing jobs, with a little under a third in tertiary occupations. Among the Jews, however, around a half or more were in dealing, retail and services. We should not understate the importance of manufacturing as a direct provider of jobs for Jews; in Manchester it was (narrowly) the largest sector for employment. Nonetheless, it did not dominate to the extent that it did in the local population more generally, probably reflecting a spectrum of factors from cultural preferences, discrimination and prior skills (or lack of[7]). It was almost certainly easier to enter the retail than the manufacturing sector, not least because with a small amount of capital, one could set up on one's own – and perhaps crucially, set one's own hours of work.[8] Immigrant Jews did not tend to have experience of factory work and newcomers would also have lacked contacts to secure a job in such an unfamiliar sector, which also depended on set hours of work.[9] Information sharing and sympathetic attitudes to the requirements of the Jewish calendar then further magnified the pull of certain areas of work which did accommodate Jewish skills and preferences, potentially creating distinctive patterns of work.

Within the tertiary sector, too, the Jews were quite distinctive compared with those around them (the lower panel of Table 4.1). In all three towns, the vast majority of people in this area of work generally were in services (especially domestic service), to the order of 80 per cent or more. Among the Jews, however, this was much lower, at 44 per cent in Liverpool, but only 20 per cent in Birmingham, and with a correspondingly inflated presence in dealing and retail. We will return to this below.

So far so distinctive as far as Jewish employment was concerned. However, there are other ways in which the Jews' occupations did reflect the economic profile of the towns in which they lived. We see this in their raised presence in manufacturing in Manchester compared with the other towns, and even more notably in their increased gravitation towards dealing and services in Liverpool. Liverpool was quite a different type of industrial town than the manufacturing hubs; in particular, its wealth was built on shipping and services rather than making goods and processing raw materials. This is reflected in the inverted prominence of the secondary and tertiary sectors in this town compared with the other two – and an even larger representation of tertiary jobs among the Jews than elsewhere (over 60 per cent of the employed population). This presents the important suggestion that in broad terms Jews did adapt their employment to fit the available opportunities, whether by moving to towns with jobs that fitted their skills, or simply by taking up what was on offer in the local employment market. Such a tendency was then perpetuated within the broader Jewish community because flows of information encouraged people to follow where fellow Jews had had success.

That said, the Jews in the sample did specialize in certain areas, some of which were to become even more distinctively identified as 'Jewish trades' in

**Table 4.2** Most common Jewish occupations: manufacture and trade (N in parentheses), 1851

| Liverpool | Manchester | Birmingham |
|---|---|---|
| **Manufacturing** | | |
| Clock and watch maker (38) | Tailor (54) | Tailor (25) |
| Tailor (13) | Cap maker (42) | Glazier (21) |
| Tobacco (12) | Watchmaker (12) | Wool/worsted manufacture (13) |
| | Shoe/boot maker (11) | Slipper maker (12) |
| | Glazier (10) | Shoe/boot maker (12) |
| **Dealing/retail** | | |
| Traveller/hawker (24) | Merchant (71) | Traveller/hawker (40) |
| Grocer (11) | Traveller/hawker (46) | Pawnbroker (29) |
| Merchant (9) | Textile products (14) | Jeweller (18) |
| Jeweller (8) | Jeweller (10) | Merchant (18) |

Source: AJDB/census database; 'Occupational structure of Britain' database.

later decades. The most popular of these in the manufacture and dealing sectors are listed in Table 4.2.[10] Clothing manufacture, and especially tailoring, was conspicuous in all three towns, but particularly in Manchester, where 70 per cent all of Jews in manufacturing were in clothing.[11] This will partly have reflected the skills that immigrant Jews brought with them – tailoring was a common trade in the communities of Eastern Europe – but it is another suggestion that they chose specific towns in which to settle because of their specialization in areas where they could find work easily. However, it is clear that it was clothing rather than the ubiquitous Lancashire textiles that offered the most opportunities for Jews at mid-century. Tailors, glovers and hatters were also prominent (as well as cap makers in Manchester – as in London[12]), as was footwear manufacture in both Manchester and Birmingham. Jews were notably absent in all three towns from food and drink manufacture – possibly linked to a reluctance to deal with non-kosher foodstuffs.

According to Williams, several of these manufacturing occupations were relatively recent additions to the Jewish portfolio in Manchester in 1851, and many of them were skewed towards the bottom end of the social scale. Cap making, tailoring, slipper making, cabinetmaking, waterproofing and glazing all became features of the occupational profile of Red Bank in the later 1840s, often on a contracted piecework basis with whole families sharing tasks that required little in the way of skill.[13] Many Jewish tailors, for example, were doing piecework for mass production rather than skilled garment making, and often in conditions akin to the 'sweated' labour which was to be the focus of much negative attention in later decades.[14] On the other hand, it is also clear that such occupations offered the potential to boost the formation of tight kin and community links, with income, skills and knowledge shared among co-religionists with similar requirements for work. It is, however, clear that some of the most distinctively 'Jewish' occupations were not ones that promoted affluence: a point to which we will return.

The only other area of manufacturing in which Jews featured across the three towns was building, principally as glaziers and also, in Birmingham, as painters. Glazing – an itinerant occupation requiring only a few sheets of glass and a diamond to cut it to size – was yet another ubiquitous trade of young immigrants in the provinces, and one that will recur in future chapters.[15] Without wishing to read too much into the categories with smaller numbers (not shown), manufacture in precious metals and of jewellery stand out in Birmingham both among Jews and in the workforce more generally (the town was renowned for the manufacture of 'toys' like buttons and brooches, and had a vibrant jewellery quarter) – though also in Liverpool; as does clock- and watchmaking in all three Jewish communities, but particularly in Liverpool.[16] Again, this reflects prior expertise among Jews from Eastern Europe. In other respects, the Jews did not capitalize on local industries: they did not enter the high-profile iron and steel manufacturing sector in Birmingham, for example, just as they were largely absent from textile production in Manchester. This suggests again that Jews, in the provincial commercial cities at least, adapted existing skills rather than embracing new areas of work, or that certain sectors remained closed shops because of prejudice, working hours or problems of skill acquisition.[17] Generally, however, it is striking how far we can characterize the Jewish population in the manufacturing sector of these three towns in much the same terms as Laidlaw did for the London-dominated AJDB: that they were 'in essence, supplying consumer-facing parts of the economy, rather than industrial infrastructure'.[18] This is in keeping with their history of peddling and small retail, though we should not overlook the growing number of large-scale manufacturers and retailers in the commercial provincial communities. We will return to these in the context of the wealth base of the three communities.

In terms of trade, Jews were concentrated in similar sectors of the economy as they were as manufacturers: clocks and watches, jewellery, clothing, tobacco, plus an array of minor trades in consumer goods from umbrellas to artificial flowers.[19] The most distinctive aspect of the Jewish profile in trade, however, was the presence on the one hand of merchants (37 per cent of all those in dealing and retail in Manchester, 34 per cent in Birmingham and 15 per cent in Liverpool), and on the other, of itinerant sellers and hawkers (around 51 per cent in Birmingham and 35 per cent in Manchester and Liverpool). This bifurcation underlies some of the geographical patterns observed in the previous chapter. Only in Manchester were sellers of textile products at all common, all selling miscellaneous or cotton goods. Generally, though, it was much less common for Jews to be engaged in selling clothing or textiles than it was in manufacturing them. Precious metals and jewellery were again common products for Jews to be engaged with, especially in Birmingham, while grocers had a high profile in Liverpool, as was noted in the previous chapter. However, in all three cases the most prevalent type of goods sold by Jews were 'minor products', a testament, perhaps, to the 'commercial versatility' of the Jews: between 35 and 54 per cent of those in dealing and retail occupations.[20] The vast majority of these were the ubiquitous itinerant small traders we will meet frequently in subsequent chapters – peddlers, hawkers and travellers, plus a striking twenty-nine pawnbrokers in Birmingham.[21]

It is worth exploring the implications of the itinerant traders a little more, as Williams utilizes them as a way of measuring the progressively more settled nature of Manchester Jewry.[22] According to his evidence, the peddling of small goods, often beyond the town, was a common occupation for those using Manchester as a base early in the century. By the 1820s and 1830s, however, it was increasingly a failing occupation, with stricter requirements for licences, and progressively greater pressure from within the community to move into more 'respectable' occupations. Some individuals accumulated enough wealth to make the transition into more static (and respectable) forms of retail; others managed to switch to urban peddling – others fell into poverty and crime.[23] The current data show that hawking had certainly not disappeared in any of the three towns by 1851 – nor, as we will see in later chapters, had it ceased to be a concern for those higher up the social scale.[24] In Birmingham a contemporary described hawkers as still of the traditional type who returned to the town on Fridays to observe the Sabbath and collect more stock, before disappearing on their weekday pilgrimages further afield.[25] The emphasis on transition from hawking has perhaps thus been rather overstated, with the greatest changes in Jewish occupations still to come. Others may have used it only at slack times of year. On the other hand, Williams's suggestion that the support networks for the older style of hawking had disappeared by the 1840s may be useful in explaining why hawkers loom so large in the Jewish charity records.[26]

The number of Jews working in service jobs was quite small, especially in Birmingham. Again, however, there were discernible differences between the Jews and those around them (Table 4.3). First, bearing out the household patterns discussed in Chapter 2, there were tiny proportions of Jews in domestic service compared with almost a third of the wider population in all three towns. Second, there was a large over-representation of financial, commercial and administrative services: mainly clerks and agents, although with a number of bankers in the Liverpool population too. Jews were also well

Table 4.3 Occupations in the service sector, Jews and town populations (% of all individuals), 1851

|  | Liverpool | | Manchester | | Birmingham | |
| --- | --- | --- | --- | --- | --- | --- |
|  | All | Jews | All | Jews | All | Jews |
| Transport | 36.3 | 1.2 | 20.8 | 1.6 | 16.9 | 2.6 |
| Storage | 1.9 | 3.6 | 5.1 | 6.3 | 5.6 | 2.6 |
| Hotels, restaurants, lodging houses | 6.8 | 2.4 | 7.2 | 6.3 | 7.0 | 10.5 |
| Entertainment | 0.2 | 0.0 | 0.3 | 0.0 | 2.7 | 10.5 |
| Other service industries | 4.2 | 0.0 | 7.6 | 0.0 | 8.0 | 5.3 |
| Domestic service | 31.0 | 10.7 | 35.1 | 16.4 | 35.4 | 7.9 |
| Financial, commercial, administrative services | 5.9 | 34.5 | 8.3 | 40.6 | 6.7 | 29.0 |
| Professions | 5.3 | 22.6 | 7.3 | 25.0 | 9.4 | 21.1 |
| Church service | 0.1 | 0.0 | 0.1 | 0.0 | 0.1 | 0.0 |
| Local government service | 1.4 | 0.0 | 1.5 | 0.0 | 1.6 | 0.0 |
| National government service | 1.4 | 0.0 | 0.4 | 0.0 | 0.5 | 0.0 |
| Armed forces | 1.0 | 0.0 | 2.4 | 0.0 | 1.0 | 0.0 |
| Owners, possessors of capital | 3.9 | 16.7 | 3.3 | 3.9 | 4.7 | 7.9 |
| Titled gentlemen | 0.9 | 8.3 | 0.5 | 0.0 | 0.7 | 2.6 |
| N | 78,586 | 84 | 54,493 | 128 | 29,667 | 38 |

Source: AJDB/census database; 'Occupational structure of Britain' database.

represented in storage jobs, relative to their population size (most were working as warehousemen); and again in lodging houses and hotels (principally as lodging-house keepers). Few Jews worked in transport service jobs in the three towns (in contrast with London) and none was employed in local or national government – although small numbers were to take high-profile positions here in future decades – or in the armed forces. However, they held their own when it came to owning capital (particularly property), and especially in Liverpool, where there was also a small cluster of people described as 'gentleman' or 'gentlewoman'. Once again, the evidence points to the Jewish community in Liverpool containing an element which was both well off and well embedded in the local society. This will be an important point to develop when it comes to thinking in greater detail about wealth and poverty in the community.

In common with later periods, Jewish occupations were quite restricted in range compared with the wider population. Vaughan and Penn found, for example, a total of 190 occupations among male Jews in Manchester in 1881 compared with 377 for non-Jews.[27] Nor was there much overlap in the most common jobs between the two groups in 1881: only 5 per cent of Jewish men had occupations that were in the top ten most common of non-Jewish jobs, and the reverse was true as well, with only 8 per cent of non-Jewish heads doing jobs in the Jewish top ten (these were, ranked from the top in terms of popularity, tailors, glaziers, commercial travellers, cap making, jewellers and watchmakers, merchants, commission agents, cabinetmaking, pawnbrokers and waterproof makers).[28] The same pattern is true in the current data set as well, supporting the points already made about the distinctive niches occupied by the provincial urban Jews and their only limited interaction with the local economy. As Table 4.4 demonstrates, the most common occupations among adults in the three towns were quite different, both from each other and from the occupational profile of the Jewish population. The exceptions are some of the categories in the clothing and textile sector. The preponderance of labourers and domestic servants in the population at large is, however, almost entirely missing among the Jews, as are the specialized metalwork jobs in Birmingham, and those in sea transport and harbour work in Liverpool. In one respect the lack of labouring jobs among Jews implies that they avoided this residual, non-specific and likely unskilled (and seasonal) occupation. On the other hand, it is another reflection of the Jewish preference for itinerant dealing as their fall-back, and their lack of contacts in a world that relied heavily on personal introductions to get daily work. Dealing may have called for greater initial outlay in goods, but it permitted greater control over their own time. The narrower range of occupations found among

Jews may well also reflect tight networks of chain migration and information flow, with people recommending co-religionists as employees and preferentially employing those from their own homeland. These occupational clusters were strengthened by the small *chevroth*, which were often based on occupation as well as common place of origin.

The final group in the Wrigley/Booth–Armstrong scheme is the one noted at the outset: those without an occupation recorded. Here, as a proportion of the population, the Jews hugely over-represented those around them. In some cases these people were unemployed (or in receipt of institutional welfare or penal services), in others they were independently wealthy, and in others still – much more commonly – they were described only in terms like 'son', 'daughter' and 'wife'. Jews were rarely found listed in non-Jewish institutions in the census, and those who were often had their regular occupation given rather

**Table 4.4** Most common occupations among all adults (20+ years), in Manchester, Birmingham and Liverpool, 1851

| Liverpool | Manchester | Birmingham |
|---|---|---|
| Domestic service, house servant (18,596) | General cotton manufacture (42,503) | Domestic service, house servant (8,359) |
| Labourer (12,691) | Domestic service, house servant (14,016) | Iron and steel products (5,521) |
| Sailor (9,932) | Clothing manufacture (other) (8,853) | Clothing accessories (5,414) |
| Clothing manufacture (other) (9,639) | Silk manufacture (8,253) | Brass industries (5,161) |
| Navigation and harbour staff (7,793) | Labourer (7,092) | Precious metals and jewellery (4,785) |
| Boot/shoe maker (6,417) | Milliner (6,439) | Clothing manufacture, other (4,754) |
| Carpentry (5,615) | Cotton manufacturer (other) (5,787) | Shoe/boot manufacture (4,542) |
| Messenger (5,365) | Messenger/porter (5,510) | Labourer (3,972) |
| Tailor (3,455) | Engine maker (5,420) | Non-ferrous metal products, other (3,958) |
| Road transport (3,401) | Tailor (3,918) | Iron manufacture (other) (3,946) |
| Plasterer (3,110) | Carpentry (3,778) | Iron industries, general (2,015) |

Source: 'Occupational structure of Britain' database. Students and people classed as 'unspecified' are omitted. Agricultural labourers are in a different category from general labourers.

than describing them as paupers, patients or lunatics. This naturally affects the way that they are categorized: one Jew who was listed in the workhouse in Birmingham was recorded as a tailor rather than a pauper, for example, while a patient in the infirmary at Broughton (Manchester) went down on the census form as a 'dressmaker'. Only one Jew was recorded as a prisoner: his occupation was given as 'prisoner and hawker'.[29] Instead, 'scholars' and 'students' loomed large for Jews with no specific occupation given.

A large proportion of the people with no occupation recorded were women and children. Their status is thus worth some more investigation, not least because of what it implies about the size and diversity of individual household incomes. As Table 4.5 indicates, just over half of all women aged twenty and over in Manchester and Birmingham were recorded with no occupation in the census; in Liverpool it was just under a third. Among Jews, meanwhile, the figure was around three-quarters in all three cities. As a proportion of all adults, the figures were very similar among Jews and non-Jews, probably because women formed a smaller proportion of the total in the Jewish population.

Few Jewish children had a recorded employment (as distinct from an occupation such as 'scholar') either: only twenty of those aged sixteen and under in Manchester (4.8 per cent), twenty-five in Birmingham (6.8 per cent) and twenty-four in Liverpool (6.1 per cent) compared with considerably over 30 per cent in the population of England and Wales.[30] These fell fairly evenly between manufacturing, dealing/selling and services. The remaining Jewish youngsters either had no information recorded or were registered as scholars, although scholars were no more prominent as a proportion of the population

Table 4.5 Women (20+ years) with no stated occupation in Manchester, Birmingham and Liverpool, 1851

|  | Liverpool | | Manchester | | Birmingham | |
| --- | --- | --- | --- | --- | --- | --- |
|  | All | Jews | All | Jews | All | Jews |
| N | 69,099 | 148 | 63,619 | 174 | 38,823 | 159 |
| % of all women over 20 | 32.3 | 73.3 | 52.7 | 72.2 | 59.2 | 76.8 |
| % of total over 20 | 32.3 | 35.2 | 28.2 | 27.5 | 30.6 | 32.2 |
| % of adult population who were women | 52.6 | 48.0 | 53.5 | 38.1 | 51.7 | 41.9 |

Source: AJDB/census database; 'Occupational structure of Britain' database. Paupers, lunatics and similar were excluded.

than in the town more generally (10 to 14 per cent in all cases).³¹ This is still noteworthy given that Jewish schooling was in its infancy at this time; in earlier decades an even larger proportion of Jewish children would likely be returned with no occupational designation, or as in work. In 1851 no Jewish children under the age of twelve had a specific occupation noted and the majority in work were fourteen or older. Occupations included watch- and cap making, tobacco manufacture, hawking, grocery and pawnbroking. Some youngsters were specifically described as apprentices or assistants.

It is well known that the employment of women and children was understated in the census: the result of seasonal and part-time work, overlaid with a reluctance in some families to admit that the household could not survive on the income of the male head alone.³² Kerschen suggests that Jews were particularly reluctant to admit that they needed the income of their wives.³³ However, this does not seem entirely plausible: they were a diverse group after all, in terms of language, cultural expectations and experiences of work. It was, perhaps, just as likely that it was the census enumerators themselves who made assumptions about the working patterns of Jews. It is also possible that Jewish wives, sons and daughters worked in less formal settings than those around them, particularly if they had concerns about keeping dependents protected from non-Jewish culture. This could have resulted in family members not being designated with their own occupational descriptor on the census form while still making a vital contribution to the family income, as we saw with occupations like tailoring.³⁴ The under-reporting of women and children's work may thus be a reflection of the lack of engagement in the more industrial areas of the economy, where women especially were more likely to have named and regular jobs in their own right. The other, less likely, conclusion, given the impoverished state of many of their most common occupations, is that Jewish families did get by on the male breadwinner wage to a greater extent than their urban peers. In the absence of data on household incomes in this sector this is hard to test, although some of the information in the subsequent section will address the state of poor Jewish households.

Overall, it seems unlikely that Jewish women really did work as little as the census suggests, but there is evidence that single women and widows were more likely to be recorded with an occupational descriptor. This is in line with the legal position of married women (whose position was likely to be subsumed with that of their husband) versus the unmarried, and also with the likelihood of regular paid work at different points in the family life cycle. Thus, 53 per cent of Jewish widows in Manchester and 45 per cent of single adult women were employed according to the census forms, compared with only 20 per cent of those married.[35] In Birmingham the overall pattern was the same, although employment among both single and married women was lower than in Manchester (36 and 15 per cent, respectively), while in Liverpool widows were particularly likely to be in work (89 per cent). However, as was the case generally, Jewish women went into a restricted range of named jobs, in which clothing and small-scale selling were prominent.[36] Even in these areas, however, they did not predominate as much as they came to do later: Williams reports that almost a third of Jewish piecework tailors and more than this proportion of cap makers were women in Manchester in 1871.[37] In 1851 only 14 per cent of Jewish cap makers were women (six individuals) and 11 per cent of tailors (also six individuals). All of the five Jewish dressmakers were female.

## Wealth and poverty

The occupational information has presented some clear patterns of Jewish employment. One of the themes to emerge is the degree of diversity across the socio-economic scale, from bankers at one end, to glaziers at the other. In this section we will push this finding a little further, to unpack what it meant for the relative wealth and poverty of the British-Jewish community more broadly. How large, for example, was the population of skilled and professional Jews, who might be called upon to invest in community funds for the poor? How unstable were the occupations of those at the other end of the social scale, who were never more than a few steps from failing to make ends meet? And – vitally – did the resources of the former stretch far enough to accommodate the needs of the latter? This last question will be best answered via an examination of Jewish charities in the following two chapters. There is considerably more to be said, however, about the affluence (or otherwise) of the Jewish population in the three sampled towns. In this section, the occupational data will be examined alongside contemporary comments about the nature of Jewish employment, health and housing conditions.

Naturally, any identification of a community 'elite' must rely on occupational descriptors which could potentially cover a very wide range of wealth. While we can safely assume that the propertied and professional were at least reasonably and securely provided for, other descriptors hid a great deal of diversity.[38] 'Tailor' is a good example: at one end of the scale this could be an unskilled worker doing piecework; at the other end, a business proprietor employing a large workforce (like Manchester's Benjamin Hyam, who was described as a tailor and clothier in the census, but ran a business empire mass manufacturing clothing which spanned several cities by 1851 and which supported his family in a well-staffed villa at Cliff Point in Higher Broughton near Cheetham Hill).[39] Nonetheless, there are several additional indicators of status which can help us to get a sense of the shape of the elite in the three towns and how they compared with each other.

First, Wrigley's modified Booth–Armstrong scheme captures individuals with supervisory or directorial positions. There were four such Jewish individuals in Birmingham and Liverpool in 1851 and five in Manchester (where they were all in clothing businesses – although they do not, ironically, include the empire-building Benjamin Hyam as he was recorded simply as a tailor and clothier). In the other two towns, master tailors and clothiers were still prominent – such as James Cohen Pirani, manager of the Birmingham branch of Hyam's 'Pantechnetheca' (and co-resident with many of his employees, as we saw in Chapter 2), and Hyam's brother Samuel, who gave a lot of time and money to the Birmingham synagogue and the Hebrew Philanthropic Society.[40] Others worked in a range of sectors, from a doll maker, to a pawnbroker employing several people. Birmingham's David Woolf, for example, had one of the largest enumerated workforces in the dataset, employing ten men as a master shoemaker. A further four people in Manchester were employed as managers to other people's businesses.

Laidlaw's classification of skill status gives further insights. The highest categories in terms of social status are the leisured, professional or managerial (there is also a label for entrepreneurs but there is no one in this category in the three sampled towns), and these are set out in Table 4.6. Those described as leisured were all 'gentlemen/women' or 'annuitants', all suggestive of private income, although the latter could cover stipends from a charity or the Poor Law (Laidlaw classes all of these as leading a 'largely leisured existence'[41]). The managerial class includes those described as managers in the previous tally, but also covers landed and railway proprietors, and several warehousemen (though not, again, including Hyam, whose understated census descriptor places him in the semi-skilled manual group). The professional class includes doctors, dentists, teachers, bankers, Jewish ministers and similar – a group which Williams characterizes as still in its infancy by 1851, partly because of a narrow market, and partly because advanced education still had little appeal for the larger part of the Jewish population.[42] This meant that the provincial Jewish 'middle class'

Table 4.6 Number of individuals described as leisured, professional and managerial in the AJDB, 1851

|  | Liverpool | Manchester | Birmingham |
|---|---|---|---|
| Leisured | 16 | 1 | 3 |
| Professional | 19 | 14 | 2 |
| Managerial | 6 | 18 | 4 |
| Total | 41 | 33 | 9 |
| % of the population over 15* | 8.3 | 4.6 | 1.6 |

Source: AJDB/census database.

* Adults were classed as over fifteen to permit comparability with Laidlaw's analysis.

was arguably only starting to emerge in our period. Laidlaw's modified Booth–Armstrong scheme widens the professional class to include bankers (seven in Liverpool, none in the other two towns) and teachers (four in Birmingham, twelve in Manchester and nine in Liverpool covering a range of subjects).[43]

One of the most striking features of the table is the very small numbers of people in these categories in Birmingham compared with the other two towns (for reference, the Jewish population in Birmingham was of a very similar size to that in Liverpool). Manchester Jewry included considerably more managers than elsewhere while Liverpool had a high concentration, relatively speaking, of people who were leisured. These towns clearly either attracted, or created, opportunities for attaining high socio-economic status. Manchester's textile trade was a draw for overseas and London-based businessmen in the 1830s and 1840s, some of whom set up provincial branches of an existing enterprise.[44] The community in Birmingham did not seem to have gained the same traction in the town in terms of professional or managerial status, or created the same pull factors for migrants by 1851; nor does it seem to have housed people who had done sufficiently well that they had moved into these ranks. This supports the suggestions about the wealth and status of the most connected households in the previous chapter. On the other hand, there were fifty-three subscribers to a dinner in aid of the Birmingham Philanthropic Society in 1850, each pledging 2s. 6d. to £5, while the 1851 electoral roll returned forty-four Jews with property valued at over £10.[45] The most conspicuous of these – men like Jacob Phillips who returned with a fortune from managing the overseas branch of his Chinese import business shortly after the census in 1851 – led lifestyles of some opulence. In 1861 he was living in 'a turreted Italianate villa' in Edgbaston with his sister and her children, plus a number of specialist household staff, and having established himself as a core (and modernizing) member of the congregation and the town.[46] Clearly, he was more of an exception in Birmingham than he would have been in either Liverpool or Manchester. Only in Liverpool was this broad elite category better represented than in the AJDB as a whole however (7 per cent), undoubtedly reflecting an elite skew in the London population – and the attraction of the metropolis for those who had done well in the provinces. Manchester was the only town to house a Jew specifically returned as a philanthropist, although this was the Unitarian convert Julia Schwabe, wife of Salis.

In the light of the evidence presented in the previous chapter, it is unsurprising to find that these occupational patterns had a strong spatial element. On Liverpool's Mount Pleasant, for example, we find a preponderance of professional and skilled trades among Jewish residents: two surgeon-dentists, a dentist, a merchant and a commission agent. There were also Jews working in skilled manufacturing, one servant and a travelling jeweller. This was quite strikingly different from the non-Jews living on the same section of the street, again, supporting the broader patterns uncovered above. In the non-Jewish population, servants were by far the largest occupational group (23 per cent of the total), followed by dressmakers, and then the rather surprising pairing of milliners and barristers. There were many individuals working in professional and managerial positions too, but alongside a much wider range of other occupations than we saw in the Jewish sample. On the less affluent Paradise Street too, also in Liverpool, Jews had a narrower range of employments, this time focused in skilled trades and especially watchmaking. Among non-Jews, meanwhile, there was again a heavy preponderance of domestic servants (27 per cent of the total), while others were described as housekeepers. The other high-profile categories on this street were shop assistants, and there was then a long tail of mixed occupations from the skilled to the unskilled (including two dock labourers).

It is clear that at the upper end of the social scale, the Jews in the provincial manufacturing towns were doing very well for themselves. When the new Jewish burial ground at Prestwich (Manchester) was consecrated in April 1841, for example, attendees included eleven families who came in private coaches.[47] Their wealth came from clothing, trade and the professions rather than high finance, but it permitted a very comfortable existence, often still in close proximity to other Jews. Williams paints a picture of shared observance and sociability between some of Manchester's elite Jewish households, and we know that many cemented these ties in business and community affairs.[48] Their wives and daughters, too, had common endeavours in charities, principally as donors at first, but also in the management of the several ladies' lying-in and domestic visiting charities (these opportunities were to grow considerably in scope in the final decades of the century). On the other hand, the communal status that went with wealth was closely guarded, and one of the key reasons for the foundation of the breakaway 'New' congregations was the closed nature of the existing oligarchy, which prevented access by newer arrivals. Nor was wealth necessarily a good predictor of communal respect: one of the biggest thorns in the side of the Birmingham congregation was Joseph Colman Cohen, one of the first Jewish property owners in the town. Despite impressive generosity to Jewish charities, his refusal to pay his synagogue seat rent and his alleged general obstreperousness – traits exacerbated in the view of Birmingham local Jewish historians by his sense of superiority based on English birth and great wealth – made for considerable tension.[49] Nonetheless, these were the families at the centre of the Jewish social network, taking the highest positions in the synagogues, instigating and directing the community's charities, and controlling access to jobs with employers who were sympathetic to Jewish observance. What is more, it seems – despite the well-publicized growth of Jewish poverty – that there was upward social mobility at least among the more traceable element of British Jewry (the British-born) in the decades following 1851.[50] The potential for community support of the poor was, therefore, on the rise. Unfortunately, so too was the level of distress.

The lower ranks of provincial Jewry might have shed the worst-paid aspects of itinerant peddling and 'slop' (old clothes) selling by 1851, but they still gravitated towards trades that caused concerns for the community elites.[51] Chief among these were glazing, hawking and the deskilled aspect of tailoring done for middlemen, and catering for the ready-to-wear market (the same market that Benjamin Hyam was feeding, in much more prosperous style).[52] These occupations recur time and time again in the minutes of the provincial congregations and charities as causes of poverty among the lower-class Jews. Here, Laidlaw's classification of skill status is helpful again. In that scheme, those working in unskilled jobs were assumed to have only an elementary level of schooling (some of the semi-skilled occupations, in contrast, would have had a short apprenticeship).[53] In the AJDB as a whole, unskilled and semi-skilled (both manual and non-manual) occupations account for 75 per cent of all adult employed Jews, largely consisting of general dealers, hawkers and costermongers.[54] In Birmingham, Manchester and Liverpool, however, the figure was much lower, at 43.5 per cent. This is a salutary suggestion that, whatever the impression received by community officers, the Jewish populations of the larger manufacturing towns were actually somewhat better skilled than in the country at large. It suggests that these centres attracted more skilled workers, gave them opportunities to acquire and work at a greater skill level than those elsewhere – or gave them access to migratory opportunities if their skills were not a good fit for the town.[55] The ready accessibility of goods for small traders to sell, and diverse markets to sell them to, would also have been an appeal – but this too may have given them some security and flexibility in the job market.

## Living conditions

Another way of thinking about living standards at the lower end of the social scale is via housing conditions. Evidence for this can be found in charity records and also in the reports on the health and sanitary conditions of the major manufacturing towns which were drawn up by national and local bodies from around the 1830s onwards.[56] Taken in conjunction with the mapping exercise reported in the previous chapter, these provide a better impression of how relatively poorly off Jews were at the lower end of the socio-economic scale. They demonstrate that, despite growing concerns from the Jewish authorities in the 1860s and 1870s, it is likely that mid-century Jewry did not live in the worst parts of the industrial towns, and quite possibly not later in the century either. However, this should not detract from the fact that some of the poorer Jews did live in insanitary and crowded conditions which affected their health and their ability to work.

The Liverpool Corporation was one of the most active in the country when it came to civic improvements – though it also had some of the hardest work to do in this area. Spurred partly by the efforts of William Duncan, a lecturer at the Liverpool Royal Infirmary School of Medicine, and from 1846 the town's first Medical Officer of Health (MOH), the corporation had taken important steps in improving the worst aspects of the urban environment in the years leading up to 1851. It had enhanced the provision for sewerage, improved paving and lighting, made moves towards condemning the worst court and back-to-back housing, and secured local acts to set up a health committee. However, new housing needs were met only slowly in the 1850s, and rents were not particularly economical for the poorer sorts.[57] W. S. Trench, Duncan's successor as MOH from 1863, recorded further improvements in housing standards and crowding by 1865, but nonetheless, the 1885 Royal Commission on the Housing of the Working Classes still noted that Liverpool was urgently in need of further housing reform.[58] Infant mortality was notoriously high and the period immediately following 1851 saw rising food prices, with several years of very high cost burdens for staples like bread and potatoes. Other basic consumables like clothing and fuel also rose in price, with little evidence for rising wages to compensate.[59]

In Manchester, too, much working-class housing had been put up in hurried fashion as migrants poured in to access new opportunities for work: the town's population had increased nearly sixfold in the sixty years to 1831 and much of this was from in-migration.[60] Some of this accommodation was shoddy, lacking cellars and foundations. The high cost of land led to high rents, with many poorly ventilated and insanitary back-to-back houses arranged around cramped courts.[61] The water of the Irwell (the main river running through the centre of the city) and the Medlock (at the very southern end of the area of Jewish settlement) was not considered to be fit for drinking. By the 1840s the town had attracted a reputation for innovative action in public health and sanitation, and improvements had been made via local sanitary and improvement acts.[62] Red Bank was one of the more deficient areas, with much cellar dwelling, unlit streets and poor drainage. The houses were not particularly small, but they were frequently subdivided; we have already noted the tendency among Jews to split the space between residence and work.[63] The town continued to attract negative attention for its housing and health conditions, largely because of the visibility of the factory workforce – but also because its status as the first provincial 'shock city' meant that stereotypes were easily perpetuated.

Birmingham, in contrast, was generally characterized by contemporaries as well situated for health. It lay on high ground with good drainage and drinking water, and although its small metalwork workshops brought certain occupational diseases connected to toxic materials and fumes, it lacked the large-scale manufacturing businesses associated with Lancashire.[64] It had also witnessed improvements in sanitary facilities, although the most effective changes did not take place until the 1870s.[65] However, the poorer (older) areas of the town were less well off, with many courts containing poor-quality housing, poor water run-off and minimal sewerage – many neighbourhoods still relied on refuse heaps or middens.[66] Not all streets had a good water supply either: the lower end of Bordesley Street, where one Jewish household lived in 1851, was one of a small handful of locations singled out in the local report to the government's Sanitary Inquiry of 1842 as receiving water only fit for washing floors. Nonetheless, despite the high prevalence of back-to-back and court housing it was common for each family to have their own house, and cellar dwelling was almost unknown.[67]

Overcrowded homes were one of the principal causes of concern for contemporaries, as they led to the spread of disease and the degradation of morals (crowding in private dwellings was not regulated in the same way as lodging houses). Although Jewish households frequently contained lodgers and kin which pushed up their average size, they were clearly not in the worst categories when it came to crowding.[68] None of the streets listed by Trench in 1865 as the most poorly off in Liverpool in this respect had more than one Jewish household living on it, and in fact only two featured Jews at all.[69] The distinction between voluntarily sharing houseroom, as we saw happened with lodgers and kin, and subdivision or subletting was ultimately determined by the census enumerator, and probably contains some room for error. The nature of housing and the amount of space and facilities available for each family probably varied too. However, if we take the enumerators' demarcations of shared housing at face value, we find that between 4 and 12 per cent of all Jewish households were affected (lowest in Manchester, highest in Liverpool).[70] This was true even on roads where sharing was otherwise common, like Manchester's Hanover Street. Only one pair of Jewish families seemed to share with each other (in Birmingham); in all other cases we must assume that they lived in close proximity with non-Jews. In each of the three towns, shared housing was fractionally more common among families with foreign-born heads, but numbers were small and we should probably not place more than passing weight on this. The correlation between shared housing and household size was also variable and not particularly high: there was evidently no straightforward relationship at work here.[71]

Generally speaking, Jews did not live on the streets which attracted the most negative attention in contemporary reports. There were no Jewish residents in the 1851 census living on any of the streets named by Duncan as the 'most dirty' in Liverpool, for example.[72] Nor were they present on the 'black spot' streets in Birmingham. There were none on either of the streets named as containing the worst lodging houses in 1851 (Slaney Street and London Prentice Street, both occupied by the 'low Irish'), although there were individual Jewish households on streets that housed prostitutes' lodging houses.[73] Localized fever hotspots did include several of the streets inhabited by Jews in Birmingham, most notably the clusters on Hurst Street and Inge Street; also Hill Street, Suffolk Street, Essex Street, Bristol Street and Old Inkleys, all of which housed smaller numbers. Jews also inhabited some of the general districts held up as being a particular cause for concern: Scotland and Vauxhall Wards in Liverpool in particular, where Jews were small in number relative to the local population, but notable within the wider Jewish community, and of course, Manchester's Red Bank. While investigations consistently found little correlation between disease rates and nationality, they did find that the less crowded and polluted outer districts were better off for mortality risks, possibly aided by the migration of doctors out to the suburbs.[74] The wealthier Jews may have similarly benefited from these trends – and the converse for those left behind.

Jews rarely lived in court housing either – again, despite living on streets where there were courts. Assuming that all court addresses were specifically labelled as such (not necessarily a dependable assumption given the fluidity over addresses at this time[75]), then no Jewish households at all lived in courts in Liverpool or Manchester and only twenty-two in Birmingham (6.8 per cent of all Jewish households in the town, and principally off Inge Street and Essex Street). Jews were also more likely to be employers of servants or business staff than their neighbours on streets that contained courts and had lower rates of lodging. Again, this lends further weight to the suggestion that Jews were comparatively better off than many of their neighbours. It also suggests that their higher rates of lodgers may have been part of their self-perceived obligations to their community rather than a necessary way to make ends meet – at least compared to some of those around them.

It was instead the Irish residents who were consistently singled out for comment in the industrial towns, living in the worst courts and cellars, in the most crowded conditions, and 'the least cleanly in their habits, and the most apathetic about everything that befalls them', in the words of Liverpool's MOH.[76] When a government inspector in 1842 deplored the 'improvidence and thoughtless extravagance' of much of the population in Birmingham, who bought small quantities of food and fuel at inflated prices, displayed drunken and ignorant behaviour, and who lacked facilities for personal cleanliness and recreation, he did not single out the Jews for comment.[77] This no doubt reflects their relatively small numbers, but it also makes the point that their ethnic background was not doing the same sort of cultural 'work' for contemporaries as the Irish; indeed, it may have been the dominance of poor Irish in certain areas which pushed Jews to move to alternative parts of town.

We also catch glimpses of the housing conditions of the Jewish poor in the records kept by the various communal charities. These became more numerous as the century progressed, in line both with the growth of the poorer classes, and the accumulation of wealth and self-confidence of those higher up. They naturally focus on those in the worst situations but they are striking in their portrayal of hardship. When representatives of the Birmingham Hebrew

Philanthropic Society visited the homes of forty of the Jewish poor in the bad winter of 1861, for example, they found 'poverty in many cases distressing to witness and distress widespread and general'.[78] This was a bad season, with poor weather exacerbating an economic downturn (Lancashire was experiencing particularly acute hardship under the 'Cotton Famine'), and the charity's committee noted that there was 'great distress now existing among some of the members of our Faith in this Town'.[79] The medical officer (MO) to Manchester's Jewish Board of Guardians, meanwhile (discussed in greater detail in following chapters), regretted the state of the homes of the Jewish poor in 1870/1, and attributed the high incidence of measles and whooping cough to 'ignorance of, or inattention to first principles of hygiene, viz. cleanliness and ventilation'. It was a shame, he said, 'that the habits of the inmates are not subjected to more supervision and control'.[80] The following year he expressed his fear that the 'close dwellings of the Jewish Poor, would render any epidemic disease a grave calamity', and an outbreak of scarlatina in 1875 was attributed to poor sanitary conditions and the large number of children present (the fatalities were among the young).[81] By 1874/5 it was noted that '[m]any' houses had to be reported as unfit for habitation to the Inspector of Nuisances, despite plans for improvement of the Red Bank area being drawn up by the town's surveyor in 1870.[82]

The MO to the Liverpool Jewish Board of Guardians went further in illustrating the difficulties he faced in a report of 1874: attendance on poor patients was always difficult, he said, because of the cramped conditions of their homes, poor ventilation and lack of linen. He reported one particularly affecting situation where a family with two small children, one ill with scarlatina and dropsy, the other with pneumonia, were living in a room eleven feet by eleven feet and eight feet high. Allowing for the furniture they only had three feet to move around in.[83] In 1872 the Manchester board received a proposal that model lodgings be erected for the Jewish poor so that better conditions could be assured; this does not seem to have gone anywhere but it indicates the level of concern about housing by later decades.[84] We do not have records that detail housing conditions in the same way for the mid-century period, nor do we have much information about the addresses of charity recipients, although where these exist they confirm existing patterns – namely the preponderance of streets like Fernie, Hurst and Inge. It is also possible that the records reflect a deterioration in living standards over time for poor Jews into the 1860s and 1870s. There certainly seems to have been a steady growth in the numbers of people calling on the resources of the community by the 1860s, both resident and newly arrived, as will become particularly clear in the next two chapters.

Importantly for our current purposes, many of these people needed assistance in getting jobs or equipment on arrival, suggesting that not all were well placed to go immediately into employment in their new setting.[85]

The earlier charity records are less expansive on conditions but do sometimes note occupations of recipients. David Jonas Cohen of Moorfields in Liverpool, for example, stated in his petition for congregational poor relief in 1841 that he had been set up in 'a little shop' by benefactors, but that it was now failing.[86] An investigation into recipients from the Liverpool Philanthropic Society in 1838 noted a polisher, a tailor earning eight shillings per week but currently out of work, a lodging house keeper lacking in lodgers, a family dependent on the wages of three daughters who worked as milliners, and several others who were out of work or whose occupation was not listed – evidently because it did not bring in enough money to affect the material conditions of the family.[87] It is notable how many families were in trouble because of a downturn in an otherwise potentially profitable line of work; it would be useful to know more about whether this was because of personal circumstances like age or ill health, because of wider cycles in trade or fashion, or whether it was because the individuals (or their trades) were poorly adapted to the local economy. The balance of incomings and outgoings is glimpsed in a few cases, such as Liverpool's Joseph Hart who received nine shillings per week (plus something from the Hebrew Philanthropic Society) but paid seven of them out in rent. His fellow townsman Joseph Hyman was a bit better off: his family brought in ten shillings per week between them, and spent just under four in rent: fairly typical for one room at this time.[88] Unfortunately, neither man had an occupation recorded, and cannot be traced in the AJDB. The situation of many others was worsened by illness and unemployment, and several were reported to have pawned their clothes. The household of Jacob Goldberg was particularly desperate: 'a sad scene of distress not a chair nor bed the wife deprived of her proper dress to furnish food for the famishing family'.[89] More broadly, it is clear from the frequent references to people suffering from a depression in their trade, or who needed assistance to set themselves up in business, that there was a considerable amount of background uncertainty over employment.

Distressing though some of these scenarios were, there is little reason to think that Jewish homes and conditions were worse than those of their neighbours. In fact, it has been suggested that the Jewish dietary laws encourage better food hygiene, and other studies point to high levels of breastfeeding, which would have decreased some of the risks of infection and gastrointestinal illness for babies.[90] Jewish males were not given to drinking, which meant that income was retained for more useful expenses, and the provision of Jewish ritual baths meant access to facilities for personal washing.[91] It is also possible that the extra tier of scrutiny provided by the Jewish charities increased the chance of material aid, although urban sanitary authorities were increasingly alert to this as well. The Jewish poor certainly do seem to have benefited from regular and prompt visits from doctors when in need, and welfare services increased with the foundation of more organized charities in the later decades of the century. Visiting committees made frequent distributions of whitewash and soap, for example, and many medical officers insisted on prompt vaccination and the separation of infectious cases, especially of school children. These measures were held up on several occasions as keeping disease and mortality lower than in the surrounding neighbourhood, as in Manchester in 1871, when cleansing and whitewashing of poor Jewish homes was judged to have prevented deaths from smallpox.[92] And furthermore, the relative lack of participation in the industrial manufacturing sector by Jews could have offered some measure of protection from the interruptions to the cotton trade in particular as well as to industrial accidents and diseases. There is one point of evidence that Jewish homes were distinctive in some regards, however: in 1883 the Visiting Committee of the Manchester Jewish Board of Guardians noted that their homes were more likely than their neighbours to be used as workshops, which decreased the standard of the housing. Non-Jews were much more commonly employed outside the home, in mills and factories, for example, pointing again to a very different experience of work – and home.[93]

## Conclusions

The common and comparative framework for the analysis of occupations and social status has revealed some novel findings about mid-century Jewry. First, it has highlighted that Jews living in the three towns did have distinctive occupational profiles, indicating that they either chose to settle in towns where their skills were useful, or that they adapted these to the local economy. Their choices were not necessarily enviable ones, but they did produce a distinctive pattern of Jewish employment, and one that points to the existence of networks of knowledge about job opportunities. Furthermore, some of these networks may have cemented kin and community ties through shared working in the home and neighbourhood. Comparison with the wider town populations, however, shows the limits to these networks and skill sets: Jews did not work in factories, on the dockside or in Birmingham's metal industry. Nor did they work in domestic service to anywhere near the degree seen in the population at large. Most of these jobs involved local knowledge, personal contacts outside the Jewish community, availability to work on Saturdays, or long habituation to the workplace. Jews did, however, play an important part in the consumer-facing market, particularly in the provision and sale of small goods, which were an important way that the by-products of industrialization were brought to the middling and lower classes. Through hard work and the accumulation of wealth, Jews were surely also participants in the *industrious* revolution, whereby leisure hours were sacrificed for the growth of income and spending power.[94]

There were further differences between the towns: Liverpool was again shown to have higher indicators of affluence than the other two, while Manchester's economic elite were focused more in the textile trade. Birmingham, once again, seems to have had quite a different sort of upper social tier, which was arguably less far removed from the bulk of the Jewish population. Many of these differences were likely due to the state of economic development in the town, as well as the history of Jewish settlement, and things could have looked quite different a few decades later. However, in all three towns it seems that even small and itinerant traders could 'make good' and move up the social scale: this has certainly been part of local community histories in both Manchester and Birmingham.[95] It also maps neatly onto the residential patterns uncovered in the previous chapter, which hinted strongly at upward mobility. Even at the lower end, in these middle decades of the century, Jews did not live in the worst slum areas, they rarely inhabited courts and cellars, and their personal and domestic habits seem to have been singled out only by the Jewish authorities themselves. However, their occupational clustering is strong evidence of internal cohesion, especially in the working classes, while the influence enjoyed by the wealthy as employers and dispensers of charity makes an argument for a network in which some individuals were particularly influential.[96] If we think of a network not in terms of homogeneity but rather as a system of information flow, patronage and influence, then the evidence presented in this chapter certainly furthers our understanding of the workings of the Jewish community at this time. There is, however, some evidence that social and economic conditions may have deteriorated over the 1860s and 1870s, and it is to this question of poverty, Jewish welfare and the wider economy that we turn next.

# Part Two

# Charity and communal networks

5

# Philanthropy, religion and community from 1840 to 1865

The foregoing chapters have pointed to the importance of religion in explaining the household, residential and occupational characteristics of the Jews in some of the large commercial towns in the middle of the nineteenth century. In this part of the book we move on to ask how this emerging model of community was translated into support for the needy across the period from 1840 to 1880. This is a crucial area of discussion for two reasons: first, because of the huge rise in international immigration to the manufacturing centres, which from around mid-century was starting to shift towards people short on economic resources and useful occupational skills. With hindsight, of course, we know that this shift was simply a foretaste of what was to come in later years, but for community leaders it represented a new and substantial challenge. The newcomers naturally turned first to co-religionists to help them settle in, and this forced the elites to evaluate their response to Jews with whom they shared only cultural and religious bonds.

Second, several scholars have used attitudes to the poor as a way to characterize the status and form of British Jewry. Both Williams and Black, for example, have stressed that welfare was a tool for the community elites in Manchester and London respectively to shape the poor – and especially poor newcomers – into a more acceptable mould of anglicized respectability.[1] Both scholars also use the development of Jewish welfare services to reflect on the wider civic status of the community elite: the ways that it encountered local authorities, for example, and the confidence with which it tackled inequality and lack of citizenship. As these examples show, Jewish welfare thus speaks to bigger questions about identity and community coherence.

These two themes will form an important backdrop to the current investigation. However, primarily, it aims to take a more comparative perspective than its predecessors, and also to situate Jewish welfare more firmly within the context of wider debates about the aims and scope of charity. This enables us to speak more robustly about the distinctiveness of Jewish ideas and practices and how far these were influenced by secular thinking. The current chapter will deal with the period up to 1865, when all three of the largest communities saw a flowering of Jewish charities. Chapter 6 will consider the later 1860s through to the end of the 1870s: a period of consolidation, reflection and greater discrimination, both within Jewish welfare and beyond.

Jewish communities in Britain trod a line between distinctive religious ideals and the wider British welfare landscape. They did this, moreover, on an entirely voluntaristic basis: they had no powers to raise taxation from their members, and Parliament had made it clear in the early decades of the nineteenth century that this was not something that could change.[2] To put it simply, the Jewish communities took on the full remit of services offered by the mixed economy of statutory and voluntary British welfare, but in the context of a limited and voluntaristic funding model which, moreover, was dependent on an often fractious and distracted (if increasingly affluent) body of donors.[3] This was, it must be said, a choice: Jews *could* access the services of both the statutory Poor Law and a huge range of voluntary charities. However, many of these had residency requirements or equivalent demonstrations of 'belonging' which ruled out newer immigrants.[4] Those that were delivered in institutions also brought challenges to Jewish worship and the observance of the dietary laws, as well as the risk of encountering the predations of conversionists – something the Jewish elite feared out of all proportion to its actual incidence.[5] The community elites thus chose to protect their own: as one of the officers of the Manchester Jewish Board of Guardians was to reflect in the 1880s, 'it might appear strange that in a city like Manchester, and in a country like England, where the poor could claim relief from the authorities, the Jews should wish to administer that relief themselves ... But they were a peculiar people, and it was to them a pride to exercise that charity towards their brethren'.[6] The analysis that follows will pay particular attention to the 'peculiarities' of Jewish ideas about charity: something that has not featured enough in the literature to date. Whatever their motivations, however, the outcome was a piecemeal but expansive – on many measures, generous – patchwork of welfare in which we can see a shifting set of emphases and priorities. However, there were also certain constants across initiatives and also across towns, which point to a common understanding as to the aims of Jewish welfare and its interactions with changing economic circumstances.

## Jewish ideas on charity and the wider landscape of welfare

Jews believed that their sense of benevolence was qualitatively different from those of other groups, particularly in its expansiveness and its compassion. One of the officers of the Manchester Jewish Board of Guardians was to reflect in 1881 that 'whereas some people considered the poor a burden ... [the Jews] thought otherwise, for in helping the poor they believed they were honouring themselves'.[7] Contemporary observers had the same sense. John Mills noted that although there was 'much destitution' in London's Jewish community in the 1850s, there was not, in his opinion, 'a single instance of that extreme want and misery' that was seen in parts of the population at large, and especially among the poor Irish. The reasons, he said, were partly the Jews' 'habits of industry' but partly 'their national charities'.[8] Doctrinally, Jewish injunctions on charity had much in common with those of other religions, but these were sharpened by their emphasis on rabbinical teachings and on the belief in the Jews' special Covenant with God.

In is important to unpick these features further, since they will be vital for our appraisal of Jewish charity in the industrial towns. The characterization of charity in the Old Testament is that it is an important aspect of the individual's relationship with God, both a joyful duty (a *mitzvah* in Hebrew) and a kindness (*Gemilut Hasadim*) which is expected of everyone.[9] As God's 'chosen people', however, this had particular resonance for the Jews – it meant that they must set an example of a godly, compassionate and observant life to those around them. The creation of wealth is not denigrated in Judaism (one factor behind the negative stereotypes of Jews as money-grubbers, no doubt), but it does carry an obligation to address social inequalities, including (in the agricultural setting of the Old Testament) by tithing one's income, leaving gleanings in the fields for the poor and sharing the produce of every seventh harvest.[10] Furthermore, Jewish legal commentaries state that it is better to give expansively and risk rewarding the odd person not in real need, than miss someone in genuine distress. This remained an important reference point for nineteenth-century British Jewry and makes their view of charity arguably more expansive than most: an editorial in the *Jewish Chronicle* in November 1854, for example (which tended to be more reflective than the records of individual charities), concluded that it was better to give relief to even a hundred imposters, if thousands of the deserving were aided at the same time.[11] This is perhaps where the idea of Jewish generosity comes from, although, as we will see, it did not dovetail well with the drive towards a more scientific approach to charity being debated by the middle of the nineteenth century.

Rabbinical authorities sharpened ideas about the precise practice of charity further, most notably the twelfth-century philosopher and legal scholar Moses ben Maimon (Maimonides). His eight-stage scheme of benevolence prioritized acts that enabled the poor to become self-sufficient without suffering loss of face. This could involve offering them work (ideally by bringing them into an equal partnership), or money to start an employment. Lower stages hinge on the willingness with which charity is given, its worth relative to what the donor can afford and the extent of anonymity (anonymous giving is more praiseworthy as it is less demeaning for the recipient and is not motivated by self-aggrandizement).[12] Generally speaking, Jews were expected to give regularly to the needy and particularly at the Day of Atonement – although not to the point of impoverishing themselves.[13] There were thus several strands running through Jewish ideals about charity, which encompassed both the benefit to the recipient and its motivation by the donor. This distinguishes it from many of the prevalent ideas expounded by both Protestants and Catholics, who (in theory at least) prioritized greater discrimination, or the act of giving for the donor.[14] It also suggests that generosity to the poor was defined by what one could afford – a factor to which we will return, but which gains resonance given the affluence of some of the elite in our period.

Jewish teachings (like other religious works, including the New Testament Gospels) also singled out several particularly 'worthy' groups of the poor: orphans, widows and – significantly for the debates of the mid-nineteenth century – strangers.[15] These were, generally speaking, the same as the 'deserving' poor in wider discourse: a group privileged in both statutory and voluntary arenas, and distinguished principally by the fact that their poverty was not their own fault. The emphasis on strangers was originally probably a call for hospitality for those without friends and family nearby, but it was to become more problematic with growing economic insecurity and forced migration for Jews in many lands. These people presented many challenges for community leaders, but in November 1854 the editor of the *Jewish Chronicle* set out a bottom line for charitable discrimination: the question 'is he any the less deserving of relief because he has just arrived?'[16] We will see that the answer was not straightforward – partly because of surrounding ideas about deservingness and belonging, partly because of the surrounding context of persecution – but that it rarely led to the community safety net being withdrawn entirely. In the process, communal charity may have given Jews a greater point of common identity than was true in British society more generally.

Beyond this, there were certain other fundamental expectations about voluntary and willing service to the Jewish community: namely visiting the sick, helping to lay out the dead and supporting those in the week-long period of mourning for close relatives (*shivah*), which were owed to everyone, rich and poor, and which carried no expectation of return. Some of these were supported via formal organizations based around the synagogue and so are occasionally visible in communal records. In other cases, though, they probably depended on spontaneous actions from friends and neighbours, which leave little mark in this pre-oral-history era. We will return to this near the end of the chapter. In sum, though, it is clear that community responsibilities for the poor loomed large in Jewish teaching, second only to the family.

Jewish charity was, on the face of it, then, expansive. It was not indiscriminate though. It was traditionally given on a scale of relief according to need, with reference to length of residence, and via a communal fund which both ensured anonymous giving and freed individuals from the need to give to beggars. These principles formed the basis of communal charity in the provinces throughout our period (none of the provincial towns had the critical mass to support institutional welfare in our period, although some individuals were sent to London for residential support). The emphasis on discrimination brought Jewish charity into line with the British welfare arena more generally, where industrial working conditions were blurring definitions of 'deservingness' and demanding new ways of thinking about the poor.

It is a commonplace in the history of social services that all forms of poor relief are discriminatory in some way, and that most of these constraints had a moral element. 'Deservingness' was a long-standing and intuitively easy idea to grasp, but its nuances were often shifting and ill-defined. By the final decades of the nineteenth century, in fact, the term 'deserving' was starting to be discarded, partly because of its outdated moral implications.[17] Even by the end of the eighteenth century, it was becoming very clear that long-accepted ideals about the 'undeserving' status of the able-bodied unemployed were no longer tenable, and that relief bills were swelling with able-bodied people thrown out of work by trade cycles and mechanization. This was not immediately reflected in welfare policies towards the able-bodied, and moral discrimination continued to be enshrined in the official ethos of the statutory 'New' Poor Law (enacted in 1834).[18] There was more room for subtlety in voluntary schemes, but there was a common ethos across the welfare sector in favour of moral betterment and self-help; of removing the taint and threat of entrenched 'pauperism' in favour of 'poverty' which could be avoided or at least deferred.[19]

For those in charge of the Jewish communities though – largely the self-appointed elites with wealth and status, rather than religious ministers – these ideas were complicated for several practical reasons. First was the antipathy to allowing Jews to be relieved outside their own community. Second was the sense that Jewish charity should be expansive, and that Jews had obligations to aid poor strangers and those without family. And finally, there was a strong desire to avoid allowing Jewish poverty to become a 'problem' in the minds of wider society, especially as the immigration of poor Eastern European Jews increased.[20] By taking responsibility for their own poor, British Jews could demonstrate their fine qualities both as Jews and as Britons, while not drawing from the resources of the state. These priorities immediately muddied the water of any clear division between the 'deserving' and the 'non-deserving'. As we will see, the synagogues and allied charities did try to put systems of discrimination in place, but these were not always implemented consistently. The question of how to prioritize within and between the settled poor and newcomers – especially those just passing through – was also the cause of much moral angst and financial anxiety. It was at least as important as the promotion of 'respectability', which other studies have made so much of, and even this was frequently a side-effect of more pressing debates about the basic triaging of ever-growing numbers.

All of these problems had become more pressing by the 1850s. From the 'relatively small' amount of Jewish poverty in Manchester in the 1820s, the numbers and types of Jewish poor had both expanded and diversified.[21] This was largely the result of restrictive laws in Russia and Poland, outbreaks of persecution and economic downturns on the Continent and improvements in transportation, which together turned a steady stream of impoverished incomers to Britain into the start of a flood.[22] Background levels of poverty were also affected by domestic economic depressions such as the one accompanying the Cotton Famine of the 1860s, which, as we saw in the previous chapter, had an impact on home conditions in the Jewish communities. This was exacerbated by the fact that so many Jews in the industrial towns worked in semi-skilled occupations in precarious areas of the economy. Finally, external events like the American Civil War had a big impact on onward migration, resulting in more people settling in the northern towns rather than trying to move on through Liverpool to America.[23] Despite the Jewish reputation for hard work and charity, then, poverty – casual, cyclical and regular – was becoming an ever more pressing issue for the leaders of the industrial communities.

## Synagogue relief

As the formal embodiment of the community, the synagogues were the obvious focal point for Jewish charity. They were easy physical locations for newcomers to find, and they were places where all social classes could meet (albeit on terms which made social distinctions very obvious given the different tiers of membership and privilege). They thus became something of a 'catch-all' provider of relief.[24] However, although their charity was at times chaotic, contradictory and restricted in terms of individual pensions, all of the synagogues had certain priorities, namely to help the 'deserving' settled poor, to aid the preservation of religious life and to do something to mitigate the hardships suffered by new arrivals. Furthermore, they went beyond financial doles to provide goods and services, and they were prepared to spend sometimes large shares of overall budgets on these schemes. On all these counts, the synagogue committees can be regarded as generous when it came to welfare. Charity was also an obvious way for synagogue leaders to expand their influence and benevolence, so cementing their position within the social network. However, in several cases, congregational schisms made it difficult to finance charity schemes from membership fees and offerings, leading to resentment between different bodies and a limit on what could be offered.

The provincial towns had a model for Jewish poor relief in London, where the synagogues had been dealing with the needy for over a century by 1850. At times this was highly discriminatory and deterrent: in 1682 the Sephardi synagogue decreed that poor Ashkenazi immigrants could only receive a maximum of five shillings in relief, and many were sent back to the Continent.[25] In 1726, however, they spent £2,786 on poor relief, largely on Sephardim fleeing renewed persecution from the Inquisition.[26] By this time the Ashkenazi community was dealing with its 'own' poor, and several innovative ideas for more unified welfare schemes were put forward, including the one that proposed self-taxing powers, and another that eventually funded one of the most important of the metropolitan Jewish charities, the Jews Hospital, in 1807.[27] However, none of the proposals gained sufficient traction to be put into operation and Jewish welfare remained a patchwork of voluntary-funded charitable efforts.[28]

All of the synagogues in the industrial towns had a small list of regular pensioners by the 1840s, principally elderly members of the congregation, who were given weekly sums of between 2s. 6d. and 5s., and occasionally more. This was roughly comparable with weekly doles issued by the 'Old' Poor Law authorities for an elderly person, and more than many received under the 'New', post-1834 regime.[29] The circumstances of these pensioners were sometimes reinvestigated to ensure that their situations had not changed, but generally it is likely that they were well known to the synagogue officers because of their long residence. The small numbers involved – only four or five from the Liverpool Old Hebrew Congregation in the 1830s, for example, and four from the OHC in Manchester in 1851 – meant that the overall impact on the community was tiny, but it demonstrates a commitment to a small and deserving core of people with an ongoing stake in the congregation even if they were not – perhaps had never been – contributors as fee-paying members.

The synagogues also gave one-off sums of anything up to a few guineas to support cases of ill health, indigence and travel expenses. These sums were initially a small proportion of synagogue expenditure: £15 6s. 9d. in Manchester in 1827/8, for example, which was made up of sums between 1s. 6d. and 2s. 6d. to 102 individuals, and represented only 4.5 per cent of the annual expenditure that year. An additional £2 11s. 11d. was spent on Passover relief.[30] Nonetheless, if we are trying to appraise the generosity of Jewish schemes in a more quantitative and comparative sense, we should note that this was considerably more than the handful of percentage points of GDP calculated to have been spent on poor relief by the British state in the nineteenth century.[31] By the 1840s this in turn had been dwarfed, when the Liverpool OHC spent almost 23 per cent of its outlay on poor relief (£217 10s. 10d. out of a total expenditure of £963 3s. 0d.) – and this at a time when congregational finances were straitened and voluntary donations down. Poor relief was matched only by the unfortunately opaque heading of 'incidental' expenses, but was exceeded twofold by the salaries of the three key synagogue officers.[32] The Old Congregation in Birmingham also devoted just over 20 per cent of its expenses on welfare in the early 1850s (£190 in both 1852 and 1853, out of a total of £924), with salaries again being the only item to outstrip poor relief.[33]

In terms of the proportion of the community being assisted by Jewish welfare sources, we are on much more impressionistic ground, largely because of the large numbers of migrants passing through all of the towns studied here. The Liverpool OHC, for example, gave out more than 250 sums in the first three months of the bad winter of 1861, ranging from a shilling to several pounds, and principally to glaziers, hawkers and tailors (together these were 72 per cent of all recipients with an occupation recorded). Accounting for multiple payments to the same individuals, this represented perhaps 160 individuals or heads of families – not far off the likely total number of Jewish households in Liverpool in 1861. Clearly, then, some of them must have been transients or short-term residents. Very few could be matched to the AJDB, but this is not to say that others had not taken up residence in the town in the intervening ten years. In Manchester too, according to Williams, only sixty-five of the 742 recipients recorded in the synagogue account books in the late 1840s were captured in the town in the 1851 census; poverty frequently accompanied transmigration.[34] Even if these proportions were small, however, they probably still compare favourably with the 5 per cent of the English population estimated to have been aided by the state or charity in 1850.[35]

In terms of individual doles too, many of the Jewish schemes can be regarded as generous. While a little under half of recipients of funds from the Liverpool congregation in 1861 received only 2s. or 2s. 6d., which was certainly not enough for a family to live on entirely, a third received five shillings or more per week and nine people were given twenty shillings and upwards.[36] Vouchers were also given out for meat, bread and groceries – presumably to ensure that relief really was spent under these useful heads (and also, perhaps, to promote support of the Jewish provisioners). Many recipients also benefited from the separate Passover relief schemes (see below), and from doles from other Jewish charities or the Poor Law. This sort of short-term support for the Jewish poor was clearly becoming an increasing burden for the synagogues over time, but perhaps in the process coming to be a key part of the community's economy of makeshifts. Its reach and expansiveness at this period of extreme want is certainly striking.

A second priority of synagogue charity was to ensure that poverty did not prevent people from participating in Jewish worship, for example by lowering or waiving fees for religious ceremonies.[37] This aid was generally directed at the settled population, but as we will see, it did sometimes extend to sojourners and even to people living elsewhere. We can also see the synagogues clinging to ideas about a moral or religious test to discriminate between applicants when deciding who to help – but again, this was not always possible in the face of need, or of religious fellow feeling. On 30 October 1836, for example, Israel Samuel was charged a reduced sum of one shilling by the Liverpool OHC for the circumcision of his child, 'the applicant being in indigent circumstances' (by contrast, another individual was charged 10s. 6d. at the same meeting simply for having a child named).[38] Saul Isaacs must have been even less well off, as he was given a guinea in aid as well as having the circumcision fee for his son waived.[39] On 31 December 1836, it was agreed that a man named Benjamin could have his child buried free of charge because he was 'a poor man' (the cost for having a young child buried would otherwise have been £3 3s. 0d., plus a variety of additional fees).[40] Prior investment in the community also counted for a lot: Mr J. C. Abraham was allowed free burial for his ten-year-old son in August of 1838 'having been many years a contributor to this Congregation tho' now in reduced circumstances'.[41] Similar examples recur both in Liverpool and elsewhere throughout the period and beyond.

The Passover *matzah* schemes can be seen in a similar light. This festival marks the Jews' escape from enslavement in Egypt: an event so sudden that there was no time to let their bread rise. For the week of the festival, Jews are thus forbidden to eat anything leavened. The distribution of subsidized or free *matzah* crackers and flour was therefore vital to enable the poor to keep the festival. Even here, though, the synagogues did attempt to discriminate on moral and economic grounds. In Liverpool, for instance, potential recipients were asked to apply in writing, and to state the size and composition of their families.[42] It is unclear how regular or thorough these enquiries were though, especially given the scale of the distribution schemes and the consequences for religious observance. The Liverpool OHC assisted seventeen families with Passover relief in cash or kind in 1840; in 1845 the Manchester OHC recorded around thirty families (11.7 per cent of the total living in Manchester at the time), and by the mid-1860s this had swelled to roughly 185 applicants (equating to 10.5 per cent of the Jewish population).[43] Most recipients were the heads of families with children, and three-quarters in the 1860s were glaziers or tailors.[44] Annual accounts from all three towns also frequently mention sums expended at the Jewish New Year, the Day of Atonement, Tabernacles and Pentecost (several of which fall close together in the early autumn and so could have a significant impact on people's income at that time of year).

The synagogues were also responsive to the more secular demands of winter, giving out food, coals and blankets to those it deemed in need. By 1854 the Birmingham congregation had specific bread and rice, and meat committees to oversee this relief, while the Liverpool OHC received a commemorative gift of £100 from the family of L. L. Mozley in 1844 to pay for coals and later also for blankets for poor Jewish residents. By the 1860s applicants to this fund had to fill in a pro forma giving their occupation, age, family situation, and the length of time they had been resident in Liverpool. Supporting signatures were also required and the application had to be certified by one of the congregational ministers, or two seat holders.[45] This was not the indiscriminate giving that could promote further indigence, then, and it also necessitated contact with several patrons who were closely connected with the synagogue. Indeed, all of the festival handouts can be seen as a valuable means of building community by drawing people into the remit of the synagogue, and establishing relationships of fellow feeling and deference. This can been seen explicitly in a few cases, for example in the Birmingham congregation's stipulation that their pensioners attend services at the synagogue. This body also cut off the assistance to a Mrs Samuel because of (unspecified) poor behaviour.[46] Further short-term relief funds were set up to dispense aid and food at hard times (as in the winter of 1861), occasionally supplemented by soup kitchens.[47] Charity like this was deeply out of step with thinking about deterrence and the promotion of self-help. However, Jews were not the only ones to flout approved modes of giving in extreme circumstances: soup kitchens were set up to help the wider body of the poor in Lancashire in the 1860s, too.[48] Furthermore, there is occasionally evidence of attempts to square practice with philosophy: the funds distributed by the Birmingham Philanthropic Society in 1861, for example, were given out personally by the committee, in order to decrease the 'anguish occasioned by the necessity of dependence on others'.[49] We can thus read the Jewish schemes as responsive both to religious instruction and some elements of the wider debates about charity, all overlaid with a layer of practical benevolence.

The casual poor presented a more troubling burden. In the legal parlance of the time, casuals were 'wayfarers' or 'homeless' persons 'in a state of destitution', but with a legal claim for statutory relief.[50] However, Englander notes that historians – like many contemporaries in fact – tend to use the term to refer more generally to the mass of 'irregular', vagrant, and unemployed people, whose claims were clearly more ambiguous. Within the Jewish populations it encompassed newcomers (whose claim on statutory welfare was minimal), transients, who were often seen by community leaders as particularly calculative in their claims for assistance, and also anyone below the highest tier of 'free' membership of the synagogue, who sometimes made occasional claims for relief. This latter group did not attract the same sort of anxiety from congregational leaders as the newer arrivals.[51] By mid-century, the scale of the 'casual' Jewish poor was starting to become a problem, but responses to this category of people were complicated by the Hebraic imperative to support strangers. These people had rarely established any sort of credit in terms of social capital beyond their membership of the imagined community of global Jewry, nor would they necessarily do so in the future if they did not intend to stay in the town. As the last bulwark before the (minimal and deterrent) aid available for the casual poor under the New Poor Law, the synagogue committees must have felt an uneasy obligation to give some assistance to these fellow Jews. On the other hand they were aware that if this were seen as an entitlement it would act as a magnet for more strangers. The congregations thus followed a range of policies at different times, from offering small amounts of aid to attempting to move migrants onwards or back to where they came from, through to refusing assistance altogether.

The problem was exacerbated by the secession of 'New' synagogues in all three towns, and also in several of the smaller communities, such as Hull and Glasgow. In each case, the breakaway groups consisted of newer arrivals who had done well financially and were frustrated at their exclusion from the existing synagogue elite. By seceding, they therefore removed resources from the original synagogue without taking with them any of the poorer members of the congregation. Thus in the 1840s, the Manchester OHC found themselves carrying the full burden of the casual poor, to the tune of £150 to £200 per year.[52] A short-lived United Board of Relief was established in January 1847 which assigned the burden of the casual poor in a ratio of 2:1 between the Old and New congregations, but by October this had broken down, partly over different attitudes to the scale of relief (the leaders of the New Congregation (NHC) advocated a much stricter and more deterrent policy – which was, on occasion, put into practice to manage the need for financial economy).[53] Between September 1848 and March 1851 the OHC gave relief in money or kind to over 2,000 people (far more than the total number of Jews living in the town at the time), most of whom were passing through on their way to the port at Liverpool.[54] Expansive this may have been, but it was not necessarily generous on an individual level: doles were deliberately kept low so as not to give any inducement to stay – a shilling or two for single men, with higher sums reserved for the most respectable, and applicants were rarely relieved more than once. At the same time, in a mode very reminiscent of the demeaning make-work schemes of the New Poor Law, some of the least eligible applicants were set to stone-breaking rather than receiving aid directly.[55] The Reform Synagogue in Manchester (founded in 1856), meanwhile, ran its own Winter Relief scheme, but there were few claimants because of the relative prosperity of its members.[56]

Efforts were also made to refer individuals to other charities, like Manchester's Society for the Relief of Really Deserving Distressed Foreigners, to which the OHC paid an annual subscription for several years.[57] By 1851, however, the system was at something of a breaking point, and notices were placed on the synagogue doors to state that all able-bodied beggars were to be sent to the Poor House; only the sick and genuinely distressed were to be relieved by the synagogue.[58] This stance lasted less than a month. It was revived in the mid-1850s but was again dropped after five years.[59] The combination of rising demand and the splitting of congregational resources was very problematic, especially in Manchester, where the schism was particularly fractious (although ultimately the shortest-lived), and critics blamed the central Board of Deputies for not taking action on a national scale.[60] However, even in these circumstances the Old Congregation could not sustain their support of a policy which sent Jews to the Poor Law authorities for aid.

The problem of transmigrants was even more pressing in Liverpool, where competition had driven down the price of a ticket to the United States to £3 by 1846, and where foreigners often ended up, lacking in resources and expecting to be put on a ship at the expense of the community.[61] In February 1838 the town's OHC called a special meeting 'owing to the great distress of the Transient poor, consequent on the unexampled severity and continuance of the weather'. Many of these people were sick, but the hospitals were too crowded to take them. The OHC approved several grants, including £1 1s. 0d. to three strangers and five shillings to a poor boy.[62] In November 1840, however, after a year of high expenditure on casuals, they pressed the 'necessity of limiting their distributions to the smallest possible amount consistent with the situation of the applicants'.[63] Further action was taken with the foundation of both a Jewish Board of Relief and a Hebrew Mendicity Society (see below) in 1846 to try to deal with the situation, but it did not remove it entirely: thirty-nine doles were recorded under payments to the casual and resident poor from the Liverpool OHC in August 1864.[64] The situation was less pressing in Birmingham because it did not lie on the cross-country route between the ports, however its market for small goods had long made it a centre for peddlers and other transients.[65]

It was often simply easier and cheaper in the long run to pay for people to continue their onward journeys, to Liverpool, direct to America, or to other towns where they had relatives. All of the synagogues made one-off doles contingent on the applicant leaving town; a policy the community in Liverpool found particularly irksome as the money often ran out on reaching the port (although they paid for people to go to other provincial towns themselves). The same policy was used to rid the congregation of troublesome members – Michael Goldston of Birmingham can have been in no doubt about the sentiments behind his grant of funds for a ticket, with any remaining money only given to him as he departed.[66] The Liverpool Mendicity Society took a harder line and would only fund journeys back to where the migrants had come from, except in special circumstances.[67] This is a particularly clear statement about the limits of responsibility felt by the provincial communities – but it was breached at least as often as it was observed. The extent to which policies like this can be seen as a means of shaping the character and perceptions of the communities is therefore very limited. Instead, it is clear that in the area of casual poverty and onward migration, the communities in many cases felt that the path of least, and most humane, resistance was to pay to make the problem go away, not quite able to countenance the moral consequences of a permanent policy of sending poor Jews to the Poor Law authorities. It was, nonetheless, a heavy financial burden, which suggests how high a priority – but also how troubling – the problem of Jewish poverty was for the synagogues. In late 1852 the congregational committee in Liverpool noted that limited resources were preventing them from revising their responses to the poor, especially given 'the constant demand on them'.[68] The casual poor often loomed large within this budget: in 1837 the Liverpool OHC spent more than four times as much on casuals as on the resident poor, although in other years this was reversed, possibly linked to cyclical unemployment and bad winters.[69]

The congregations did also, with some reluctance, support some cases living elsewhere. These were usually people with a prior connection with the community, or who belonged to a town without options for Jewish welfare. Again, then, this suggests certain deep-held beliefs about responsibility for other Jews which could override aspirations to economy. The Birmingham congregation thus gave twenty shillings to a poor family in Derby to support them in sickness in February 1849, their case probably given weight by the fact that it was supported by the head of the only known Jewish family in that town in 1851.[70] The Liverpool OHC, however, refused an application to pay for the burial of the son of a previous member in June of the same year on the basis that too much time had passed since he paid any dues.[71] The congregations were also approached if Jewish strangers died in the town: claims that were again met as long as it could be proved that the person in question was definitely a Jew and that they had no family to take on the burden. Cases like these show that even Jews living in towns with few or no co-religionists could still access the aid of the wider community – and also that Poor Law and hospital authorities were alive to the importance of ritual (and rapid) burial for Jews. Of course, this also had the benefit (for them) of passing on a financial burden.

Figure 5.1 puts some of the above in context by illustrating the amount of money spent by the Manchester OHC on the poor from 1827/8 to 1848/9. It shows a steady rise in both the number of applicants and the amount of money spent on them, especially from 1843. The only point at which the two trends depart from one another is in 1844/5, when the total spent seems to have significantly outstripped the numbers of people relieved; that is, each person received a larger sum. This is supported by Figure 5.2, which shows a rise in relief per person in that year and also in the proportion of congregational outlay which went on poor relief. This is surprising given that it was precisely the time at which the

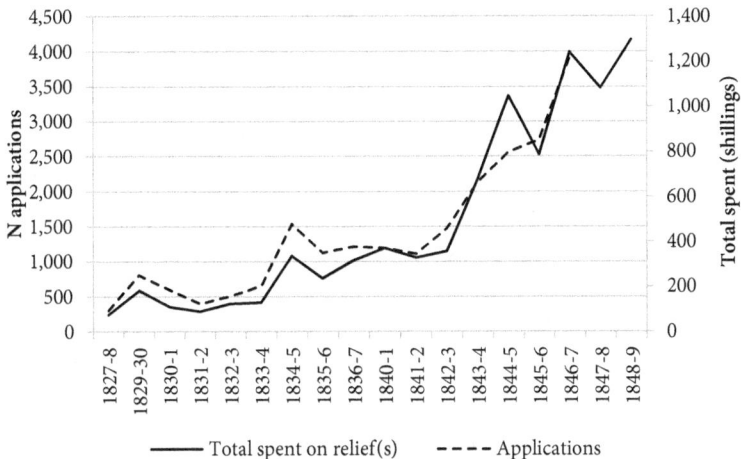

**Figure 5.1** Expenditure on the poor by the Manchester Old Hebrew Congregation, 1827/8–1848/9.

Source: MLIA M790 2/6/1, Williams papers, 'Voluntary agencies'.

**Figure 5.2** Expenditure on poor relief per person, and as a proportion of total congregational outlay, Manchester Old Hebrew Congregation, 1827/8–1848/9.

Source: MLIA M790 2/6/1, Williams papers, 'Voluntary agencies'.

secession by the New Congregation removed some of the income from seat rents without removing any of the burden of the poor. It is possible, however, that this made the outlay on relief more prominent within the expenditure burden, although it does not explain the increased generosity to individuals.[72] Another explanation is that it was a backlash or catch-up from the apparent retrenchment on amounts given per head in 1842 (see Figure 5.2). The impact of the harsh winter of 1848/9 is also evident in raised expenditure. Numbers of applicants and the amount expended on relief were highly correlated, with a coefficient of 0.973, suggesting that outlay was largely a simple response to need.

The wide-ranging nature of congregational relief, and the heavy burden of casuals, indicates that the synagogues were effectively the residual provider of welfare support. Until the foundation of the Jewish Boards of Guardians in the 1860s and 1870s (see Chapter 6), there were no other organizations dealing with such a large cross-section of the Jewish population, or with a similar sense of responsibility for ensuring that basic religious rites were met. By providing this sort of safety net – which can be regarded as generous relative both to total expenditure and to the proportion of the population relieved at times – the congregations were not only carrying out a paternalistic and humanitarian role as befitted their status as guardians of the Jewish faith, they were also ensuring that the reputation of the Jews for looking after their own was upheld. This even extended in extremis to those who were not paying members of the synagogue, in itself a significant statement about social responsibility and community. The synagogues were not acting alone, however: their welfare efforts were shared by a growing number of Jewish charities. Most of these were founded as responses to evident and specific need, some particular to Jewish poverty, others very much in line with wider philanthropic efforts.

## Jewish charities

When it came to charities, the provincial communities again had a powerful model in London. These were, broadly speaking, absolutely in line with the legacy of eighteenth-century philanthropy, targeting orphans, the elderly, pregnant women, the blind and other typically 'deserving' groups, and seeking both to relieve and to reform.[73] Some catered for specific Jewish needs, such as circumcision and Hebrew education; others gave loans, which was a typical (and increasingly popular) way to encourage independence among the poor. They were funded by voluntary donations, including some very sizeable gifts by community notables like Sir Moses Montefiore.[74] The provincial congregations were no less charitable, but their later period of development means that we can see more clearly the ways in which their leaders were taking on wider nineteenth-century points of reference about philanthropy. These included debates about self-help and the consolidation of charity, as well as the requirements of Jewish observance.

Liverpool Jewry were very quick off the mark in this area, likely a reflection of their longer settlement, greater levels of wealth, and the lively charitable ethos of the town more generally. Liverpool's Hebrew Philanthropic Society was founded in 1811 and was the model for later equivalents in Manchester (1826), Birmingham (1838), Hull (1848) and Glasgow (1858). The similarities between modes of charity in the different towns is striking, although not unusual for the time given the sharing of ideas and practice both within the Jewish community and beyond.[75] Monetary doles formed the principal mode of relief of these societies – very much in the traditional mould of voluntary charity at this time. The Liverpool Society, as the town's earliest demonstration of community responsibility for welfare beyond the traditional remit of the synagogues, was quite possibly a particular indicator of pride and status for donors. It also had the important functions of helping new arrivals to bed into the community and form attachments to it.[76] Support for the societies in both Liverpool and Manchester was high and their balance sheets showed a healthy surplus in their early years, although all of them struggled in later decades.[77] They also spent sums on one-off extras to existing pensioners, including items like bedding and linen, medical equipment and even sometimes arrears of rent; also on casual relief, within certain strict limits. The Birmingham Society gave out coals and blankets after careful inspection of applicants' homes, and all would-be recipients needed a note of recommendation signed by three members of the committee.[78] In Manchester, subscribers earmarked part of their funds for material relief for cholera patients during the epidemic of 1832.[79] In an also-typical expression of the charitable ethos of the times, the Birmingham Society stated early in its life that its 'great object' was 'not so much to assist men in distress, as to keep them if possible, from coming to that condition': prevention rather than cure of indigence.[80]

Discrimination and personal enquiry was again key to the way that the Hebrew philanthropic societies presented themselves. In Birmingham cases were reviewed and reconfirmed every few months, and applications were often rejected by all three societies because there were alternative sources of income or because the applicant was not seen as a reliable prospect. This was not a guarantee of rigour, however: a document produced by the Liverpool Society in 1852 reported that a visiting committee had belatedly revealed considerable discrepancy between recipients' claims and their actual situation. Recipient 'A.B.', for example, had claimed to have a large family, but in fact they were giving him support (this was a common disqualification for relief – in 1869, for instance, the Birmingham Hebrew Philanthropic Society made a grant to one individual only on the condition that no money was forthcoming from his relatives[81]). 'C.D.', meanwhile, had 'means of ample sustenance with trifling assistance'.[82] However, the Society was willing to aid people who had income from other charitable sources too, like Mrs E. Benedict, whose weekly four-shilling dole from the Society was supplemented by 3s. 6d. per week from the synagogue and Passover *matzah* as well.[83] The doles were – like those from the synagogues – evidently seen as a contribution towards subsistence rather than a stipend someone could live on entirely.

A rare set of charity applications survives for the Liverpool Philanthropic Society, which give us some more insight into the type of work the charity did, and the type of applicant it attracted. These consist of seventy-nine petitions for relief, written in the 1830s and in 1851 by forty-six individuals, fifteen of whom have more than one application surviving.[84] The most common reasons given for the petitioners' situations was that they had a large family to support, that they or a family member was in poor health, that they were elderly, or that they lacked work, the latter sometimes specifically linked to the 'badness of trade'. These were all common reasons for applications to the Poor Law among the population more generally too.[85] Notably, one applicant said that the reason he could not secure work was that he refused to work on the Sabbath. The formulaic phrasing in many of the petitions – which echoes that found in pauper letters and applications more generally – means that applicants likely knew well how to cast themselves to increase their chance of success. This does not down-weight the facts behind their poverty, however, even if it was not always the whole story. Only nine applicants definitely secured weekly sums, two were rejected for reasons that are unclear (both petitioners were elderly and long-term residents in the town and one was noted to have been relieved by the Society in the previous year), and three were old subscribers to the charity. Two had relief from other sources, including one who got eight guineas from the congregation. In neither case was the outcome of their application to the Philanthropic Society recorded; neither can be found in the AJDB. The reasons for Jewish poverty were thus very similar to those in the population more widely, albeit sometimes exacerbated by the restrictions of working on the Sabbath and the paucity of alternative means of support.

Charitable responses to sickness and accidents, meanwhile, were sympathetic but piecemeal, often relying on the generosity of Jewish doctors in the town.[86] Individuals were provided with money, food and medical goods; occasionally they were sent out of town to convalesce. Hospital inpatients might receive doles or food, and at least one individual in Birmingham – Abraham Wineberg – was supported after an accident which prevented him from working.[87] Efforts to assist poor married women in childbirth and sickness were more organized: a United Sisters Charitable and Benevolent Society was founded in Manchester in 1847 and Liverpool Jewry hosted a Ladies Benevolent Society from 1849 which was a powerful force in fundraising. Both were in line with the growing model of female-led charities focusing on women and children, and which flourished further in the provincial Jewish communities in the 1880s and 1890s.[88]

Responses to life-cycle poverty, on the other hand, were mixed. Many of the recipients of the schemes noted above were elderly, and most of the others were the heads of families with young children; two of the key periods of life when the balance between income and outgoings was particularly fragile. We have already seen that older people, and also occasionally lone children, often lived with relatives, which may have prevented, or supplemented, requests for external aid.[89] It was only the elderly, however, who were singled out for specific charitable relief. In Liverpool a Hebrew Provident Society was founded in 1850, which gave out pensions of at least five shillings per week to a limited number of people 'of good character' who had been resident in Liverpool for at least three years and were over the age of sixty. Vacancies in the pension list were advertised at the doors of the synagogues, and applicants had to have their credentials corroborated by two householders.[90] Oversight did not stop there: pensioners needed permission to leave the town for a month or more, or they risked losing their relief. The Barned Annuity Fund also gave out money to permanent residents of Liverpool who were old and infirm.[91] In Manchester and Birmingham there was no specific provision for the elderly beyond their presence on the pension lists until 1860, when the Birmingham Philanthropic Society resolved that it would support three poor people aged sixty or over with pensions of five shillings per week. Again, there were residence requirements: recipients had to have lived in the town for at least five years and were balloted by the Society's members from a list of those eligible. A substantial sum was raised to establish an alms house in the 1860s, but this seemed to come to nothing, and a proposal to set up a home for the elderly in the town in 1875 was rejected.[92] Whether for logistical or financial reasons – or because it behoved the family to be the first carers of the elderly – the town was clearly not ready for an institutional commitment to the elderly.

Widows and orphans, in contrast, are strikingly absent from the Jewish charitable landscape at this time, especially given that they were also groups specifically identified as worthy of charity in Jewish teaching (non-Jewish foundlings were apparently sometimes left at synagogue doors, in the belief that they would be cared for).[93] Widows were often the recipients of more general doles, but orphans are very rarely mentioned in the charity records. Those that do appear were often sent to the Jewish Orphan Asylum at Mile End, London (later at Lower Norwood), and the existence of this well-funded institution may have been the reason that no specific provision was made in the provinces.[94] It has also been suggested that Jews had low levels of child abandonment and family desertion, perhaps a function of their closely integrated society and the weight placed on family life. The emphasis on hygiene in the dietary laws and high rates of breastfeeding also reduced the mortality of both children and adults.[95] However, charity records make it clear that Jewish adults were not immune to the threats of the urban environment, and increasing numbers of families were left truncated because the breadwinner had gone elsewhere to find work. The absence of orphans except as isolated cases therefore strongly suggests that they were receiving assistance from relatives, perhaps in the form of houseroom, as was hinted at in Chapter 2. Widowed men with children – who were often particularly vulnerable to difficulties since men lacked the social networks that women did, and also had less flexible jobs – appear even more rarely in the records.[96] This raises the possibility that Jewish communal life gave men a more functional informal support network than was the case in the population at large, even when a large proportion of the community consisted of relative newcomers.

The rise in family desertion by breadwinners in later decades made responses to these cases more ambiguous, but in the 1850s and 1860s deserted wives were generally treated kindly, even when their case was morally ambiguous. Birmingham's 'Mrs Michael', for instance, whose husband was in Warrington gaol, still received relief from the Hebrew Philanthropic Society, as did Mrs Lazarus Robinson, whose husband was refusing her maintenance.[97] Perhaps more unusual still was the case of Manchester's Mrs Aaron whose husband had renounced the faith (and apparently also his family of three children). They were sent to Birmingham for onward travel to London and had their lodgings paid for.[98] Presumably they were felt to be the innocent parties and not to be penalized for their breadwinner's deficiencies. By sending them on, the community was also relieving themselves of a long-term burden.

The Hebrew philanthropic societies were followed by a host of other charities, mainly geared to the giving of small doles, but sometimes also maintaining a short list of regular pensioners. The records rarely coincide sufficiently to establish how often individuals got regular aid from more than one charity, and recipients can unfortunately almost never be traced to the AJDB either because of the timing of the records, or because they did not stay in the town. While no individual grant necessarily gave a reliable income (usually a couple of shillings per week), they could be a valuable tide-me-over at pinch points. Several societies also increased relief during the winter, or at times of economic downturn. Ten members of the Liverpool Philanthropic Society petitioned the charity in 1838, for example, to meet 'the wants and increased necessitie of the distressed … consequent on the protracted severity of the season' (the OHC also noted 'great distress' at that time), and Birmingham's Philanthropic Society called a special meeting in December 1839 to consider distributing coals to the distressed poor (they voted £5 for this purpose and repeated it in subsequent years, when blankets were also given out).[99]

There were clearly some well-understood but flexible and often unwritten ideas about individual deservingness at work here. Occasionally, cases were recommended by an officer of the charity which seems to have been enough to assure the applicant's status; in others brief notes on sickness or extreme want makes their condition clear enough to see why they were relieved. In others, we must speculate that individuals were well enough known to the charity that their deservingness was a given, or that investigations took place but were not recorded. The Liverpool Hebrew Philanthropic Society did state in 1852 that its 'immediate object' was 'the relief of the resident Hebrew poor during the winter Season', dependent on 'personal enquiry into the individual necessities of each applicant'.[100] This was the same year that it recorded several discrepancies in the condition of its recipients, however. Investigation was probably more likely for new arrivals; in later decades, home visiting was to become a much more organized aspect of relief generally.

There were other recognizable limits to the charities' remit. Most refused to pay off applicants' debts, for obvious reasons to do with encouraging thrift and responsibility. This could, however, be quietly trumped by high standing in the community, in line with the 'face-saving' aspect of Jewish ideas on relief. Mr Isaac Lewis, a seat holder in the Birmingham congregation, for example, was allowed three guineas' relief 'to extricate him from impending embarrassment' in 1854.[101] The prior investment in community social capital was evidently worthwhile at times like these, especially given that old age or misfortune could strike even relatively well-off people at some point in their lives.[102] Others were rejected because they had sufficient income or assistance from elsewhere, as we saw above, again reinforcing the importance of encouraging independence. The Birmingham Philanthropic Society was also clear that it did not aid cases of insolvency, though it did help some individuals threatened with court action for non-payment of rent. Possibly this was seen as misfortune rather than mismanagement; perhaps it was simply less expensive, or a way to avoid Jews attracting notice in the courts.[103] Transgression of religious rules was also a problem: Lewis Stern's application for a loan from the Birmingham Philanthropic Society was turned down because he was not married under Jewish law (he was also not a resident of the town; there is no clue as to which was considered to be more important in refusing his application).[104]

Residence was always an important way of limiting relief and was a clear response to anxieties about sojourners taking advantage of the community's resources. Both the charities for the elderly described above, and the Hebrew schools (until the 1870 Education Act disallowed it), insisted that recipients had lived in the town for several years before they got assistance. Birmingham's Philanthropic Society resolved in October 1829 that none of their funds could be sent out of the town unless it was for the relief of a member, and in 1870 they restated that no one living in the town for less than twelve months could receive coals or blankets; ditto for loans – the latter particularly understandable since loans were supposed to improve applicants' economic standing and integration into the industrial economy. It was also harder to police the repayment of loans made further afield.[105] Residence was clearly a way of demarcating people who had social capital in the community and thus would repay the investment made in them. 'Belonging' was a marker of status for the elite as well: would-be charity committee members often had to have been resident for a certain period, as did those wishing to become Free Members of the synagogues.[106]

The Liverpool Mendicity Society – or to give it its full title, the 'Society for the Suppression of Mendicity, and for the more effectual relief of deserving Casual poor', which was founded in 1846, had arguably a finer line to tread along the margins of 'deservingness'. The Jews of Liverpool were not the only ones to establish such a society – the community in Hull followed suit in 1860 and proposals were mooted in Manchester and Birmingham too.[107] It is no coincidence that the two port towns on the transmigratory trail particularly felt the need for such a charity, but they were following a more general trend in rehabilitating casuals and beggars at around this time: the middle decades of the nineteenth century were the peak time for the foundation of societies to eliminate mendicity and rehabilitate beggars of the more 'deserving' type.[108] The Liverpool Society was careful to shape its rationale from the outset to address fears of imposition and casual almsgiving, stating that its remit was people in need of assistance through old age, illness or misfortune rather than transmigrants or 'chancers'. Indeed, like mendicity societies more generally, it hoped to eradicate the need for indiscriminate almsgiving to beggars altogether by taking on responsibility for a more unified scheme which involved giving tickets for money or goods rather than cash. This, it was hoped, would remove the attraction of the town for circulating 'sturdy beggars' and would allow proper investigation of each case while promoting self-sufficiency and industry.[109] These aims thus took in the Jewish imperative to help strangers and the needy, but on a community rather than a personal basis. The Society was even able to bake in an unusual degree of co-operation between the two synagogues: the presidency was to rotate between the two senior wardens, who oversaw a Board of Relief which met daily except on the Sabbath and festivals.[110] This is strikingly similar to the cross-denominational appeal of urban mendicity societies to middle-class supporters in pre-famine Ireland.[111] No applicant could expect relief more than twice per year, and only once per six-month period. The maximum level of relief was set at twenty shillings per individual, or forty shillings per family. However, the provision for people who had arrived in town so recently that they had missed the daily sitting of the board indicates that the Society's remit also encompassed those with no prior claims on the town.[112]

The Mendicity Society in Liverpool struck a chord with applicants: by the start of May 1846, it had relieved fifty-seven people and given out £18 11s. 6d.; in June alone it dealt with thirty-nine applications and disbursed £16 6s. 0d.[113] Demand remained high even though the average grant per applicant fell from six shillings to five, and the OHC was convinced enough of its utility to promise a grant of £50 – although only as and when it was needed from a shortfall in subscriptions (the New Congregation never did commit itself to a donation although some of its members did).[114] Money was also given out to eighty-two people to cover loss of income over the High Holy Days.[115] In 1847 the Society's Board of Management called for retrenchment and greater scrutiny of applicants, stating that their aim was to 'relieve' not to 'maintain'. In fact at one stage they went further and said that they wished to give out sums which were just enough to prevent applicants from getting sums from other authorities.[116] It is unclear whether this was to keep people off non-Jewish charities, or to promote self-sufficiency. The system of discrimination also remained in place: 286 of 900 applicants were turned away in 1846/7 because they were 'undeserving', while another seventeen were granted relief but then subsequently lost it because they were judged to have sufficient means to do without.[117] Very few had a trade, the vast majority instead 'had been compelled to seek a precarious mode of existence'.[118] The Society fell into abeyance at the end of the 1840s, perhaps because of growing financial difficulties. It was resurrected briefly in 1853, and was then relaunched as a loan society, with money left after a special appeal for charity funds in 1861.[119]

The Society was popular with both applicants and supporters (at least at first), but judgements by historians have been lukewarm. Williams claims that it was a problematic influence on perceptions of the community from outside, at a time when it was fighting for full political emancipation.[120] Kokosalakis characterizes its aims as 'naïve' and based on 'spuriously contrived principles of individual worthiness and unworthiness', rather than an appreciation of the more fundamental and external causes of poverty.[121] This is perhaps unfair insofar as society generally was not yet fully aware of these structural factors and still tended to characterize the poor in personal and moral terms. However, it is true that the Jewish mendicity societies seem not to have made as much of their desire to rehabilitate mendicants via hard work as did equivalents outside the community, and Kokosalakis is certainly correct in his judgement that no single voluntary society could make much impact on the effects of mass immigration, even at this relatively early stage of that story. In fact this soon became clear to most of the charities involved. Birmingham's Hebrew Philanthropic Society stated in 1849 that they would no longer relieve casual strangers 'in consequence of the great imposition' that it brought, and the following year they decided not to assist the synagogue in sending away casual strangers any more either except in special circumstances.[122]

By the 1860s, all of the communities had pivoted to a more acceptable and easier-to-police type of scheme: the giving of loans. This was clearly a self-help measure, and although this emphasis was not new, it was taking on greater momentum by the mid-nineteenth century (Samuel Smiles's influential book *Self-Help* was published in 1859). Savings banks, friendly societies, insurance schemes and loans were all ways to encourage the poor to plan for self-sufficiency rather than accept demeaning doles which taught them nothing about taking responsibility for themselves.[123] Jews were thus once again acting with reference both to wider ideas about the poor here, and to long-standing rabbinical teachings on the value on loans and offers of employment which made the poor self-sustaining.[124]

In Liverpool, the tone was set by the Mendicity Society's shift towards loans for the resident Jewish poor from 1861, under the title of the Liverpool Hebrews' Free Loan Society. In its first year, it made thirty-five loans totalling £92 10s. 0d. of which £61 6s. 0d. had been repaid.[125] Loans were to be interest-free and for sums of between ten shillings and £5, lent to 'deserving applicants' who had been in Liverpool for at least twelve months.[126] Sureties were required and repayments had to commence within a week of the loan being made. If the recipient went into arrears of even one week, the balance of the loan became the immediate responsibility of the sureties.[127] These strict terms were apparently acceptable to borrowers, who for the most part made their repayments promptly and regularly, and so were at least exposed to the desired message about 'the principles of honesty & industry which are so essential to their improvement'.[128] The Society soon became more ambitious about the role that it could play in helping the poor to raise themselves 'from a position of penury to that of modern comfort', as they put it; a sentiment also very much in keeping with the times.[129] Birmingham's Hebrew Philanthropic Society adopted a resolution in September 1858 to commence a formal loan fund with similar terms to those adopted in Liverpool, and although the records rarely give the reasons that a loan was required, the fund was again popular.[130] Thirty-four loans were given in 1862, bringing, the Society proudly proclaimed, 'a spirit of self-dependence and industry, holding out a helping hand to those, who, without such friendly aid, would have fallen lower in the scale of want; and teaching them that it is far better to labour to raise their position, than to be dependent upon the bounty of others'.[131]

Furthermore, the fund had turned previous recipients into donors to the charity: perhaps the ultimate mark of success, both practically and ideologically. Both the loan fund and the provision of pensions for the elderly (noted above) were part of a bigger rethink about the aims of this charity, whose committee had resolved that their current system of relief 'be altogether abolished'.[132] In a similar spirit, the Manchester Hebrew Philanthropic Society started a sewing machine fund in 1868 alongside a loan scheme. Applications were forthcoming by spring of the following year, accompanied by the names of at least one security and a certificate of competency from the manufacturer. In July 1869, the chairman of the Society visited the houses of the first two recipients, and 'found their condition materially benefited'.[133] Clearly these schemes were reaching only small numbers of people but they indicate the directions in which Jewish charity was travelling at this time, and the ways that it was adapting in response both to the changing profile of the poor and to wider fashions in charity.

Community leaders also tried to promote economic self-sufficiency through voluntary-funded elementary schools. This was by no means a novel idea either; schooling had been used to shape the morals and identity of the poor since the British Sunday School movement of the late eighteenth century and before, and authors on philanthropy had been singling out the training of the young as a way of improving society for at least as long.[134] The provision of education has also been highlighted by historians as a key plank of the Jewish communities' efforts to shape their poor (and especially the newly immigrant poor) into respectable British citizens, thus raising the status of the community as a whole.[135] By teaching children in English and by introducing a strong secular emphasis to the curriculum alongside Hebrew and Scripture, the schools could create a channel whereby British values were carried back into the homes of the working classes. The Manchester Jewish Board of Guardians was to make this link explicit in 1872 when it noted that 'though [immigrant] parents on account of their ignorance of the language and trading customs of this country, often continue to be objects of charity, the children, by the aid of the education afforded by our excellent schools are brought up to be useful members of society'.[136] As a side-effect, children could also be guided towards trades with better prospects than glazing, hawking and low-end tailoring. This latter point contrasts with the traditional view of charity education, which was designed to prevent habits of indigence, but not to improve socio-economic standing in ways that might disrupt society.

The Jewish schools, which were getting under way in the industrial towns by the early 1840s, thus had an important integrative aim for the community as a whole. They were exclusive in that they were designed to prevent Jewish children being taught in secular or Christian schools, but they encompassed a 'commercial' education as well as a religious one, and charged a sliding scale of fees according to need.[137] This is arguably little different from the formative aims of the schools catering for Irish Catholic children at the same time. However, while these apparently deliberately focused on the creation of a Catholic identity while downplaying Irishness, the Jewish schools aimed to reinforce the duality of a British Jewish identity.[138] They also tried to create a cross-class bond with religion by educating the poor alongside the better off, to the supposed enrichment of both. As could perhaps be predicted, this was less popular with wealthier families, and the withdrawal of their children put school finances on a sometimes precarious footing; in Birmingham separate education for poor children 'whose habits &c have not yet been improved' was introduced in 1853.[139] Standards of teaching also attracted poor notice at times, especially in Birmingham.[140] Nonetheless, by mid-century more than three times as much was being spent on the school in Manchester than on the (newly reunited) congregation, and approximately eight times the amount spent on the casual poor at the same time.[141] Within a few decades, each of the three towns had provision for several hundreds of pupils and the results of pupil examinations were reported frequently and favourably in the Jewish press. Associated book and clothing charities furthered the aim to integrate, anglicize and provide material support for the children: Williams calls these a 'wheel within a wheel of assimilation'.[142] The aim to raise poor children up out of their parents' limited occupational milieux was only partially fulfilled though – apprenticeship schemes were small in scale, although they did stick to their ambitions to place children in more prosperous trades than many of their parents and which made provision for the Sabbath and festivals. Boys were bound into the boot trades, picture frame making and tailoring; several girls went into clothing trades.[143] All three towns also used the schools to reinforce religious and personal behaviour, by insisting that parents attend synagogue regularly, comport themselves well and keep their children clean and tidy. The schools were thus an agent for the promotion of values that were seen as desirable across the denominational scale, as well as – as the Liverpool OHC had hoped in 1850 – 'largely contribut[ing] to the comfort and wellbeing of our co-religionists of all classes'.[144]

Liverpool, Birmingham and Manchester had a particularly rich set of Jewish charities, funded by a growing elite and catering to rising numbers of the poor. They were not alone, though, in responding to the needs of co-religionists. When the new chief rabbi solicited information on the various Jewish congregations under his remit in 1845, he asked about the charities they operated. The small congregation of Brighton, then numbering 150 individuals, had none, but relieved the casual poor from the congregational funds. In Bristol there was also a fund for relieving the transient poor, while Falmouth had a benefit society for the sick. At the same time, by way of comparison, Birmingham Jewry already housed a school, its Hebrew Philanthropic Society and the Benevolent Book and Clothing Society. Hull had a Philanthropic Society but it operated on a contributory benefit model, and Plymouth and Glasgow both reported schemes delivered by *chevroth*. Meanwhile, a large tail of small communities (among them Leeds, Cheltenham, Cardiff and Newcastle) housed no Jewish charities.[145] This evidence suggests strongly that while Jewish charity was a fundamental response to need and to religious obligations, it was in the conditions of the industrial economy and its attendant levels of migration that the Jewish economy of welfare became most vibrant and mixed.

## Conclusions

The charitable efforts of the mid-century congregations were clearly a combination of prevalent ideas about poverty and its relief, and the maintenance of Jewish identity. In their emphasis on discrimination, self-help and assistance rather than maintenance, Jewish charity was in line with wider thinking as well as religious imperatives about the relief of the poor. However, their attitude to casuals was more expansive than was common beyond the faith, the stance on the rehabilitation of mendicants was arguably less stringent, and support was more heavily skewed to outdoor relief than was fashionable. There was also a strong element of social control – or at least, social reshaping – at work, especially in the arena of elementary education, but this was not the whole story. Compassion, commitments to religious observance and a pragmatic if sometimes desperate eye to the balance sheet all played their part too, as did an underlying set of aims to encourage independence without loss of face, which were shared with the charitable arena more widely.

If we return to our theme of social networks, we can see the social obligations acknowledged in the welfare schemes as a strong indicator of a transpatial or imagined community, especially when it involved people who had not (yet) proven their investment in the town. The Jews were by no means alone in looking inwards for aid: it is a common feature of minority culture, and is often given with an eye to the outward appearance of the group in the eyes of the majority. However, British Jewry contained a much more heterogeneous group of people than arguably any other minority at the time, making this commitment all the more powerful evidence of the reality of the imagined community. It is very hard to judge what the immigrant poor themselves felt about receiving welfare from within the community rather than the Poor Law or other charities; no doubt this varied considerably depending on their own priorities for keeping the Jewish laws.

The giving and receiving of aid was also an important way of establishing links between different groups of people. This was certainly an uneven relationship. In theory, Jewish teaching preached that charity should not be demeaning, and that by participating in Jewish life, the poor could still contribute as equals to the community as a whole. In practice, it seems unlikely that this could ever be truly achieved, especially since social distinctions were so clearly preserved in the structure of the synagogue membership. However, it did establish the community as the primary welfare safety net for those who could fashion a claim on it, and one that reinforced the importance of religion as part of people's identity. We have already met examples of people for whom charitable work was one of several ways of reinforcing their focal position within the network of community governance: the Mozley and Samuel clans in Liverpool, for example, and the Aaronses in Birmingham. They often had strong visions for the shape, outward appearance and safety of the community, and felt a strong moral obligation to give time and money to help bring it to fruition. Ties of religion, family and business thus also became links that aided the flow of information, patronage and material aid – as well as personal satisfaction. This, in turn, shaped relationships within the network, as some people were identified as influential, worth cultivating as business associates, friends or patrons, and whose social and residential preferences could be aped for further advantage and status. These were also the people who decided the definition of deservingness, thus shaping the form and outward projection of the community. Yet charity was also a means of cementing ties beyond the imagined community: individual Jews were active in supporting non-Jewish hospitals and other charities, and the Birmingham Philanthropic Society claimed in 1841 that it had aided a few members of other creeds.[146] Non-Jews in turn frequently supported local Jewish charities, either as donors or by participating in fundraising dinners: as one of the officers of the Portsea Hebrew Benevolent Society stated at an annual dinner in 1841, 'in true charity there could be no distinction between one sect and another'.[147] In their models for charitable welfare too, Jewish leaders could be said to be aping their peers outside the religious community, quite possibly using them as a way to further cement their adherence to middle-class ideals about respectability and responsibility. Occasionally – as in the case of Manchester's Society for the Relief of Really Deserving Distressed Foreigners – this extended to the sharing of charitable aid with non-Jews. Generally, however, Jews preferred to found their own charities, in line with their desire to help their own poor.

This is not to say that community leaders were always successful in their aims, or that the poor passively acceded to their aspirations. The flowering of the *chevroth*, for instance, represented a separate model for charity and mutual aid based on nationality as well as faith. Their members were effectively bypassing the place envisaged for them by the community leadership.[148] Jewish charity officers also came to worry increasingly about the duplication of services and varying definitions of deservingness within their offering – hence the pivots in priorities at different times, and the moves towards united boards of relief which were to come to greater fruition in subsequent decades. They were also not always able to maintain the standards of behaviour they required in recipients, which explains the occasional reiteration of rules on synagogue attendance and respectable appearance. Nonetheless, it is undeniable that community leaders were able to formulate priorities for the behaviour of the poor in ways that the poor themselves could not.

It is notable, too, how similar Jewish charitable efforts were in different places, partly because they communicated among themselves and via the Jewish press, partly because they were all responding to similar ideals. In other cases, we can see local priorities, like the active debates on philanthropy in Liverpool which probably influenced the early foundation of Jewish charities there, and the wider emphasis on education in Manchester. The demographic characteristics of the individual communities also had an impact, such as Liverpool Jewry's larger cadre of leisured and wealthy families, and the presence of newcomers in Manchester, some fighting for influence in the synagogue, many others claiming a need for assistance. Hull and Liverpool also had unique patterns of poverty because of their ports, though none of the communities covered by this study were immune to the challenges of immigration and transmigration.[149] On the other hand, the presence of individuals from all synagogues on the charity committees and donor lists suggests that charity could be a unifying influence within the community at large, even in this period of rapid growth. Again, this was something the editors of the *Jewish Chronicle* reflected on, noting in March 1858 that although poverty was unlikely ever to disappear, 'among so small a community as ours, where it is possible to become personally acquainted with all requiring relief, examine into their cases, and control them to some extent, it is our firm conviction that, with judicious management, imposition may be prevented, and pauperism reduced to its lowest ebb'.[150]

In many ways, this sums up the aspirations of nineteenth-century charity more generally; it is probably true that it was only in communities as small and tightly bounded as this one that there was any chance of it becoming a reality.

What we cannot see so easily from the available records are the informal ways that Jews supported each other. These may very well have been the first routes through which aid was received – in the form of small loans, gifts, credit, childcare and the like – and which probably readdressed the uneven relationship between donors and recipients visible in the more formal records.[151] We do have the odd glimpse of these forms of assistance, for example, in the reference in the Birmingham synagogue minutes that people were sent to attend the dying, and the provisions to support people with material aid during the week-long period of mourning.[152] Both the more formal modes of aid and the more informal ones of friendship and neighbourliness are important for defining community relationships, within the faith community and – importantly and yet more invisibly – without. They underpinned the benefits of mutual membership of the community: in Avery-Peck's words, they 'brought to all Jews an otherwise unattainable level of security and safety – political, economic and social'.[153] Thus, aid to co-religionists could have had benefits considerably beyond the material: important when attitudes within society could be unreliable and potentially distrustful.

For all its benefits and good intentions, however, the picture we have gained of Jewish charity in the middle decades of the century is one of duplication and unplanned growth. We have also seen that the burden of charity was growing seemingly exponentially in the face of relentless levels of immigration. In subsequent decades the need for coherent planning became increasingly pressing, and models for how to go about it increasingly numerous. It is to these wider influences, and their impact on the Jewish welfare agenda, that we turn next.

6

# Consolidation, reflection and discrimination: Jewish charity from 1865 to 1880

By the mid-1860s, things were quite different when it came to thinking about welfare, both within the Jewish community and beyond. Within, the most pressing change was in scale, principally due to rising levels of immigration, especially once the outbreak of the American Civil War restricted onward movement. It is worth reiterating that this is something that affected the manufacturing centres much more than the older provincial Jewish settlements, because of their thriving labour markets and their location in or near the ports. Indeed, by the end of this period, immigration was starting to turn small settlements in towns like Leeds and Glasgow into large hubs of provincial Jewry.[1] The change in immigration also, however – as we saw in the previous chapter – brought about a qualitative change in the types of people asking for relief, and prompted difficult thinking about who should be relieved and on what scale. This was sharpened by growing unease by the 1860s at the organic and overlapping way in which Jewish charity had developed, lacking in any overall rationale or method. 'Nemo', writing to the *Jewish Chronicle* in 1869, for example, noted that the current administration of Jewish charity nationwide 'keeps some on the very verge of starvation, it enervates others, it pauperises the many: and in few instances, if any, raises, if it even reach, the respectable and industrious poor, who strive with all their main and might to keep the relieving officer from their door'.[2] With the fight for emancipation now won, the Jewish elite turned in earnest to the growing 'problem' of the poor, who more than ever, were threatening the stability and reputation of the community at large. They were also increasingly confident about tackling other areas of perceived inequality which were now inconsistent with their legal status: the treatment of Jewish workmen in employment legislation, provision for Jewish children under the Poor Law, and the status of Jewish elementary schools.

These discussions were also affected by changes in the wider welfare landscape. Two key aspects of this shift concern us here. The first was embodied in what has been called the 'Crusade against Outdoor Relief' of the 1870s and was revealed via a tightening up of the offer from the Poor Law. From its inception in 1834, the New Poor Law had been conceived of as a deterrent service, catering for truly destitute paupers in workhouses. However, several decades later, an alarming amount of relief was still being delivered 'outdoors', especially in parts of the industrial north.[3] In 1869, the head of the Poor Law Board, George Goschen, thus issued a circular calling for a retrenchment in policies on outdoor relief. This move sits somewhat awkwardly with the growing awareness that un- and underemployment were often the result of external factors rather than personal qualities, especially in manufacturing areas where the employment market was closely related to trade cycles, and the circular was not uniformly implemented across the country. Nonetheless, large numbers of local unions did review – and slash – their outdoor relief rolls in the 1870s, leading to a sharp fall in the numbers assisted outside the workhouse.[4] This placed the Jewish emphasis on outdoor relief increasingly out of step with the statutory authorities, and also made it more likely that any Jewish paupers turning to the Poor Law would receive their relief in an institution. This raised again the old problems concerning religious worship and the dietary laws.

Goschen's circular heralded a second important shift in thinking, which is arguably even more key for our current concerns, and this was a call for a greater coordination of relief efforts between statutory and voluntary bodies. This was part of a move towards putting voluntary charity on to a more 'scientific' and philosophically reflective footing. If the Poor Law was to deal even more stringently with the indigent who had not prevented their condition, charity should complement this by offering a united safety net for the truly deserving poor.[5] Disastrous economic downturns like the Cotton Famine of the early 1860s had brought an indelible trauma especially in the industrial north-west, and had challenged long-held ideas about the causes of poverty. However, the united front envisaged by Goschen and others also meant that the poor could be properly triaged in order to aid the promotion of self-help among the deserving, and the removal of the intransigent to the workhouse. As we saw in the previous chapter, these concerns were not entirely new, but they accelerated in the 1860s and coalesced around a sense of accountability, casework and professionalism.[6]

The London-based Charity Organisation Society (COS) was the most notable outcome of this shift in thinking.[7] It was founded in 1869 and had two key aims. The first – in line with Goschen – was to co-ordinate charitable activity so that overlaps, lacunae and impositions by the canny and instrumental poor were eliminated. Instead, applicants for aid were to be thoroughly investigated so that their case could be referred to the most appropriate source of assistance (the

COS did not dispense relief on its own account as this would not encourage a spirit of independence[8]). The second aim was to promote social betterment via conversations between the classes. Casework and 'friendly visiting' would make the better-off more aware of the condition of the poor and encourage both compassion and deference.[9] This was a live point for the Jewish communities too, where the rich were starting to move into different parts of town than the poor and so were not confronting their condition personally.

We have seen that some of these concerns had been exercising the Jewish communities for some time, and several efforts had already been made to unify their charitable efforts. Manchester had set up its short-lived Board of Relief in 1847, for example, which was, in Williams's words, one of 'the earliest provincial attempts to attempt to apply more or less systematic procedures to the relief of the casual poor of the community'.[10] Liverpool's Mendicity Society had brought both of the town's synagogues into its managing committee and was also one of several charities to stress home visiting to establish levels of need. In London, too, the three major synagogues had entered into a formal arrangement for a joint relief scheme as early as 1834, and the *Jewish Chronicle* had been calling for greater unification of Jewish charities for some time by the 1860s.[11] There were also local reference points for unified action outside the community, such as the Liverpool Central Relief Society which was set up in 1863 and which was affiliated with the COS, and the efforts of philanthropists like Liverpool's William Rathbone (whose work was referenced by the founding committee of the Liverpool Jewish Board of Guardians).[12] Nonetheless, by the late 1860s, as 'Nemo' demonstrated, there was still a perceived need for greater systematization and co-ordination of Jewish relief.

There are, therefore, reasons to expect that the Jewish communities might reflect some of the wider ideas and practices circulating in the field of welfare, and others – among them, the need to preserve Jewish practice – which would suggest a different set of priorities. The most prominent of the changes to Jewish welfare in this period was the move towards rationalization, accompanied by a greater degree of personal investigation into the nature and merits of individual cases. In fact, the Jewish community put these changes onto an organized footing considerably before the COS took form, when in 1859 the three largest Ashkenazi synagogues in London founded a metropolitan Jewish Board of Guardians.[13] They also began to think more carefully about which groups of the poor were deserving of relief and which should be referred to other providers, including the Poor Law. These metropolitan efforts have been well studied, but the course taken in the provincial towns has not. The rest of this chapter will investigate local Jewish responses to charity between 1865 and 1880, and, in particular, how far they reflected the wider emphases on consolidation, casework and a philosophy of charity on the one hand, and targeted retrenchment on the other. It will also examine the evidence for growing confidence and assertiveness when it came to the equal treatment of Jews within welfare, education and employment legislation.

## The foundation of the Jewish Boards of Guardians

The London Jewish Board of Guardians was founded in 1859 in response to the increased demands for assistance over a particularly bad winter, and was initially envisaged for the poor with no prior claim on the community.[14] The influence of more sustained thinking about the modes and aims of charity are also very evident though, for example in the prolonged campaign of support run by the editor of the *Jewish Chronicle*, Abraham Benisch, an adherent of scientific approaches to charity. Cesarani describes the *JC* as the 'midwife and preceptor' of the London Jewish Board of Guardians, so significant was Benisch's influence.[15] In September 1856, for example, one of his editorials stated that '[o]ur whole system of dispensing charity is wrong … we obey, in our benefactions, impulse more than principle. It is not the sound laws of economy which we observe, but those of stagnant routine'.[16] Some years after the foundation of the Board, another editorial stated approvingly that it 'evidently proceeds on the correct view – that mendicancy is only a symptom … of a deeply seated moral disease, with which it is in vain to battle while the disease is not removed'.[17] This language is very reminiscent of wider debates about the nature of poverty. The paper continued to report on the business of the Board as it expanded over the following years, moving from relief for the immigrant poor to sanctioning grants for emigration and to repay loans (unlike the COS the Jewish Boards of Guardians did give out grants), to granting loans, visiting the poor and investigating and improving sanitary conditions in Jewish homes. By the 1880s it was, in Lipman's words, a 'comprehensive agency for social work' for Jews in the metropolis.[18]

The ambition, remit and successes of the London Board formed a powerful model for the provincial communities: the committee of Birmingham's Hebrew Philanthropic Society recommended in August 1864 'establishing a general system of relief on the plan of the London Board of Guardians'.[19] However, local events like the Cotton Famine were also important spurs to action for the industrial towns, coming off the back of increased pressure on local Jewish welfare services because of rising immigration.[20] The community in Manchester was the first to found a board of their own, in 1867, followed by Birmingham in 1870 (records unfortunately do not survive until the 1890s) and Liverpool in 1876. They were emulated in other provincial towns too: Leeds in 1878 and Hull in 1880.[21] The local boards were autonomous (much like the provincial branches of the COS), but they did exchange information and practice. The Manchester Board noted 'with pleasure' in its ninth annual report (of 1875/6) the institution of the Liverpool equivalent, as well as its own role in sending them information.[22]

There are several reasons why Manchester was the first of the provincial communities to form a Jewish Board of Guardians. One was the political slant of the town as a whole and the confidence of the upper tier of the Jewish business elite within it. Another was the unmistakeable emergence of a Jewish 'ghetto' in Red Bank by that time, which caused alarm because of its poor conditions, depressed occupational profile and visibility to outsiders. A third was the energy brought by the Reader of the Old Congregation, Samuel Landeshut, who had already made moves towards the consolidation of Jewish charity by 1867. During the Cotton Famine, he restyled the town's Hebrew Benevolent Fund (founded in 1855 to provide winter relief) into a consolidated provider of welfare, hoping in the process to unify the community behind a single relief agency, while taking the pressure off the synagogues (this at a time when unity was being threatened by the foundation of the Manchester Reform movement).[23] The charity gave out the familiar range of aid, from money to bread, meat, potatoes and blankets, but importantly, it anticipated the move towards home visiting as a way of determining both need and eligibility which was so vaunted by the COS at the end of the decade. It is evident from the names recorded in the ledgers that this was carried out by members of the committee, including Landeshut himself.[24] Unfortunately, there is no documentation surviving to indicate the nature of the visits; it seems likely that they were principally to ascertain levels and veracity of need rather than aiming for the more expansive 'befriending' advocated by COS leaders, but they did result in some applicants being rejected or found to be 'doubtful'. In 1863 the charity used the money left over from a special appeal specifically to help promote independence among the poor, making loans of up to £10, and later in the 1860s renting out sewing machines and other work tools.[25] It also gave medical advice and goods and assisted with emigration. The range of assistance was thus very similar to the combined efforts of synagogues and charities in earlier decades, but the emphasis on home visiting and the centralization of several functions in one body give an indication that this was part of a wider rethink.

The sums given out in cash by the fund were not large, suggesting that like other charities, the aim was supplementation rather than substitution of income: over a third of those receiving financial aid received only 1s. 6d. per week and a further quarter got 2s. or 2s. 6d. The duration of relief was not often recorded, but seems to have varied from a few weeks to thirteen or seventeen weeks at a time, likely reflecting perceived levels of need and the nature of individual circumstances. Almost two-thirds of recipients were married, but they had children of very different ages: there was no dominant family 'type' who were assisted (no ages were recorded for adults so it is impossible to see how many were elderly). Sixty per cent of applicants lived on Fernie Street and Verdon Street or their Backs, and of those with occupations recorded, 42 per cent were glaziers. This is very much the snapshot of want seen in the records on residence and occupation in earlier chapters and points to the vulnerability of working-age adults and their families to economic hardship. The same charity had 262 applications to its Passover Fund in 1868, and upwards of 250 in 1869; the vast majority were given relief.

Under Landeshut, this society clearly developed a sense of an enlarged remit and set of aims, but Williams's judgement that it lacked the resources and staffing to cope with both investigating and relieving the levels of poverty seen in the community in the 1860s seems sound.[26] In Birmingham, too, the Hebrew Philanthropic Society was starting to think about new modes of relieving poverty: in 1870 it added to its aims 'the function of becoming guarantee to manufacturers for work given to Jewish workmen', and several sources recorded the odd instance of assisting workmen to purchase licences to operate.[27] These efforts accompanied the various loan schemes which were often used to set up businesses, and other self-help initiatives like the contributory insurance scheme operated by the Manchester Hebrew Sick and Burial Benefit Society (founded in 1860), the amalgamated Birmingham Loyal Independent Israelite Society and those run by the *chevroth*.[28] Self-help and independence clearly continued to form a key aim of Jewish welfare schemes, although they had yet to be consolidated in the way leaders were starting to envisage.

Running parallel to these developments, however, was the ongoing simmering of ill feeling between the different synagogues over the burden of relief. The total cost of synagogue charity was still about the same in the 1870s as it was in the 1830s and 1840s, although since the numbers of poor had risen considerably, it was a less significant element in the Jewish economy of makeshifts.[29] This reduction in generosity was probably the result of a combination of increased demand, ongoing concerns about who to relieve, and reluctance to commit to large outlay when it was felt that other congregations were not doing the same. Despite attempts to institute joint schemes in all three towns, the Old congregations were still complaining of a disproportionate burden: the Liverpool OHC contributed about three times as much as the New in 1874/5, for example (in line with its membership and levels of poverty, but not, it said, its income). Squabbles continued over the amounts the two synagogues should contribute to the Joint Relief Fund in the late 1860s, and by 1870 it was clear that the problem of unified relief required a better solution.[30] In Manchester, too, Landeshut's efforts at unification foundered, partly over differences between the synagogues, although this time of a different nature: they could not agree over the potential use of the Reform prayer book in the Orthodox burial ground should a Reform pauper end up in need of charitable interment.[31] It must be said that the foundation of the Jewish Boards of Guardians did not entirely eliminate these issues: the Manchester OHC was to complain that it was the only synagogue making a regular grant to the Board – 10 per cent of its income, or £200, which it claimed it could ill afford, especially since its social composition had changed with the withdrawal of many of its wealthier members to the suburbs.[32] Nonetheless, the establishment of the boards did ensure that the synagogues were able to hand over their status as place of both first and last resort for charity.

The provincial Jewish Boards of Guardians certainly had expansive aims. The Birmingham Board recorded that it hoped to 'assist in ameliorating the condition of the Jewish poor, resident or casual, by temporary relief, assistance to procure employment, by making grants of money, the distribution of seasonable relief at the festivals and during the winter months, and by visiting at their houses'.[33]

The remit of the Manchester Board was similar, adding that relief was available 'irrespective of the religious practices or opinions of the applicant', and also that 'temporary, exceptional or continuous' relief could be allowed, according to circumstances and resources.[34] The Liverpool Board expanded further in 1878, stating that its aims were: to make further discrimination between the 'worthy and the unworthy'; to look 'to the alleviation of distress for the moment and its prevention in the future'; and – strikingly given surrounding debates – to promote 'the elevation of the Poor from a condition of unspeakable misery to a state of independence and happiness'.[35]

Expansive though they were compared with the COS and many other charities, these statements of intent also indicate that there were limits to who could be relieved. Both the Manchester and Birmingham boards committed themselves to the support of casuals on a discretionary basis only, for example, with no relief for beggars. The casual poor thus still occupied a contested space:

in 1869 the Manchester Board reported that 'every possible attention has been paid to the poor of this city [in the preceding year] whilst the least possible encouragement has been extended to casuals & tramps'.[36] We will see that there were instances where the boards did relax their intentions further for the sake of reducing the long-term burden on relief; in the case of deserted wives and emigrants, for instance, to which we will return. However, on the whole they remained wedded to their belief in a unified and discriminatory system at least in theory; this took up far more emphasis than the notion of 'friendly visiting' which so preoccupied the COS.[37] The Manchester Board was to stress on several occasions that its registers were open to public scrutiny so that anyone could check the 'trustworthiness of applicants for Charity'. The fact that this also opened up the personal circumstances of those applicants does not appear to have been a problem; perhaps, in fact, it was meant partly as a deterrent to the 'undeserving'.[38]

Their initial remit set out, the Jewish boards did not reflect much more on their philosophy in their annual reports and committee minutes. We can see changes of emphases in their actions and the new schemes that they launched, however, and their members were sometimes more expansive in letters and speeches reported in the Jewish press. These show an ongoing sense of exceptionalism as well as an awareness of debates about the nature of poverty and its relationship with the dreaded condition of pauperism. Thus, Lionel Louis Cohen, president of the London Board, expounded to the collected supporters of the Manchester Board in 1873 that '[a]n individual was not a pauper because at a time of exceptional distress he asked for exceptional relief'.[39] This attitude was in line with COS thinking in the emphasis on temporary relief to produce permanent benefit. However, there were grey areas when this involved unemployment, which seem not to have troubled the Jewish boards, perhaps because their poor had such different prior experiences of work.[40] The Rev. Morris Joseph of Liverpool also spoke to the distinction between paupers and the poor when he lent his voice to the initial proposal to establish a Jewish Board of Guardians in the town in 1875, noting that '[i]t was their duty as "merciful sons of merciful fathers," to strive by personal effort to raise the condition of the poor and to make the paupers an object all but unknown in their midst'.[41] This sentiment can be traced through later debates over the treatment of the immigrant poor.

In terms of particularism, other comments show that the idea of Jewish distinctiveness was still live in the new schemes. The Manchester Board recorded in 1877, for example, that because its founding principles were 'entirely different from those adopted by parochial Boards of Guardians [that is, the Poor Law authorities], it is impossible to compare the state of our poor with that of other denominations'.[42] The voluntary status of the Jewish Boards of Guardians also makes the comparison difficult to sustain, but the deep-rooted pride in Jewish charity is still clear. Joseph was thinking along the same lines when he suggested that by founding a Jewish Board of Guardians in Liverpool, his fellows would not only 'improve the condition of the poor', but would also 'excite the admiration of their fellow-townsmen for the wise manner in which they dealt with the distressed'.[43] Lionel Cohen was also live to the different presentations of poverty in different settings, warning his Manchester brethren that 'it was necessary to pursue this modern science of charity carefully and watchfully: not to apply axioms too closely to one district which answered in another, but to regard with care what existed; not subverting, but moulding it to the circumstances and the period in which we lived, and the people among whom we lived'.[44] His use of the word 'science' in relation to charity is noteworthy.

The first priorities of the Jewish boards were to appoint investigating officers, actively discourage ad hoc almsgiving and – at least in theory – prevent applicants being able to solicit funds from a number of different sources, many of which had different criteria for applications. From the start, they worked with other charities and the synagogues as well as giving out money on their own account. This was again not without precedent: Birmingham's Ladies Society had applied to the town's Hebrew Philanthropic Society in September 1860 for a grant for their own work, rather than relieving the poor individually themselves, for example (the matter was left open for further discussion), and the president of the Birmingham OHC referred cases to the Philanthropic Society on at least one occasion.[45] However, this was now baked into the composition of the boards' central committees, with officials from the other major Jewish charities and the synagogues serving as ex officio members. The boards also took over the festival relief schemes (not within the remit of COS-approved practice, replacing as it did any impetus to self-help[46]). This removed a huge administrative burden from the synagogues although they still contributed financially. However, the attitude of the synagogues to the new bodies remained ambiguous. They dragged their feet over their financial contributions and they worried that the existence of the boards would discourage people from making voluntary contributions to their own coffers.[47] In Manchester there was opposition from the Reform congregation, and both they and the new Spanish and Portuguese synagogue (est. 1872) initially declined to make a grant, although individuals from the Reform congregation were actively involved. This was to cause financial issues for the boards, who frequently noted the tardiness of the congregation in paying their subscriptions.[48] Further donations came from individual members, including some large and repeated gifts, and in Birmingham, the Benevolent Book and Clothing Society noted in March 1866 'That this Committee recognise the usefulness of the Board of Guardians and wish to support it as far as practicable'.[49]

The Jewish Boards of Guardians rapidly set up professional and efficient systems for investigating and supporting applicants. Their relief committees met several times a week to receive applications, which would then be investigated, often by a paid official.[50] Relief could take the form of one-off or repeated ('fixed') doles, usually lasting a couple of months, or a wide range of the usual material forms of aid. A medical officer was appointed to hold surgeries in the poor localities and make home visits if requested by the committee (the poor could not request a visit themselves, presumably to restrict over-enthusiastic demands – several of the MOs reported the popularity of the medical services, and even that some of the poor used them as a covert way to bring themselves to the Board's attention[51]). In addition, the committees made emergency payments for those sitting *shivah* or who came to their attention outside regular meetings, and they gave business loans and rented out occupational equipment. In subsequent years, many of the local boards set up industrial funds, like the earlier Manchester Benevolent Fund.[52] Finally, they assisted onward or return migration, principally of new arrivals: a project which was to become increasingly onerous as the years progressed. The new boards met with a rapid response from the poor: the first annual reports of the Manchester Board recorded that it had 'entertained' 535 applications for relief, more than two-thirds of them from 'casuals'.[53]

The boards were also keen to develop the loan and apprenticeship schemes already in operation in the three towns, as a way to foster self-sufficiency and the promotion of useful work skills. Both had an uneven reception, however, despite the fact that they were familiar to the Jewish poor. Whether the terms of the boards' schemes were stricter, whether potential applicants were put off by the more rigorous investigation, or whether newer waves of immigrants did not see their value is debatable, though there is evidence of all three factors playing a part. The boards certainly did tighten up their terms over time to cover residency requirements and a more stringent demand for loan sureties. This apparently resulted in loans being (according to the Liverpool Board again) 'confined to trustworthy persons, with the natural result that the re-payments have become far more regular'.[54] Greater discrimination was also exercised: only £47 10s. was lent in 1877/8 compared with £134 9s. the previous year, with the largest amount being £10.[55] In Manchester too, increasing discretion was exercised over applications for loans, with eighteen of forty-four applications turned down in 1878/9.[56] This scheme was particularly slow to take off though: the Board reported that few of the early applicants were of a type 'who under any circumstances are not likely to be permanently benefited'.[57] The equipment hire schemes also turned out to have an unwelcome level of risk: the scheme in Manchester was abandoned only a year after its launch, in 1874, when it was decided that it was too financially precarious a prospect for the Board to continue, despite some early successes with the hire of sewing machines. The loan scheme was relaunched in June 1873, with a much larger fund behind it, but it was not until 1880/1, when it was restyled in friendlier terms, that it became popular (the condition that the money could not be used to redeem pawned clothing notwithstanding).[58]

The apprenticeship schemes were also conceived – like their predecessors – to equip their recipients with the power to better themselves and to avoid the creation of a pauperized subclass.[59] Unfortunately, as they were to repeat in their annual reflections year on year, the Jewish Boards of Guardians found it very difficult to persuade parents to forgo the boys' immediate earnings in less desirable – but readily available – jobs. Some of the earlier schemes, including the one run by the London Board, had overcome this by negotiating an increasing scale of wages over the course of the apprenticeship. In Manchester, too, the Board's industrial committee granted special allowances to parents in the early years of a child's apprenticeship rather than paying the fee themselves and expecting the money to be reimbursed once the youngster was employed. This policy was not followed in Liverpool, where, at the end of the first year of its scheme, the Board reported, regretfully, that it had had no applications.[60] It was, however, undaunted, citing similar experiences in other towns, and noting that the whole idea was as yet unfamiliar to the poor. It also lost no time in pointing out that the majority of the recipients of relief in that year had been glaziers, hawkers and tailors – precisely the trades that it hoped the rising generation would be able to avoid. The Board remained optimistic, although their first success story was not in fact reported until 1779/80 when one boy was apprenticed to a firm of upholsterers. The committee reported their hope that the poor are 'at least becoming alive to the advantages which apprenticeship holds out to their children'.[61] However, by 1881/2, the Board was still expressing regret that there had been no further progress: 'It is evident that the benefits offered by apprenticeship have still to be appreciated by the great majority of the poor.'[62] In Manchester too, the Board cited lack of interest from parents in 1877, despite early successes with the system of direct payments.[63] It could also be difficult to find masters prepared to take on Jewish apprentices: a problem that had been reported in the *Jewish Chronicle* since the early 1850s.⁶⁴

The expansiveness of the various schemes operated by the boards meant that finances were always precarious. The Liverpool Board reported that it was running with a deficit after only two years, and the following year its income was compromised by a poor economic situation which curbed the generosity of donors.⁶⁵ It had in that year received almost £280 in subscriptions and an additional £65 in donations at the Jewish New Year and Passover. The synagogues had assisted it to the tune of £80 from the Old Hebrew Congregation and £35 from the New, with a further £20 donated by the committee of the soup kitchen. In the same period, it had spent over £250 in relief and had given out approximately £85 at the various major festivals. Additional sums were spent on the provision of kosher meals to hospital patients (over £27), money on 'goods' and groceries, surgical instruments and almost £50 on loans; all areas of aid previously met via the patchwork of Jewish relief agencies in the town.⁶⁶ In Manchester 133 fixed pensioners were supported in 1868, and the committee also gave out 880 4 lb. loaves of bread, 1635 pounds of meat, 840 hundredweights of coals and 42 of rice and 44 loads of potatoes, and spent £22 13s. 1d. on groceries. It also assisted 107 emigration cases, gave 'goods' to a further forty, made seven loans, paid for four hawkers' licences, spent more than £4 on assistance for sitting *shivah*, helped three cases with clothing, redeemed eleven pledges for pawned goods and (unusually) helped out three families with their rent. A total of £266 19s. 3d. was also spent on 'general' relief and additional sums went on subscriptions to medical institutions and the London Jewish Workhouse, stimulants, wine and cod liver oil, nursing and midwifery tickets. In total, 884 applications were considered, a staggering 689 of which were from casuals and 195 from the resident poor, and 45 were refused.⁶⁷

The boards were clearly performing a much-needed service, but it came at a high monetary cost. The committee in Liverpool felt moved to remind readers in 1878 that '[i]t is obvious that the amount of good that the Board can do must entirely depend upon the pecuniary support it receives. It is also, it should always be remembered, the servant of the entire Liverpool Community; for it performs the work of charity which belongs primarily to each and all of its members'.⁶⁸

With a discernible note of exasperation, the report went on to cite the iniquity of 'persons' who utilized the charity for the poor 'and yet [did] not contribute a single shilling to its funds'.⁶⁹ In 1881 it again regretted that its financial position had prevented it from taking up its deserved role as 'one of the most powerful and prosperous' of Liverpool's Jewish institutions, and the president threatened to resign because of the 'inadequate support' given by the community.⁷⁰ The

Birmingham Board was able to maintain a healthier balance sheet at least in the early years: in 1872 it had an income of £822 2s. 1d. and outgoings of £732 19s. 9d. And while applications were again skewed towards casuals – 355 compared with 104 residents – it was the latter who got the lion's share of the grants: 1795 compared with 398.[71]

Residency status was an important point for the Jewish Boards of Guardians, as it had been for its predecessors: relief for residents was compared with casuals in the annual reports and money spent on the latter was kept as low as possible. Residents could often access more generous scales of assistance: the founding rules of the Birmingham Board stated that the clerk could give out five shillings to residents but only two shillings and sixpence to casuals applying for the first time – the latter similar to doles given out by the Jewish charities decades previously.[72] The first annual report of the Manchester Board also stated that 'principal attention' had been to those resident in the town for a year or more. The implications were made clear:

> This will clearly prove that the Board held out no premium to the Poor of other towns to settle here nor to foreign Poor to emigrate to this city; but that it has been careful to carry out strictly and as far as possible the principal [sic] upon which the institution has been founded, viz. to care for the Poor of the city, and to discourage vagrancy.[73]

The Liverpool Board, too, was at pains to stress that it assisted more long-term residents than newcomers: an unsatisfactory balance of seventy-six to eighty-eight in 1876/7 had shifted to eighty-three against fifty-nine by 1877/8 and was even more pronounced when it came to the sums handed out: over £215 for residents compared with just under £70 for newer arrivals. The committee reflected that this indicated the slowing of inward migration 'and any fear that the establishment of the Board might attract poor to the Town is thus finally dispelled'.[74] This does seem rather like wishful thinking given the ongoing scale of immigration, which more than filled the spaces left by those who became independent or moved on.[75] Some of the figures cited earlier also show that in other years numbers were dominated by casuals.

Figure 6.1 shows the numbers of people relieved by the Jewish Board of Guardians in Manchester from 1868 to 1876 in several different categories. It demonstrates a fall in total numbers over time, at least until 1875, but the trajectory of the fall was particularly noticeable among those resident in the town for less than six months. In the boards' own terms, this must be judged a success, and given the ongoing scale of migration must have represented a deliberate

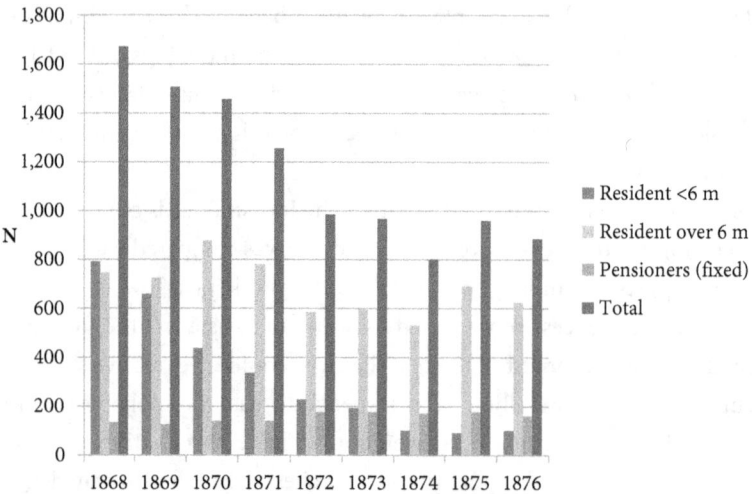

**Figure 6.1** Numbers relieved by the Manchester Jewish Board of Guardians, 1868–76.
Source: Cohen, 'Problem of Jewish Poverty Relief', Appendix J.

change in policy. Even at the low point of 1874, however, when the Board reported that want was falling among longer-term residents who were now only applying for relief in exceptional circumstances, it was still assisting 800 people, and reduced numbers could sometimes disguise longer periods spent on relief.[76] Nonetheless, it is notable that a fall in relief among the longer-term residents was also taken as a sign of a different type of success: that independence and self-help were now being more fruitfully promoted. Numbers of fixed pensioners remained fairly stable, though they were seen as an expensive category. Since they were mainly 'aged and helpless' there was, however, little that could be done to ameliorate this.[77]

It is thus difficult to characterize the boards' practices as either generous or deterrent. Individual doles remained unremarkable – although higher for residents – but in terms of absolute outlay the commitment to relief is very striking. We can certainly see an underlying theme of self-help, which would make sense of the size of the pensions, and also of the sense that a drop in outlay represented a moral success. As ever, much of the policy was dictated by the balance sheet, and with ever-growing demands on their schemes, and a static set of income streams, the Jewish communities needed a new strategy. By the 1870s, this emerged in discussions over ways to redraw their limits. First the boards targeted repatriation and onward migration schemes; the former were seen as philosophically preferable because it would also act as a deterrent to other would-be immigrants. Naturally, this was a particularly live issue for the communities in the port towns, especially as other congregations often paid for poor Jews to reach them. They called on other charities to help them where they could: in June 1880 the Liverpool Board agreed to send one family to Germany providing the German Society agreed to assist; in August 1881 it joined with the (non-Jewish) Foreign Aid Society and the Jewish Ladies' Benevolent Society to support another family in their onward journey to America – although this was a course that flouted their stated aims.[78] The Manchester Board, meanwhile, secured an arrangement in 1869/70 to purchase passage for emigrants at a charity rate through an agent.[79] This significantly reduced the burden on the Board's finances while also reducing the problem of the transient poor. Things were only to get worse though – by 1880 the annual report of the Liverpool Board made specific reference to the persecution of Russian Jews, which was already producing 'many thousands of fugitives' in Liverpool, en route to America.[80] By this time the Mansion House Fund was supporting those who could not support themselves, but many were choosing to stay in Liverpool rather than go home.[81]

The last option was to refuse relief altogether to specific groups of people. Jewish charities had for years been trying to put immigrants off coming to Britain because of the pressure they put on welfare services and the image of the community. This was clearly a battle that was impossible to win. Refusing relief to people *in situ* was difficult to countenance because it not only involved excluding part of the 'imagined community', it also involved sending them to the Poor Law authorities. In London, the line was eventually drawn at medical relief, which, other than the provision of kosher food, was not deemed a specifically 'Jewish' matter. From 1879 the Board's medical services were thus handed over to the Poor Law authorities.[82] In the provinces, it was deserted wives and children who were targeted.

Family desertion was not an issue that the earlier charities had had to face on any great scale. In the more pressured circumstances of the 1870s, however, things were quite different, and this group of the needy now carried considerable emotional baggage for the Jewish Guardians. The issue was that with escalating immigration – and also, perhaps, as knowledge increased about more comprehensive schemes of relief within the Jewish communities – more and more immigrant wives were being left behind in towns where relief was thought to be readily available, while husbands moved on to find work. It was the old fear of the instrumentalism of the casual poor, writ large. Some of these wives expected to be sent on to America by the Jewish authorities – a course the boards debated as both expensive and unmerited, but ultimately sometimes cheaper than taking on a long-term burden.[83] Fundamentally, these dependents, though 'deserving' in the most customary use of the word, had no claim on the Jewish charities beyond their religion, and were tainted by the presumptuous and irresponsible actions of their husbands. Could the boards, though, actually take the final step of turning them away?

The decision to close off one of the streams of relief in London was perhaps made easier by the fact that the Board was already accustomed to working with a range of statutory services; plus the Poor Law medical services were (theoretically at least) divorced from the more stigmatizing aspects of the workhouse regime.[84] In towns like Liverpool and Manchester, it seems to have been harder to make the same decision, and any resolve to do so – as we saw in the earlier policy towards casuals – tended to collapse in the face of actual need. This was despite the fact that it was only the statutory authorities who had the ability to impose fines or threaten imprisonment for deserting husbands.[85] The Manchester Board took a middle way by deciding early on only to give relief in kind to deserted wives, but towards the end of 1879 this was firmed up into a ruling that any woman requiring aid for more than fourteen days was to be offered the workhouse. This was, however, repealed three months later.[86] In both Manchester and Liverpool special committees were convened in the summer of 1880 to consider how to deal with deserted wives. In 1877/8 the Liverpool Board debated a proposal to give no further relief but rejected it, noting that the issue was 'one of extreme difficulty'.[87]

The treatment of deserted immigrant families underlines the boundaries of 'belonging'. In reporting an (apparently short-lived) fall in the numbers of deserted wives in the late 1870s, the Manchester Board stated with a touch of pride that of these women 'there is fortunately not a single native case'.[88] The resident poor were evidently still thought of in different terms than the new arrivals, and perhaps more significantly, as the core in whom the character of the community as a whole was invested. This suggests that the rise of immigration may have increased a spirit of solidarity across the entire resident community, rich and poor.

Things were different when immigrants could be seen to settle in and become 'respectable'; it was the transients who only claimed from the community and did not envisage giving back who were the particular problem. Thus, an address from the chairman of the Manchester Board in May 1873 described immigrants as consisting of two groups: first, those fleeing countries where they suffered prejudice, and whose 'intellects and deportment' were as a result 'so deficient and so inferior when they came here that it was with the greatest difficulty in the world that they could find the means of obtaining their livelihood'. However, they rapidly learnt English and 'as they were naturally thrifty and well disposed, they soon made their way and ultimately became good citizens'. These, then, were people worth investing in as they would prove their worth as useful British Jews. The second group, he said, arrived with a trade, but the means could not be found to support them. The answer, he said, lay with a new proposal for an industrial fund, which could lend out tools and so on.[89] They too, then, had the potential to be good citizens. Moreover, Lionel Louis Cohen, the President of the London Board and guest of honour at the same meeting, cited the foreign origins of so many of the settled members of British Jewry as a reason for their underlying sympathy, giving them 'a lingering sympathy for the foreigner'. But, he went on to say, 'while they must not proscribe these persons, it was their duty at the same time to hold out no stimulus to helpless poverty to flock to this country' ('Hear, hear', said the assembled audience).[90] The attitude towards foreign immigrants thus held at its heart a near-unresolvable tension between compassion and shared origins on the one hand, and fear of imposition and tainted reputation on the other. As an editorial article in the *Jewish Chronicle* put it: 'Jewish sentiment will always revolt at the idea that any of its members should without their fault, merely in consequence of misconduct of which they are the victims and not the accomplices, be deprived of those rights which Providence adjudged to them when it allowed them to be born into the community.'[91] Therein lies both the key motivation and the key reservation behind Jewish charity in the 1870s and 1880s.

## Co-operation and consolidation

The Jewish Boards of Guardians did not take over the full remit of the mixed economy of Jewish welfare, but they tried to prevent duplication by sharing information and passing applicants between themselves and the various charities. Several of the other societies also made grants to the boards to support their work, and in Birmingham, moves were made towards a fuller consolidation of the largest Jewish charities: the Hebrew Philanthropic Society, the Educational Society and the Board of Guardians (by then four years old).[92] This was finally effected in 1880, in recognition 'that the present system of relieving the Jewish poor is by no means perfect'.[93] Thenceforth, applicants would be investigated by a single set of officers and their details would be recorded in one set of registers, although the funds and investments of the three bodies remained separate. This is undoubtedly the closest any of the profiled Jewish communities came to either the COS or the Jewish Board of Guardians ideal, taking in as it did, the moral impact on the poor as well as the unified approach to casework.

The Jewish charities also sought out co-operation with wider civic bodies, from the Poor Law authorities to the sanitary departments. The sick were sent on to local hospitals, Poor Law infirmaries or Jewish welfare institutions in London for treatment, or to convalescent homes and seaside resorts where they could recover from illnesses.[94] The boards' medical officers liaised with the town authorities on the improvement of Jewish homes, although they were not able to prevent outbreaks of epidemic disease in the poorer Jewish areas despite seeing hundreds of patients per year (and the sanitary and civic improvements of the 1860s and 1870s notwithstanding). Their prompt actions sometimes put them ahead of the local sanitary authorities. On an outbreak of cholera in Manchester in August 1883, for example, the Board wrote to the town corporation asking what action was being taken and making suggestions for the circulation of posters and handbills, presumably to notify local residents of the precautions they should take. The corporation agreed to the circulars and to provide bags of disinfecting powder, although they were concerned to avoid creating a sense of panic. They also agreed to send a representative to the Jewish quarter to hear any complaints.[95] The Jewish MOs also continued their own campaigns of vaccination, cleansing and whitewashing especially at times of epidemic disease, when their actions were frequently noted to have prevented worse outcomes for Jewish residents.[96] It cannot be denied, however, that the health of the Jews in the poorer areas was potentially compromised by poor-quality housing, as we saw in earlier decades too. The MO to the Manchester Board cited in 1868/9 'the close, dirty, ill-ventilated and ill-drained habitations of our poor' as a key cause of premature death and diseases like fevers and diarrhoea, the latter of which had caused the death of twenty-two Jewish children that year. Another troubling cause was 'the meagre condition of the parents', although this was partly outweighed by the promptness with which they sought medical assistance for their children, including those 'who would not accept charity under another form or who would be refused because of sufficiency of earnings'.[97] The MO suggested sending a memo to the Board of Health to request action regarding the state of the housing and their sanitary condition; a sign of their growing confidence in demanding action from civic authorities.

The attitude of the Jewish boards towards co-operation with the local workhouses was more ambivalent. They seem to have regarded institutional medical facilities as a useful extension of their own services, and the Poor Law generally as a safety valve of last resort. The workhouses were, however, generally viewed with disdain, partly because their use could be taken as a failure by the Jewish community to look after their own poor, but also because they overrode family bonds and the ease of Jewish worship. One of the ongoing aims of the boards, like the earlier charities and the synagogues, was thus to ensure that Jewish patients in non-Jewish institutions were able to access kosher food and religious services.[98] With a greater centralization of casework under the boards, it was arguably more likely that the Jewish authorities would know when one of 'their' poor was sent to an institution. On the other hand, with growing populations and so many people passing through, others likely encountered the non-Jewish welfare services without coming to the boards' attention – at least until they were released or died and the financial support of the Jewish authorities was requested.[99]

The practical concerns about Jews' use of the workhouse came to a head in Manchester in 1867, when the Jewish Board of Guardians became concerned about the terms of what would become the 1868 Poor Law Amendment Act. Specifically, they challenged its ability to cater for kosher meals and the observance of the Sabbath and festivals for Jewish indoor paupers, and whether it could accommodate the needs of orphan Jewish children. Jewish patients in the Manchester workhouse had already been attended by their own medical officers, but now the Board of Guardians wrote to the local Poor Law authorities asking that provisions be made 'which would permit the poor of the Mosaic faith to participate in the benefits of parochial relief without doing violence to their religious opinions'.[100] The ensuing negotiations with the Poor Law Board in January 1869 eventually secured a satisfactory set of provisions: Jews were not singled out by name in the legislation, but under its more general provisions Jewish indoor paupers could now be excused from labour on the Sabbath and leave the house to attend services at the synagogue; they could receive kosher food as long as the Jewish boards provided it; and they would have provision made for relief on the Jewish festivals as long as that was provided by the Boards of Guardians (this to avoid opening a floodgate to applications from Catholics for relief on their own festivals). Similar, voluntary, arrangements were subsequently entered into with the local hospitals, although all drew the line at reserving wards for Jewish patients, as had happened in some of the London medical institutions.[101] The Poor Law Board also confirmed that Jewish inmates (specifically including children) could access religious teaching from a Jewish minister, like members of any other creed. Finally, any deserted or orphaned children would be permitted to remain in the house or go to the Jewish Hospital or Jewish Orphan Asylum in London (at public expense) rather than go to a parish school.[102] These concessions speak volumes to the confidence and persuasiveness of community leaders in Manchester (as well as the receptive attitude of the local authorities), and they managed as a result to secure greater concessions than those in London, where negotiations over outdoor relief for Jews foundered in the 1870s.[103]

The concessions secured in 1867 were observed as far as possible, and board minutes continue to note instances of Jewish inmates of workhouses and hospitals, usually on the occasion of their release. The provisions for children were sometimes difficult to fulfil: in November 1878 the Manchester Board heard that it was hard to find industrial schools willing to accommodate those referred to them because of their religious requirements. No action was proposed at that time and it is difficult to estimate what numbers were ever involved.[104] A handful of children were sent to the Jewish Orphan Asylum with the costs shared between the local authorities and the Jewish Board of Guardians, and the latter did send in kosher food for Jewish patients in both hospitals and workhouses.[105] The problems did not entirely go away despite the terms of the 1868 Act, however: in their annual report of 1874/5 the Manchester Board was still noting that the Jewish poor were 'debarred by the Practice of their Religion from entering the Parochial Workhouses'.[106]

The confidence of the provincial Jewish communities extended into other areas of welfare too. The Manchester Board again led the way here, keeping a lively eye on regulations as to working hours which might disadvantage Jewish workmen keeping the Sabbath, and on the provisions for universal education under the 1870 Education Act. Its members called a special meeting in February 1871 to discuss several cases where Jewish tailors had been prosecuted and fined under the Workshop Regulations Act of 1867, and noted that an amendment had been successfully seen through parliament in June.[107] The build-up to the 1870 Education Act caused some debate because of the potential for discrimination against the teaching of minority religions: representatives of the Birmingham Hebrew School Committee attended a meeting in London on the matter, but reported that no further action was required since there is 'now little reason to apprehend that the Jews will have anything to fear from the Bill'.[108] We have already seen that it did remove the ability of the Jewish authorities to impose residency requirements on parents, and it also brought the need for further adjustments to ensure that the Jewish schools were eligible for funding. With those provisos though, it ultimately did not bring restrictions on religious teaching as long as the curriculum was deemed to be broad enough. Many of these causes were supported in the pages of the Jewish press too, and urged on the attentions of the Jewish Board of Deputies, but the influence of the now well-established and confident provincial communities is striking.

## Conclusions

Richard Titmuss observed in the mid-twentieth century that welfare is an excellent reflection of the cultural and political characteristics of an era.[109] The Jewish communities in the manufacturing towns prove this point very effectively during the period from 1865 to 1880. In each case the growing scale and composition of need forced community leaders to think again about how to relieve the poor, and in doing so they developed an increasingly coherent set of reference points. In earlier decades the provincial congregations had embarked piecemeal on an expansive set of voluntary schemes which were characterized both by benevolence and by a desire to regulate behaviour. This had produced an overlapping patchwork of charitable services, all well intentioned, but forming no particularly well-conceived whole. The Jewish voluntary sector (like that beyond it) thus offered a valuable safety net for the poor, but one which might see them investigated several times – or not at all – and which (so people came to think) gave them mixed messages about self-help and moral deservingness.

In subsequent decades, Jewish charity increasingly reflected a system of prioritization based on 'deservingness' alongside a desire to apply wider models of charity. In this respect their benevolence reflects, Titmuss-style, their taking on of British modes of thinking. However, the changed landscape of Jewish relief was also an expression of the cultural and political world of European Jewry. European trade cycles had as important an impact on the scale of poverty as domestic ones, as did policies of discrimination and violence against Jews in Central and Eastern Europe. This brought immigration on a previously untold scale, which pushed communal resources to breaking point, both economically and philosophically. Most of the new arrivals were poor, strikingly 'foreign' and ill adapted to modern urban life. Add to this the sense that Jews had a duty to care for their own and preserve religious practice, together with the economic crisis of the 1860s at home – and the Jewish authorities were faced with a potent mix of challenges.

The first of these related to sheer numbers, which forced them to discriminate more heavily between applicants. Second, and relatedly, the tacit acceptance of responsibility for co-religionists was pushed to its utmost, especially when it was combined with the realities of transient sojourners and abandoned families. Third, it raised the alarming problem that the hosts of poor and very obviously foreign Jews might undo the hard work British Jewry had been putting into their campaigns for acceptance and emancipation. It is the latter that has attracted the most attention in the literature to date, but in the current analysis, we are as interested in the balance between material resources and the conceptualization of belonging and obligation for fellow Jews. The records of the Jewish Boards of Guardians suggest that both loomed equally in their thinking and practices. With hindsight we know that all of these problems were to become much more pressing in the decades that followed, but it is in the 1860s and 1870s that we see community leaders confronting them for the first time, and their responses are very revealing both as to their sense of the wider imagined community and their place in civic society more generally.

Contemporary debates about the nature and purposes of poor relief added a layer of reflection to this pressing situation. The more acculturated and politically conscious of the Jewish elite had long been aware of shifting trends in charity and welfare – according to Williams the ethos of the New Poor Law underpinned the harsher attitude of members of Manchester's NHC to the Jewish poor in the 1840s and 1850s, and Rozin characterises Jewish philanthropy generally as embracing influences from Benthamism to social Darwinism and economic laissez faire.[110] If the 1840s had brought about a rethink of poor relief with reference to state centralization and deterrence though, the 1860s ushered in an era where the intentions and investigation of charity became as important as the relief given, while the state both tightened up its treatment of the able-bodied poor and, with increasing provision of infirmaries and schools, became more expansive in its responses to the sick and the young. We can see these imperatives very clearly in the ways that the Jewish charities of these years were conceptualized and operated. Perhaps just as important, however, were local priorities – the centralization and casework emphasized by Liverpool's Central Relief Society, for example, and the focus on elementary education and political activism in Manchester. In other respects many of these priorities built on earlier practice, from domestic visiting to the provision of business loans and occupational tools, many of which were designed to raise poor Jews out of ignorance and poverty, but which were now brought into a more streamlined whole.

The upshot for Jewish welfare was a higher level of consolidation, investigation and discrimination than had been seen before. The highest-profile outcome was the Boards of Guardians, which have not had sufficient attention paid to them in the provincial context. The comparison with the aims and structure of the Charity Organisation committees is unavoidable, but in many ways the boards trod their own path, principally by giving out relief on their own account, supporting schemes which more or less guaranteed entitlement in the form of Passover relief and clothing for school children, and – because of their ambiguous attitude to the Poor Law – by considering all types of paupers. It is not quite true to say that the boards acted in role of both Poor Law and voluntary charity for their communities, as they clearly regarded the statutory services as more residual. Nonetheless, their remit was broader than any single area of welfare in wider society.

That said, the Jewish boards did attempt to delineate boundaries to their work, recognizing that they could not be a welfare net for all. Part of this recognition lay in the fact that some of the newer categories of applicant were seen not to be as 'deserving' as others, bringing huge financial demands with no guarantee at all that they would stay and become respectable citizens (a concept to which we will return in the concluding chapter). Ultimately, however, the boundaries of their work were never fully established either within or across towns, since these involved giving up responsibility of co-religionists who were in need. However, we can see a clear difference in attitude to the resident versus immigrant poor: while the boards relieved both groups, they treated the former in more generous terms and were anxious to separate them out in their statistics. Money spent on their 'own' poor, or those who stayed on and became self-sufficient, always seems to have been considered better spent, their sympathetic attitude to fellow immigrants notwithstanding. When it came to it, the 'imagined' nature of the transpatial community – while strong – could not trump the bonds of relationships that were based on residence and social capital. Benevolence, organization and deterrence therefore existed in a shifting and somewhat uneasy balance in the 1860s and 1870s, together with an anxious eye to what the growing problem of immigrant poverty was doing to perceptions of the faith from outside.

It is extremely difficult to judge the success of the provincial Jewish Boards of Guardians and their satellite charities. They were certainly well used; numbers of applications and amounts handed out were high in total, and in both Manchester and Liverpool where minutes survive for this period, it was felt that they caused a fall in Jewish mendicancy. However, on the other hand, they could not make much of a dent in levels of migrant poverty in the larger Jewish communities, and certainly not – despite their occasional claims – in immigration itself. Nor were they able to stick consistently to the remit and exclusions that they had asserted so confidently at their foundations. Certain priorities remain throughout their work, however, most notably in the focus on self-help via business loans and apprenticeship to promote more secure modes of employment for the local workforce. In 1882 the Liverpool Board of Guardians noted that '[h]ow to assist the Jewish poor by utilizing their industrial capacities is a question of the first importance, and is at least as momentous as the task of supplying their wants by pecuniary assistance'. However, it recognized that it could not achieve this on its own, and called for every Jewish employer 'who had the welfare of his poorer brethren at heart' to help.[111] This, of course, was a problem that went with the increased geographical separation of social classes over the ensuing decades: the better off only came across the poor via their charitable work, as a mass at the back of the synagogue (assuming they worshipped there rather than their own prayer houses), or as employers. In fact, the boards had some of their lowest success rates when it came to utilizing the industrial capacities of their poor: apprenticeship schemes were only slowly taken up, and later waves of Jews were characterized by equally unskilled and precarious trades as those who had gone before.

The extent to which the boards achieved a unification of charity was also variable; in fact this seems rapidly to have been dropped as an overt priority, perhaps because the committees realized they could work productively with other bodies to achieve their aims. The boards may actually have had more impact in cementing charitable networks among the elite than in the face they presented to the poor, although behind the scenes communication may have improved. In terms of community networks, then, this could have delineated even more markedly the divisions between rich and poor. On the other hand, both Williams and Kokosalakis have suggested that the boards helped to unify the different congregations in Manchester and Liverpool respectively, while providing a vital means of 'containing' and integrating newcomers. Together with the Jewish school the Jewish Board of Guardians in Manchester comprised 'the community's cultural earthworks'.[112] It is easy to lose sight of these concrete benefits when faced with such problematically large numbers of transmigratory poor in the committee minutes.

We know almost nothing about the way that the charity of these years was received by the poor, or whether its messages of self-help and discrimination were taken on. More work on the use of alternative facilities like the Poor Law and non-Jewish charities would be helpful here, especially in the light of the growing population of immigrants and transients: Jews were almost certainly targeted by Christian and secular societies too.[113] Unfortunately this is difficult as Jews are rarely identified as such in the records of these bodies. With more digitization and record linkage this may become a more viable prospect. It would also be advantageous to build in the growing welfare resources offered by the *chevroth* and other self-help groups, both to test the remit of the Jewish welfare network as a whole, and to examine whether it began to compartmentalize into subcommunities.[114] As already noted, the final part of the welfare puzzle – informal aid given by friends, neighbours and informal congregational bodies – is sadly the most invisible, though that should not prevent us noting its undoubted, if unquantifiable, importance.[115]

The transient nature of much Jewish poverty also makes it difficult to estimate its scale at this date. Contemporary discussions have led scholars to characterize the social pyramid of British Jewry at this time as 'diamond shaped'; that is, with small numbers of very wealthy and very poor, and a large majority of people in the middle. A relative paucity of resident poverty is not incompatible with the heavy demands placed on the Jewish charities from migrants. However, several historians have highlighted the Jews' tendency to upward mobility, thanks to their vaunted work ethic and business-orientation.[116] These factors give Jewish poverty quite a different character from that of the other obvious migrant minority, the Irish, who were as a group less well skilled, more distinctly 'othered', and apparently less inclined or able to move up the social scale. The Irish also lacked the sizeable cadre of wealthy residents which was well established in the Jewish communities by the middle of the century. In terms of experiences of welfare, Jews were more reluctant to use state and voluntary services than groups like the Irish (and were, perhaps, lucky in having such a range of well-funded alternatives), and remained further removed from institutional welfare except in London.[117] This meant that they were less affected by the Crusade against Outdoor Relief than they were by the concurrent changes in thinking about voluntary welfare. It also brought them good notice from legislators compared with other immigrant groups like the Italians and Hungarians.[118]

One final point to note is the growing confidence of the provincial Jewish leaders in asserting their political rights. Perhaps more significant is that they were often able to secure them without having to make the sort of concessions Irish community leaders did in the way that they balanced their ethnic identity with their Britishness. The key difference here may be the fact that by the 1860s and 1870s, British Jewry had proved that their primary allegiance was to the practice of their religion within the British state; there was no distant alternative such as the Catholics had in the Pope. In many ways, with all the conflicts and painful rethinking that this brought, this is the most accurate way to characterize the welfare systems of British Jews in the 1860s and 1870s.

Part Three

# Conclusion

# 7

# A community of British Jews?

This book started by asking what evidence there is for a community of Jews in British industrial towns in the decades around the middle of the nineteenth century. Having examined evidence on household arrangements, spatial residence patterns, employment and charity, we are now able to come to a greater appraisal of the bonds between members of this 'imagined community' and the ways that they experienced the social, economic and cultural effects of the industrial period.

Part I gave the empirical evidence, based on the 1851 census. Chapter 2 showed that large proportions of Jews lived with other Jews, both kin and non-kin, suggesting a strong preference to live with people with whom they had something in common. This is a pattern uncovered for other migrant groups too, but it is especially notable here because of the comparatively small numbers of Jews in the provincial towns and their considerable heterogeneity. Networks of information flow and family assistance must have been especially strong therefore, for lodgers in particular, to exert such a strong preference for Jewish households. The census data also show less evidence of the 'calculated reciprocity' found by Anderson for Preston. This, I suggest, was because of a sense of responsibility not only to family but also to co-religionists, especially those from the same geographical locale, which was based on both religious tenets and fellow feeling. The tendency to cluster together in households is, if anything, most striking in the smaller communities like Leeds, where we find large numbers of single Jewish workers living together in mixed lodging houses. This is perhaps the most compelling evidence for the existence of a community network, and one that could be profitably extended to other small religious minorities.

The evidence for geographical clustering in the three largest communities, presented in Chapter 3, is also persuasive. While Jews did not dominate specific streets in the way that they came to do later, there were unmistakeably parts of town in Liverpool, Manchester and Birmingham where Jews were highly likely to have Jewish near-neighbours. As expected, they often clustered around the 'Old' synagogues – later foundations tended to follow the outward migration of the wealthier members of the community. Again, the evidence suggests that there were common information flows between Jews, and benefits (economic, personal, cultural) to living in close proximity. This is suggestive of a meaningful community because living near fellow Jews – whom one also met at the synagogue and at the shops dealing in kosher goods – made it more likely that these would be the people one would call on in times of need. As Wirth observed of urban Jewish communities in the 1920s, institutions like synagogues were not only physical foci for worship and community governance, they were also powerful signals to newcomers of the 'transpatial' society of international Jewry. They meant that strangers, even before the days of the Continental ghettos, 'will be capable of firstly, recognising the symbolic structure of the society and knowing how it works, and secondly, will be able to use it as an entry point into the local society'.[1] This coding of the built environment is particularly relevant for a community which we can see was starting to fragment geographically along socio-economic lines even in 1851, and where mobility generally could be high.[2] Nonetheless, while only a fairly small proportion of Jews had family elsewhere in the town, tracing these links shows that such households were often well connected, with the potential for aid and support nearby. Other records also show that these families were often central and high-status 'nodes' in the social network, exercising influence via their economic status but also in the administration of the synagogue and Jewish charities. Many others, of course, had kin sharing their homes.

The occupational information presented in Chapter 4 demonstrated another way in which the Jews were quite different from those around them; more so, perhaps, in the industrial and manufacturing towns than in London and the older places of settlement. It confirmed that Jews participated relatively little in the heart of the industrial economy – but that they were active in making and disseminating smaller consumer goods. This is a previously overlooked aspect of their involvement in the industrial and consumer revolutions and is worth reiterating. Furthermore, the comparative approach demonstrated that Jewish occupations were differentiated according to the local economy, showing evidence of adaptation or the deliberate selection of employment markets with a good fit for existing skills. Finally, despite the emphasis on 'dead-end' occupations, the Jews do not display many of the common social indicators of poverty, including court residence and shared accommodation, even when living alongside people with higher markers on these scales.

Part II focused on a different and more qualitative measure of community: charity. This is significant because, unlike the measures considered in the earlier chapters, it encompassed people who did not necessarily have much social capital invested in the community. This type of network is thus not necessarily about a two-way flow of kinship, knowledge or resources, but a more uneven one which recognizes a cultural bond at a more fundamental level. This was not unusual for British charity, but in the Jewish case it was based on a very specific sense of religious distinctiveness and obligation, which led Jews to take a more expansive view of deservingness than was fashionable in wider society. The desire to anglicize and 'improve' both native and foreign poor was undoubtedly one motivating factor, but Chapters 5 and 6 stress that this was not incompatible with a striking sense of compassion for co-religionists. This is perhaps the most concrete evidence of shared bonds across the whole social network, even including very new arrivals. Local studies reveal specific examples, like Birmingham's David Barnett, a jeweller and general merchant, who gave preferential cut prices on his stock to local Jewish hawkers. All of the Jewish businesses in the town shut on the day of his funeral in 1854, indicating the position of esteem he held in the social network.[3]

However, there were limits to Jewish charity. We see these debated in the 1850s and early 1860s in the face of growing levels of immigration, but they really came into force in the later 1860s and 1870s under the Jewish Boards of Guardians. At this stage, ever-growing levels of immigrant poverty, claims by transmigrants and deserted families, and problems of finance and local economic depression combined to force charity officials to set boundaries. In the industrial towns it was deserted wives who fell on the wrong side, while attitudes to people only passing through were also tightened up. This contrasts in certain respects with the position in London, revealing the necessity to consider local factors as well as national ones in the organization and conceptualization of charity. The commitment to the Jewish poor and the anxieties provoked by the need to draw boundaries around who could be helped is, again, a strong marker of community, which goes beyond interpersonal ties and flows. At the same time, though, charity was a way to reinforce status positions within the network, and to enforce religious conformity, at least in the larger communities. Overall, Part II also demonstrates that the actions of the different communities make the most sense when set alongside a fuller understanding both of Jewish teachings and of wider discussions in the field of welfare and local politics.

The sources and methodologies available inevitably focus attention on people who maintained a link with their religious community. It is simply not possible to take in those who turned instead to other local or cultural networks for their sense of identity and assistance, and in an ideal world this would be addressed further. However, it should not downplay the evidence we have uncovered. It is clear from the living arrangements and charitable practices of provincial Jews that shared religion did provide one of the most relevant and useful points of identity and support for many people, and that it brought people within the network together in different ways. These ties were further reinforced by the common experience of migration and urbanization, either recent or as part of the shared history of the Jews.[4] In fact, if we are thinking about the impact of wider social and economic changes in this period, then it seems likely that for the Jews it was immigration that was the principal disruptor of earlier household and community relationships rather than industrialization or urbanization per se. Shared ethnicity then provided new immigrants with networks that could help them find housing and work, shared culture and practice, and, should they need it, economic assistance. It is worth stressing that by taking up these opportunities newcomers were exerting a voluntary preference – they did not *need* to live in 'Jewish' parts of town or seek out Jewish charities, given the lack of official restrictions in British society. Jews *could* have given up their religious ties and looked to secular charities, the neighbourhood or the Poor Law for aid; the fact that so many did not points to the benefits of maintaining their cultural bonds, both for personal and religious fulfilment and for material assistance. It would be naïve to ignore the possibility of underlying religious or cultural discrimination at work here too, but this does not seem to have been as entrenched as it was in some other parts of Europe, especially where Jews were clearly contributing to local society and to the maintenance of their own poor.

In the rest of this chapter we turn to two further ways of thinking about the coherence and characterization of British Jewry, which return us to some of the research questions set up at the start of the study. These are the extent of religiosity and the impact of secularization on British Jewry; and the ways that Jews negotiated a path to an identity which encompassed both religion and nationality. Both have formed important strands in previous discussions of British Jewry, but the foregoing discussions have given us a new perspective by privileging a more fully contextualized and comparative approach. They also provide an excellent way to set the industrial case studies in a wider setting of provincial and British Jewry, allowing us to draw broader conclusions and set up some possible future agendas for research.

## Becoming British Jews

According to Endelman, it was the end of the eighteenth century when Jews started to feel that they belonged to the British state, as acculturation and integration shifted up a gear.[5] Even by the mid-nineteenth century though, their relationship with their British home was complex. On the one hand, historians emphasize Jews' desire to 'blend in' and acculturate: to describe a Jew as a Briton was a point of praise and one that acculturated Jews frequently used to describe themselves.[6] This explains their attempts to make foreign immigrants appear less foreign, Adler's campaign to clothe the outward forms of worship in attire which was familiar to Protestants, and the push for political emancipation and legal equality in the mid-nineteenth century. On the other hand, one of the chief ways in which Jews asserted their entitlement to Britishness was by holding themselves aloof from its welfare services, as a way of demonstrating that they were not a drain on the state's resources. Much of this can be linked to the legal informality of the Jews' readmission to Britain in the late seventeenth century, which left them (so they believed) vulnerable to re-expulsion at any time; the ultimate failure of the Jewish Naturalization Act of 1753 served the same purpose.[7] It explains the energy behind their efforts to fund a complete range of charities in the larger towns, and their defensiveness to charges that particular traits or social problems were 'Jewish' ones.[8] Taking responsibility for their own was thus a way of signalling to the wider world that Jews had taken on British ideals and responsibilities. According to Williams, it was only the community elite which had 'earned' the right to mediate with wider society because they were the only section to demonstrate middle-class British values.[9]

We see these trends in the actions of the larger provincial congregations too, but over time we can also see them increasingly willing to enter into collaboration with local authorities and institutions. This was partly a recognition that they could not achieve everything themselves, but it also shows a growing confidence in their entitlement to state services and equal treatment under the law. Since it often called attention to Jewish particularity, this also demonstrates an acceptance of their role in British society. The campaign by Manchester community leaders in the 1860s and 1870s to protect working hours, for example, highlighted that Jews had specific demands for their employment, and that they did not keep the Christian Sabbath. The dietary laws and the preference for Hebrew religious education also set Jews apart and created problems when they entered workhouses or other non-Jewish institutions. The very practice of looking after and at times directing their own poor (for example, into particular areas of work) could further encourage cultural isolation.[10] However, in other ways, Jewish institutions were designed to be assimilatory, like the Hebrew schools, which provided a wide curriculum, were supported by charities which provided respectable clothing, and which proved to be adaptable to the non-sectarian provisions of the 1870 Education Act.[11]

I would stress, therefore, that any desire to 'blend in' was nuanced by ideas about religious exclusiveness and practice, social class and wider aspirations to citizenship. All were changing over the period spotlighted here, and industrialization and urbanization, the waning of formal religious practice, religious emancipation and the extension of the franchise all formed a backdrop to the ways that Jews learned to balance their religion with their British culture. It is important to note, though, that the two were not mutually exclusive, given the relative liberality of the British state to religious minorities.[12] Much of Jewish observance – the personal morals, the way that it extended to family governance and gender roles, even its outward forms once Adler and his adherents had started to make headway – looked essentially familiar to Christians.[13] While negative cultural stereotyping remained alive, philosemitism was strong in many circles, any sustained campaign from evangelical Protestants to convert the Jews had petered out (the anxieties expressed in the *Jewish Chronicle* notwithstanding) and the state had shown repeated willingness to endorse the powers of bodies like the Jewish Board of Guardians.[14] One of the reasons that Jewish emancipation was so comparatively long in coming was that it involved loosening the importance of the Christological oaths rather than because the Jews per se were seen as a threat. As Endelman points out, Jews did not *need* to convert or assimilate in order to be accepted, as they did in other countries, either before or after emancipation.[15] Furthermore, many of the most obvious signs of 'otherness' had been muted by the start of the nineteenth century: many middle-class Jews had long left off their distinctive dress, men their beards and women their head coverings, and had become fluent in English. This was to change as time went on and rates of immigration from Eastern Europe increased: in 1879 a note in the *Jewish Chronicle* referenced the 'dialect peculiar to Eastern Europe' which was among those used in the 'minor' synagogues in Manchester.[16] Nonetheless, the evidence suggests that this had not yet revived and redirected the cultural perception of British Jewry in wider society as it was to do in some sectors later on.[17]

In order to judge the desire to 'blend in' we also need to interrogate more closely what it means. 'Blending in' is really a shorthand way of describing adaptive cultural behaviour, but a host of nuances from assimilation to acculturation and integration are often elided under this heading. In fact, they refer to different places along a spectrum of attitudes and practices. Crudely speaking, acculturation refers to the taking on, or adaptation to, local practices, ideas and cultural reference points. Assimilation implies a greater degree of absorption into this culture and thus a greater loss of the minority identity. Integration, meanwhile, implies a sufficient level of adaptation to allow individuals to operate fully in the majority culture. While all imply that the original culture cannot remain unchanged, acculturation and integration can more easily accommodate a process of partial change or adaptation where two cultures coexist, and do not necessarily imply that the outcome is negative. Indeed, the process can bring growth or enrichment as long as one is prepared to see culture as adaptive – not always an easy point to entertain, especially in the face of persecution.[18] By learning to adapt their behaviour though – as many seem to have done – Jews could operate in a range of environments, from business to personal.

It is also easy to overlook heterogeneity within the minority culture when talking about assimilation.[19] This is prescient for the current case, where there is a temptation to refer to the majority of Jews in Britain as immigrants. Not only is this not accurate, it also bundles together a great variety of prior experiences of religion, culture, tolerance and restriction. The urban German Jews who settled in Manchester in the 1840s were a voluntary diaspora who were ready to adapt in order to maintain their status.[20] The later waves of Eastern European Jewry also came voluntarily, but from a situation of more extreme restriction and persecution. They were less likely to speak English and thus less likely to engage rapidly in adaptive behaviour; they were more used to already thinking of themselves as 'other'.[21] Given the relative weakness of the Jewish communal authorities in Britain compared with the Continent (and arguably especially so outside London), we can see how decisions about religious identity were essentially personal.

It is therefore unwise to make overarching statements about the acculturation and assimilation of British Jewry in this period. The evidence shows that among the community elites (who were often the longer-term settled and most embedded) there were many who felt their British identity very strongly. Some had already started to anglicize their names by our period; the Samuel and Yates families in Liverpool both commissioned family crests based on those used by English families of the same name. Indeed, Kokosalakis reads the community records as revealing 'a strong desire to set their roots as deeply as they could in the social and economic structure of English society'.[22] We see this in the position taken up by the Jewish press too: one correspondent to the *JC* asserted in 1876 that '[i]n this free and enlightened land we are essentially Englishmen, as much as in feeling and in practice as his Grace the Archbishop of Canterbury, Cardinal Manning, and Gladstone himself'; another, writing in the earlier Jewish paper *The Voice of Jacob*, under the heading of 'the British Jew' stated that 'it seems even as if a happy predisposition, rooted in the character of the Jews at large, had facilitated the transfusion of the peculiarities of the English into their minds, blending them with their own'.[23]

The communities in the industrial towns felt increasingly able to contribute to this sense of blended Jewishness and Britishness. While they referred points of order and debate to the Chief Rabbi (and had participated in his election), they were not always receptive to taking direction from outside.[24] Offended by Adler's 'apathy' to their proposed reforms in the form of worship in 1851, the committee of the Liverpool OHC minuted that a potential invitation to visit was 'totally uncalled for' (they eventually toned this down to state that they could not receive him 'owing to a variety of untoward circumstances'). In the event, their hand was forced as the Chief Rabbi requested a visit himself and was received.[25] Indeed, the only real challenge to Adler's authority over his long period of tenure came from Manchester, where for a short time there was another rabbi – Dr Solomon Marcus Schiller-Szinessy – whose qualifications equalled Adler's own.[26] Over time, the *Jewish Chronicle* also became increasingly responsive to news from the provinces and the role of these congregations in British Jewry. In the 1870s, a series of articles called for a greater unification in the funding and provision of synagogues over the country, and for more English-speaking preachers. Such officers would, it was felt, engage the young and old alike, and also – tellingly – 'enhanc[e] the standing of the Jewish community in non-Jewish eyes'.[27] The paper was a unifying force for co-religionists in other ways too. Towns with small congregations, like Glasgow, used its columns to appeal for support, for example, to build a new synagogue, or to help a family in extreme need. In fact, we can read the building of new synagogues – many of them impressive structures in prominent locations – as another illustration of the confidence of the communities' stake in British society.[28]

Several of the provincial communities went further in their public statements of their loyalty to the British state; a position that would have served them particularly well amid contemporary concerns about the external allegiance of ultramontane Catholics. In February 1863, the Birmingham Benevolent Education Society voted that the school children be given a free dinner to commemorate the wedding of the Prince of Wales, for example, while the Jewish poor were to be given a gift of meat.[29] Even earlier, Liverpool's OHC had opened up the synagogue for Queen Victoria's coronation in 1838 and voted £5 to be distributed among the poor in a demonstration of their loyalty and pride in the new monarch.[30] In Manchester trustees of the Jewish Board of Guardians all had to be British-born or naturalized, presumably as the greatest possible testament to their trustworthiness and appreciation of ideas about poverty.[31] Members of the provincial communities were active in promoting political emancipation, and individuals served on a range of political and cultural committees: a clear way of demonstrating citizenship by participation.[32] Membership of these bodies clearly brought status both within the community and beyond, and allowed them to mix with philanthropic and civic-oriented individuals on equal terms. In these ways, the message of national loyalty and acculturation *alongside* Jewish identity was spread among rich and poor alike. Once again, it is much harder to access the reactions of those lower down the social scale to these messages, or to reach the range of their contacts in daily life. It is unfortunately difficult to see how this can be addressed without knowing much more about their business and personal dealings, but it is certainly an area which should be prioritized for future work.

At the same time, it is clear that the Jewish elites at least felt part of an international faith community, formally linked via trade links, family businesses and the growth of print culture, and more intangibly, by bonds of shared religion and heritage. Cesarani believed that the nineteenth-century diaspora no longer felt attached to a common origin in the Land of Israel, but noted that British Jewry remained quick to come to the aid of co-religionists abroad.[33] They raised money for Syrian Jews affected by the notorious 'Damascus Affair' of 1840, for example; for the Jewish victims of a fire in Smyrna in 1841 (the contribution from the 'small but warm-hearted' community in Manchester was particularly praised by *The Voice of Jacob*[34]); and later, for the Jews of Eastern Europe. In 1871 the Anglo-Jewish Association was founded to defend Jewish interests on the international scene, and the *Jewish Chronicle* always devoted considerable space to foreign Jewish affairs.[35]

We should not overstate the degree of harmony within British Jewry, however, despite the increasing number of bodies who claimed to speak for large parts of it. We have seen that internal schisms were relatively common; that the Ashkenazim and Sephardim remained quite separate from one another; and that the emergence of the Reform movement was a divisive affront to Orthodoxy, leading ultimately to the excommunication of the West London (Reform) congregation.[36] New groups of immigrants could change the character of a local community, and Laidlaw has shown that British-born male Jews were unlikely to marry foreign-born women (although foreign-born men were equally likely to marry British as foreign women), suggesting that there were distinctions – 'cliques' in social network terminology – within the wider community.[37] We see this most clearly, perhaps, in the growth of the *chevroth*, where nationality was joined with religion in the assertion of identity, worship and self-help. This was a clear message to the existing elites that newcomers had their own ways of expressing their ethnicity – and often that they felt alienated from the ritual, exclusiveness, and perhaps also the social control mechanisms, of the older congregations.[38] Nationality or length of residence in Britain could lead to long-lasting stratification within the Jewish community, as Williams demonstrated for Manchester, and which also seems to have been the case in Hull, where a visitor commented in 1878 on the 'racial groupings' among the Jews which separated Germans from Russians, and both from the British-born.[39] British Jewry never managed to marshal these smaller groups of more recent incomers to fall in with their own ideals on common practice, and this was probably exacerbated by strong attachments to different cultural and linguistic traditions. This is a salutary reminder that Britishness mattered to a greater and lesser degree to different groups of British Jews, and that they negotiated their identity in different ways.

## Religious lives

It seems, nonetheless, that religion continued to be a vital aspect of identity for a large body of Jews living in Britain. The evidence presented in this book suggests that this went beyond doctrinal practice (though that was important), to offer status, friendship and material assistance. This should not surprise us given the centrality of religion to the fabric of people's lives in this period, but the specifics add considerably to our appreciation of how immigration, acculturation and religion combined. We have seen, for example, the huge demand for places in synagogue on the High Holy Days, the ways that recipients of relief were expected to take part in aspects of Jewish practice from attendance at synagogue to watching the sick, the demand for places at the Hebrew schools, and the assumption that notices posted on the synagogue doors would attract widespread notice. It seems scarcely credible that community leaders would spend so much time trying to secure concessions for Jewish workmen to keep the Sabbath if this was not a popular demand: apparently 400 Jews in Manchester were eligible to take up the proposal to substitute a half day on Friday for Sunday closing in the 1867 extension of the Factory Acts.[40] We might also recall the petitions for relief which referenced restricted working hours and the need for support during the period of mourning, too. The Liverpool Jewish Board of Guardians cited a deep-seated attachment to the dietary laws when they pursued an arrangement to have kosher food sent to hospitals. 'It is certain', they minuted in 1878, 'that in many cases if Kosher food were not supplied, the patients would either take the ordinary diet with a reluctance which would have an injurious effect upon their condition, or refuse it altogether'.[41]

The view of religion uncovered from these sources, therefore, stresses its cultural aspects as much as doctrinal or welfare ones. In some cases, practice was probably linked to conditions of relief, but in others – like the applications to have marriage, circumcision and burial fees waived, and the applications for handouts at Passover – this clearly went much deeper. The rites of passage were a fundamental way of staking one's sense of belonging, and the alternatives were a very definite statement of rejection.[42] Applying for Passover relief also demonstrates a greater involvement in practice: one did not *need* unleavened bread and flour unless observing the festival, and although the extra material aid would have been a boon for those in need, it did attract personal investigation and an expectation of religious compliance. Many parents who were not on relief also chose to use the Jewish schools when there were alternatives (especially after the 1870 Education Act). This strongly implies that they found the Jewish education and the company of co-religionists a positive advantage. This reminds us – as Kokosalakis stresses so heavily – that observance is only one aspect of feeling part of a religious community: it also brought shared cultural and national bonds, a social life and emotional security.[43]

Furthermore, some people whose observance had lapsed later came back to the faith or acknowledged its support. One man named Jeffreys whose wife and children were baptized Christians still felt able to approach the Manchester Jewish Board of Guardians in 1873 for aid – and was granted it on his agreement that he would be buried among Jews when he died.[44]

However important these more intangible aspects of belonging were, perceptions of practice remained high profile for community leaders. This was partly because of the importance of respectability, which has been mentioned already, but there was also an underlying code of Jewish ethics at work. This is known as *maris ha'ayin*, or 'appearance to the eye', and it directs Jews to be conscious of *perceptions* of their actions, even if in fact they comply with Jewish laws.[45] For example, the Birmingham congregation was quick to investigate an allegation that there had been an irregularity over the slaughter of kosher meat in 1852.[46] In Hull, one of the butchers licensed to sell kosher meat was suspended in 1863 because he was found to have tampered with the certifying seal on the goods.[47] In both cases, proper observance was clearly at risk, but so was the reputation of the community. *Maris ha'ayin* could be applied to protect Jews within the framework of British law too: in Manchester the Jewish Board of Guardians moved to stamp out 'irregular' marriages carried out by immigrant rabbis in 1871 because they were illegal in Britain. The Board also resolved that no one married 'irregularly' could receive relief.[48]

It is undeniable that community cohesion and religious practice were easiest in the larger communities, which housed the largest array of Jewish services. In towns like Liverpool, Birmingham and Manchester Jews could, if they chose, mix largely with their own. There were very few Jewish butchers in the provincial towns in 1851 (the authorities certified non-Jews to sell kosher meat), but there was a wide range of other provisioners and shopkeepers. In fact, in Birmingham in 1851, a Jew could, apparently, 'if she wished, have dealt almost entirely with her co-religionists', from the purchase of clothing and food, to utilities, furnishing and care of her teeth.[49] In the smaller communities, like Leeds and Sheffield, Jews would have had to rely far more on the services provided in the neighbourhood, and on meat certified by slaughterers from elsewhere.[50] This may have played its part in the waning of strict practice, although Jews in some of the smaller communities, or in towns where there was no formal organization of Jews, were able to call on the services of others nearby. The Hull congregation served individuals from York to the north-west, to Boston, seventy-five miles to the south, for example, while Jewish families in Dudley and Wolverhampton had a (sometimes fractious) relationship with the community in Birmingham.[51] Others – like Leeds and Glasgow – were on their way to becoming large centres for provincial Jewry with all the services that brought. The Jewish populations in the provincial towns also had high rates of immigrants who had left their homelands *because* they were Jewish. For some, this meant that religion inevitably remained a key part of their identity – although it made others wish to shed this association as quickly as possible. In places like Leeds and Manchester, these incomers could inject a new tone of religious Orthodoxy into the poorer neighbourhoods.

For outsiders too, culture went along with practice in their descriptions of British Jewry. The philosemitic clergyman John Mills, for example, recorded high levels of Sabbath and High Holy Day observance in 1853 (the former, he said, was kept by 'most' and the latter by '[e]very Jew who has the least feeling of Judaism'), but also distinctive forms of dress, behaviour and cultural customs in synagogue and at home.[52] He also noted some of the ways in which strict observance had to be mitigated by the practicalities of life in a mixed environment: many Jews did not keep the laws prohibiting shaving or restricting dress after the loss of close relatives, for instance, 'as business frequently compels them to mix among other people'.[53]

This returns us to the question of whether British Jews participated in any wider trend towards secularization. This is ultimately very difficult to untangle because of the way that religious practice was constantly altered by the changing composition of the provincial communities. There is certainly evidence of *acculturation*, particularly at the top end of the social scale, where successful business usually meant mixing with non-Jewish associates.[54] Contemporaries also called attention to lack of practice: in Bradford in the 1840s and 1850s, religious observance was said to be rare, while the *Jewish Chronicle* noted in April 1859 that there were 'hundreds' of foreign-born Jews in London, Liverpool and Manchester who did not belong to a congregation or support communal charities.[55] Mills concluded his observations on London Jewry by citing a petition drawn up by the principal metropolitan synagogues which stated that there were many people who did not attend synagogue even when they lived close by. '[T]hus', they said, wistfully, 'the national band is daily becoming weaker; the children of the wealthy seldom hear the word of God from the preacher or precentor.'[56] It is also possible that the congregations and charities had to enforce conditions like visiting the sick on their poor because they would not otherwise have carried out this important act of Jewish charity; parents may have sought out the Jewish schools because they felt uncomfortable dealing with non-Jews because they were native English-speakers rather than because they were Christians. In 1845, the Chief Rabbi found that only half of the communities in Britain had a ritual bath (*mikvah*) (although others used public baths or sea bathing for the same purposes).[57] He did not, however, ask questions about Sabbath observance and *kashrut*, which Susser interprets as indicating that 'in general, there were no great fears that these aspects of Jewish life were not being maintained'.[58]

When discussing assimilation or secularization historians have not tended to make a distinction between changed practice at an individual level and at a community one (which could be altered by the outlook of newcomers). It was hinted at in the testimony of Israel Napthali, a Jewish convert to Christianity, however, who was employed by Manchester conversionists in the 1840s to work as an agent among the Jews. According to him, there were many Jews in that town who knew very little of their faith and were open to conversion. He also, though, identified a mass who were traditionally observant (although 'extremely ignorant and excessively bigoted'), as well as the Eastern European immigrants, who were more knowledgeable and thus harder to convince to abandon their religion.[59] The key point here is the different influences at work on patterns of religious observance. For some, acculturation meant more relaxed or selective practice, but without necessarily bringing loss of Jewish identity; a feature Kokosalakis describes taking place in Liverpool, where Jews experienced 'a gradual loss of attachment to certain of [the] symbols and rituals [of Judaism]' but without loss of ethnic affiliation.[60] Endelman also points to a 're-ordering of personal priorities' in this period rather than a total loss of religion: 'Judaism became only a part of their sense of self' but one which was still very present.[61] Others – including many of the waves of newcomers from Eastern Europe – brought new levels of Orthodox observance (to the extent that they rejected the state of worship in the established synagogues), while others still – like the acculturated and urban German immigrants of the 1840s – had a deep attachment to a more liberal and Reformed attitude to worship which arguably combined more easily with urban and British values but nonetheless was a frame for self-definition.[62] The overall shape of Jewish feeling and observance is thus tangled up not only with secularization and acculturation, but also with the level and nature of religiosity of different waves of immigrants. Historians of British Jewry have tended to focus almost exclusively on acculturation, seeing changed practice as reflecting adaptations to British life. However – as Endelman points out – this did not necessarily map on to assimilation, which tended to lag behind changes in patterns of worship, implying that Jewish identity went deeper than religious observance.[63] However – although seemingly an obvious point – the way that this mapped on to the history of immigration in individual towns has still not been properly integrated, and is worthy of further investigation.

This line of enquiry raises pertinent questions; however, it seems to lead down a rabbit hole of further enquiries with – as yet – few concrete answers. An alternative way of thinking is to join practice more deliberately back up with the question of *community* rather than strict observance. In a sense, it does not matter where the boundaries of Jewish adherence lay, or who chose to drift away from it: this study has clearly identified that for many people these bonds were functional and reassuring parts of their social network and personal identity. In this respect, there is little evidence that the Jews in the industrial towns lost touch with their religion – Judaism was internalized as part of ethnicity just as Christianity seems to have remained a core part of Victorian Britishness. For those wishing to take up their place as British Jews, the challenge was to demonstrate how their religion carried the same traits of respectability and citizenship as Protestantism. For others, community started to fragment into subcultures based on place of origin, neighbourhood and shared social and mutual-benefit networks. Increasingly, 'community' could mean several different things for the Jews of provincial Victorian Britain.

## Conclusions

This study has developed a comparative approach to the history of British Jewry in some of the largest industrial towns in Britain. By situating trends and actions much more firmly in their wider economic and social context, it has broadened our view of the Jewish family and household and the development of Jewish occupational structures and residence patterns, and explored forms and reactions to charity in a way that allows us to interpret welfare as a way of expressing both Jewishness and Britishness. It also advocates, per Kokosalakis, that the discussion of religion should pay careful attention to shared ethnicity as well as formal practice. While we cannot capture practice across the broad community of British Jewry, we can see many ways in which a shared sense of culture and tradition gave an enduring quality to religious identity and action. Communal charity is just one example; it not only provides care for the needy, but also makes a statement about belonging, *and* reflects the standing of its donors. In the words of one Liverpool representative at the foundation of the local Jewish Board of Guardians, 'charity could exalt a community as well as a nation'.[64]

It seems undeniable that British Jewry stood on the edges of industrialization itself, but that is not to say that it was not deeply affected by the wider social, economic and cultural changes in this period. In the period covered here, British Jews managed to balance the demands of secular influences, immigration and a new scale of urban life, but this balance was increasingly difficult to manage and contain for community leaders. With the increased scale of immigration, newcomers made their own, vibrant communities and created 'Jewish' parts of town like the Gorbals in Glasgow and Leylands in Leeds. At the same time, this changed the ways that townspeople encountered poorer Jews, and arguably started to create a greater sense of alienation and foreignness. Jews had until this point largely escaped being characterized as a 'residuum' or 'underclass', as the Irish all too often were – despite the fact that they often lived alongside Irish neighbours.[65] Mills specifically contrasted the conditions of the poorest religious Jews with the misery of the Irish, noting that 'the British Jew is not brought up in idleness, whatever his wealth may be; nor the poor, entirely to depend upon charity'.[66] By the 1880s, however, attention started to be drawn to a Jewish residuum in the East End of London, and this was followed up with new ways of thinking about the Jewish quarters in places like Leeds, Glasgow and Manchester too. The scale of Jewish settlement changed out of all recognition: Liverpool Jewry numbered 5,000 individuals by 1897 compared with less than 900 in the AJDB in 1851; by 1914 Manchester housed 30,000.[67]

Our period thus ends on a note of confidence and pride in the status of British Jewry on one hand, and on the other, a growing awareness of the challenges posed by immigration and lack of cohesion with the modern workforce. These were common challenges for all of the industrial towns, but on differing scales, and played out before a backdrop of different priorities, attitudes and cultural histories. At the same time, new communities were springing up, seeking their own identities and relationships with Jews in other towns; meanwhile, some of the existing communities, like Manchester, were increasingly pushing against the oversight of centralized London offices like the Chief Rabbinate. It would be valuable to know more about the composition and organization of the smaller provincial communities in this period, in order to enlarge this picture of identity and urban social networks. Similarly, to complete it we really need to know more about Jewish relationships with non-Jewish friends and neighbours, and a greater appreciation of what worship in their homes looked like. This may never be entirely possible given the sources available, but it is worth keeping in the forefront of our minds. It would also be worthwhile considering the Jews more overtly against comparably small ethnic minority groups, like the Italians, to unpack further the ways that they were othered and accepted. What this book has been able to highlight above all, however, are the ways that Jews reacted and adapted to life as Britons in the most rapidly growing towns in the country, the varied ways in which their religion gave them identity and social bonds, and the value to be gained in setting Jewish history firmly within the social and economic context of daily life.

# Notes

## 1. Introduction

1  D. Rabinowitz, 'Community Studies: Anthropological', in *International Encyclopedia of the Social and Behavioural Sciences*, ed. Neil J. Smelser and Paul B. Baltes (Oxford: Elsevier, 2001), 4 vols, 2387; C. J. Calhoun, 'Community: Toward a Variable Conceptualization For Comparative Research', *Social History* 5, no. 1 (1980): 105–29.
2  Gerard Delanty, *Community* (London and New York: Routledge, 2003), 2–3. Interestingly, Delanty (a sociologist) characterizes the nineteenth century as the century of community, compared with the crisis of the twentieth century (4).
3  Calhoun, 'Community', 106. See also Delanty, *Community*, 9–10.
4  Keith Wrightson and David Levine, *Poverty and Piety in an English Village: Terling, 1525–1700* (Oxford: Clarendon Press, 1995), 75.
5  Anna Davin, *Growing Up Poor: Home, School and Street in London, 1870–1914* (London: Rivers Oram Press, 1996); see also Michael Anderson's *Family Structure in Nineteenth-Century Lancashire* (Cambridge: Cambridge University Press, 1971) for a more qualified example of a close-knit working-class community in nineteenth-century Preston. Also J. Connell, 'Social Networks in Urban Society', in *Social Patterns in Cities*, Institute of British Geographers Special Publication no. 5 (London: Institute of British Geographers, 1973): 41–52.
6  Steven King, 'Migrants on the Margin? Mobility, Integration and Occupations in the West Riding, 1650–1820', *Journal of Historical Geography* 23, no. 3 (1997): 284–303.
7  Benedict Anderson, *Imagined Communities*, rev. edn (London and New York: Verso, 2006). Another classic study of Britain is Linda Colley's *Britons: Forging A Nation, 1703–1837* (New Haven and London: Yale University Press, 1992), which identifies shared Protestantism as a key definition of belonging.
8  John Scott, *Social Network Analysis: A Handbook*, 2nd edn (London: Sage Publications, 2000), 21.
9  See Laura Vaughan, 'A Study of the Spatial Characteristics of the Jews in London 1695 & 1895' (MSc diss., University College London, 1994).
10  Ferdinand Tönnies, *Community and Association*, trans. Charles P. Loomis (London: Routledge and Kegan Paul, 1955). Tönnies did not devise this theory but he clarified and popularized it.

11  Calhoun, 'Community', 113.
12  For example, see Calhoun, 'Community', and the overviews provided in Tamara Hareven, 'The History of the Family and the Complexity of Social Change', *American Historical Review* 96, no. 1 (1991): 95–124; Neil J. Smelser, *Social Change in the Industrial Revolution: An Application of Theory to the British Cotton Industry* (Aldershot: Gregg Revivals, 1959).
13  For example, see Peter Laslett, 'Introduction', in *Household and Family in Past Time*, ed. Peter Laslett (Cambridge: Cambridge University Press, 1972), 1–89, and the Introduction and references to Anderson's *Family Structure*, 1–4. For more recent contributions, see Barry Reay, 'Kinship and the Neighbourhood in Nineteenth-Century Rural England: The Myth of the Autonomous Nuclear Family', *Journal of Family History* 21, no. 1 (1996): 87–104; Naomi Tadmor, 'Early Modern Kinship in the Long Run: Reflections on Continuity and Change', *Continuity and Change* 25, no. 1 (2010): 15–48.
14  Anderson, *Family Structure*.
15  Steve King and Geoff Timmins, *Making Sense of the Industrial Revolution* (Manchester: Manchester University Press, 2001), 275.
16  For example, see Emma Griffin, *Liberty's Dawn: A People's History of the Industrial Revolution* (New Haven and London: Yale University Press, 2013).
17  Katherine Lynch, *Individuals, Families and Communities in Europe, 1200–1800: The Urban Foundations of Western Society* (Cambridge: Cambridge University Press, 2003), e.g. 101.
18  In Britain, the Sephardi congregation was longer established than the Ashkenazi and was also, as a body, much wealthier. They maintained separate synagogues and separate welfare schemes for their 'own' poor. By the early nineteenth century, the Ashkenazim were starting to dominate numerically. It was they who gave the outward migration to new provincial centres in the early nineteenth century its character, and so attention in this book is invariably skewed in this direction. The Sephardim, however, coming from lands where it had been illegal to practise Judaism, were often more accustomed to living and working among non-Jews. The first provincial Sephardi congregation was established in Manchester in 1874 (Bill Williams, *Making of Manchester Jewry, 1740–1875* (Manchester: Manchester University Press, 1976), 240–56, 319–24).
19  Jewish immigration to Britain had seen a notable upswing between 1750 and 1815 when 120 to 150 new migrants arrived per year, predominately from the German-speaking lands, Amsterdam and Poland. Rates then slowed with the impact of the Napoleonic Wars, quickening again with the Continental upheavals of 1848 and then a combination of improved transport links and periods of persecution. It was between these years that the provincial industrial communities started to grow, in a trajectory which took on ever-quickening momentum in the subsequent decades.

By the late 1850s to 1881, 500 to 1,000 foreign Jews were entering the country each year, notably from Poland and Russia (Vivian D. Lipman, *Social History of the Jews in England, 1850–1950* (London: Watts & Co., 1954), 8; ibid., *A History of the Jews in Britain since 1858* (Leicester: Leicester University Press, 1990), 12).

20  For example, see Colin Pooley and Jean Turnbull, *Migration and Mobility in Britain since the Eighteenth Century* (London and New York: Routledge, 1998).

21  King, 'Migrants on the Margin?'

22  Petra Laidlaw, 'Jews in the British Isles in 1851: Birthplaces, Residence and Migrations', *Jewish Journal of Sociology* 53 (2011): 29–56 (48).

23  This is a major theme of Williams's work on Manchester Jewry in the nineteenth century (*Making of Manchester Jewry, passim*).

24  For example, see Frank Felsenstein, *Anti-Semitic Stereotypes: A Paradigm of Otherness in English Popular Culture, 1660–1830* (Baltimore and London: John Hopkins University Press, 1999); Bryan Cheyette, *Constructions of 'the Jew' in English Literature and Society: Racial Representations, 1875–1945* (Cambridge: Cambridge University Press, 1993).

25  Todd Endelman, *The Jews of Georgian England, 1741–1830: Tradition and Change in a Liberal Society* (Philadelphia: Jewish Publication Society of America, 1979), 86–117. On the Irish see, for example, Mervyn Busteed, *The Irish in Manchester c. 1750–1921: Resistance, Adaptation and Identity* (Manchester: Manchester University Press, 2016); John Belchem, *Irish, Catholic and Scouse: The History of the Liverpool Irish, 1800–1939* (Liverpool: Liverpool University Press, 2007); Roger Swift and Sheridan Gilley, eds, *The Irish in Britain: The Local Dimension* (Dublin: Four Courts Press, 1999). On the impact of the 'Eastern Crisis' on perceptions of Jews, see Cheyette, *Constructions of 'the Jew'*, esp. chapter 1. Anti-Jewish feeling was also stoked by fears about 'aliens' in the context of mass immigration from Eastern Europe in the 1880s and beyond (see Colin Holmes, *Anti-Semitism in British Society, 1876–1939* (Edward Arnold: London, 1979).

26  Rev. Moses Margoliouth, *The History of the Jews in Great Britain*, 3 vols (London: Richard Bentley, 1851), Vol. 3, 159–60.

27  W. D. Rubinstein, *A History of the Jews in the English-Speaking World: Great Britain* (Basingstoke: Macmillan, 1996), 59.

28  On these attitudes to the Irish, see Mary J. Hickman, *Religion, Class and Identity: The State, the Catholic Church and the Education of the Irish in Britain* (Aldershot: Avebury, 1995). She contends that the more negative ideas were projected specifically onto the Catholic Irish, although there was long-standing antipathy to Catholics in Britain more generally. More recent readings of Irish immigration have tended to stress a more positive story of internal ethnic solidarity – see, for example, Belchem, *Irish, Catholic and Scouse*. The editors of the *Jewish Chronicle* took up an anti-Catholic stance in the 1840s and 1850s as a way of demonstrating

their Englishness, although David Cesarani notes that this rather perversely meant associating themselves with Evangelical Protestants (*The Jewish Chronicle and Anglo-Jewry, 1841–1991* (Cambridge: Cambridge University Press, 1994), 20–1). Lucio Sponza (*Italian Immigrants in Nineteenth-Century Britain: Realities and Images* [Leicester: Leicester University Press, 1988]) reads a similar story of apathetic acceptance into British reactions to Italian immigrants in this period.

29  For example, A. D. Gilbert, *Religion and Society in Industrial England: Church, Chapel and Social Change, 1740–1914* (London and New York: Longman, 1976), xii, 77; C. D. Field, 'Counting Religion in England and Wales: The Long Eighteenth Century, c.1680–c.1840', *The Journal of Ecclesiastical History* 63, no. 4 (2012): 693–720; David Newsome, *The Victorian World Picture: Perceptions and Introspections in an Age of Change* (New Brunswick, NJ: Rutgers University Press, 2007).

30  See Callum G. Brown, *The Death of Christian Britain: Understanding Secularisation 1800–2000* (London and New York: Routledge, 2001).

31  Gerald Parsons, 'A Question of Meaning: Religion and Working-Class Life', in *Religion in Victorian Britain, Vol. 2: Controversies*, ed. Gerald Parsons (Manchester and New York: Manchester University Press, 1988), 64–7. See also Asa Briggs, *Victorian Cities* (Harmondsworth: Penguin, 1968), 63, 68. More than half of the total attendance in Bradford, Leeds, Oldham, Wolverhampton and Sheffield was at non-conforming places of worship, and between 40 and 50 per cent of those in Birmingham, Manchester, Salford and Newcastle. Catholics were also prominent in Liverpool (30 per cent) and Manchester (20 per cent). Parts of London were equally affected.

32  Brown, *The Death of Christian Britain*, 145–69. He maintains that this discursive Christianity remained strong up to the 1950s. See also Parsons, 'A Question of Meaning', 77–9.

33  Lipman, *History of the Jews*, 28.

34  The contemporary observer John Mills stated that '[e]very Jew who has the least feeling of Judaism, attends the Synagogue on the Day of Atonement' (John Mills, *The British Jews* (London: Houlston & Stoneman, 1853), 174).

35  Birmingham Jewish Local History Study Group, 'A Portrait of Birmingham Jewry in 1851', https://www.jewishgen.org/jcr-uk/Community/Birmingham/articles/birmingham-vic2.htm. Originally published in A. Newman, *Provincial Jewry in Victorian Britain* (London: Jewish Historical Society of England, 1975). The Census of Worship counted eighty-two attendees at the Friday night service at the main synagogue in Birmingham, 185 on Saturday morning and forty on Saturday afternoon. See Chapters 3 and 4 for more on occupations.

36  Todd M. Endelman, *Broadening Jewish History: Towards a Social History of Ordinary Jews* (Oxford and Portland, Oregon: Littman Library of Jewish Civilization, 2011), 43. He makes a similar point about the more acculturated

Continental Jews for whom assimilation was largely the result of 'apathy and carelessness' (Endelman, *The Jews of Georgian England*, 7).

37 From 1836, Jews secured the rights to register marriages which took place in synagogue (Rubinstein, *A History of the Jews*, 72).

38 Todd M. Endelman, *The Jews of Britain 1656 to 2000* (Berkeley and London: University of California Press, 2002), 59–60.

39 Using a conveyance like a carriage – or in the modern era, a car – constitutes 'work' and is thus banned on the Sabbath.

40 The laws of *kashrut* (which produce food that is *kosher*) are laid down in Leviticus and Deuteronomy. They cover foods that are permissible and those that are taboo, and also set out rules for ritual slaughter of permitted animals and prohibitions on combinations of certain foods (meat and milk must not be combined in the same meal, for example).

41 Kokosalakis described Judaism as 'a special kind of religion which cannot be understood apart from the history, the ongoing life and the social experience of the Jewish people … Judaism is an ethnic folk religion *par excellence* …' (N. Kokosalakis, *Ethnic Identity and Religion: Tradition and Change in Liverpool Jewry* (Washington: Universal Press of America, 1982), xxii). John Mills also stated that 'The Jewish idea of religion is national; that is, in his estimation his faith and his nation are synonymous. To profess the one is to belong to the other; and to change the former is to deny the latter. Thus there is no line of demarcation between religion and nationality' (Mills, *British Jews*, 67).

42 The most famous collections of rabbinic interpretations are known as the *Talmud* (which contains most of the Jewish laws) and the *Midrash*. Although these were based on the teachings of rabbis, a formally qualified minister is not actually necessary for worship to take place as long as a member of the congregation is capable of leading it.

43 Eugene C. Black, *The Social Politics of Anglo-Jewry, 1880–1920* (Oxford: Basil Blackwell, 1988), 38–41.

44 Black, *Social Politics*, 26–7; Lipman, *Social History*, 23–4, 38–40; Endelman, *Jews of Britain*, 115–21. The Chief Rabbi did not have the same authority as his equivalents on the Continent, but he was the acknowledged leader of the community as whole.

45 Black, *Social Politics*, 26.

46 Black, *Social Politics*, 39; Rubinstein, *History of the Jews*, 71.

47 Cesarani (*Jewish Chronicle*, 25) claims that the Board of Deputies was 'ignored by most of the Jewish population'. See also Black, *Social Politics*, 40–1. Attitudes were improved once its proceedings started to be reported in the Jewish press, and once community notable Sir Moses Montefiore had taken the reins in 1835 (Rubinstein, *History of the Jews*, 71–2). The provincial seats were often taken up by allied members who lived in London.

48 Cesarani, *Jewish Chronicle*. The paper was launched in 1841 but was initially short-lived; another Jewish paper, *The Voice of Jacob*, was founded in the same year but merged with the *JC* in 1848. Together they were possibly the first minority community journal in the English-speaking world (Rubinstein, *History of the Jews*, 91). Two of the early recruits to the paper's editorial team were Jacob Franklin of Liverpool and Dr Morris J. Raphall, later minister of the Birmingham Hebrew Congregation (Cesarani, *Jewish Chronicle*, 8–9).

49 Cesarani, *Jewish Chronicle*, 31.

50 These organizations were joined in the early 1870s by the London United Synagogue (a joint body representing the main metropolitan Ashkenazi congregations) and the Anglo-Jewish Association, founded to organize aid for Jews overseas (Todd M. Endelman, 'Communal Solidarity among the Jewish Elite of Victorian London', *Victorian Studies* 28, no. 3 (1985): 491–526).

51 Lipman, *Social History*, 37.

52 Endelman, *Broadening Jewish History*, 30–1.

53 Ibid., 31–3.

54 For example, see Scott, *Social Network Analysis*; Stephen P. Borgatti, Ajay Mehra, Daniel J. Brass and Giuseppe Labianca, 'Network Analysis in the Social Sciences', *Science* 323, no. 5916 (1990): 892–5. Also Connell, 'Social Networks'.

55 John Scott, *What Is Social Network Analysis?* (London and New York: Bloomsbury Academic, 2012); Stanley Wasserman and Katherine Faust, *Social Network Analysis: Methods and Applications* (Cambridge: Cambridge University Press, 1994).

56 Network theory has been used to address the question of how village networks responded to the influences of industrialization and urbanization. See Scott, *Social Network Analysis*, 77; Borgatti et al., 'Network Analysis', 897.

57 Borgatti et al., 'Network Analysis', 892–5; Lynch, *Individuals, Families and Communities*, 68. Lynch cites church membership as one such 'inspiration' for an active network of 'invented kinship' (68–102).

58 Connell, 'Social Networks', 44.

59 Rubinstein, *History of the Jews*, 70.

60 Connell, 'Social Networks', 44.

61 Ibid., 46–7.

62 This tardiness is often attributed to the fact that there were few areas of discrimination that directly affected Jews or which could not be got round, and also that they were small in number. Municipal office holding was allowed under the Jewish Disabilities Removal Act of 1845. The first Jewish MP to be elected was Nathan Rothschild, for the City of London. The House of Commons was prepared to allow him to take a modified oath so that he could take his seat, but the Lords consistently overruled this until 1858, when the need to take a Christological oath was lifted. Rubinstein, *History of the Jews*, 73–6.

63  Chaim Bermant, *The Cousinhood* (London: Macmillan, 1971).
64  Cecil Roth, *A History of the Jews in England*, 3rd edn (Oxford: Clarendon Press, 1964); Lipman, *Social History*. For an excellent overview of the historiography, see Todd M. Endelman, 'English Jewish History', *Modern Judaism* 11 (1991): 91–109 and the introduction to Endelman's *Broadening Jewish History*; also David Feldman, *Englishmen and Jews: Social Relations and Political Culture, 1840–1914* (New Haven and London: Yale University Press, 1994), 7–9.
65  Almost all of the communities studied underwent secession by some of their members, commonly because of dissatisfaction over access to positions of influence; occasionally because of personal differences. 'New' congregations were formed in 1839 in Liverpool, 1844 in Manchester (and again briefly in 1869) and 1852 in Birmingham. The schisms in Manchester and Birmingham were short-lived, as were equivalents in Glasgow and Hull, but in Liverpool it endured. (Williams, *Making of Manchester Jewry*, 132–4, 137; Kokosalakis, *Ethnic Identity*, 71–4; Birmingham Jewish History Society (BJHS), *Birmingham Jewry, Vol. 2: More Aspects, 1740–1930* (Oldbury: Birmingham Jewish History Research Group, 1984), 13–14.) For one example of several in Hull, see Israel Finestein, 'The Jews in Hull between 1766 and 1880', *Jewish Historical Studies* 35 (1996–8), 38, and on Glasgow, A. Levy, *The Origins of Glasgow Jewry, 1812–1895* (Glasgow: A. J. Macfarlane Ltd, 1949), 43–4.
66  Rubinstein, *History of the Jews*; Lloyd P. Gartner, *The Jewish Immigrant in England, 1870–1914* (London: Allen & Unwin, 1960).
67  For these criticisms, see Endelman, *Jews of Britain*, 2; Todd Endelman, 'Jews, Aliens and Other Outsiders in British History', *Historical Journal* 37, no. 4 (1994): 959–69.
68  Williams, *Making of Manchester Jewry*. Endelman states, of Williams's book, that 'he made the parochial disputes of a provincial, culturally undistinguished Jewish community relevant to both students of the Victorian middle class and students of Jewish assimilation in Western Europe and North America' ('English Jewish History', 93); Endelman, *Jews of Georgian England*; Feldman, *Englishmen and Jews*.
69  Rubinstein, in contrast, finds some of this work 'deliberately adversarial' and calls instead for a refocusing of attention on the relative tranquillity of the experiences of British Jewry (*History of the Jews*, 32–3, and 22–33 generally).
70  Kokosalakis, *Ethnic Identity*. Some examples of local studies are M. Freedman, *Leeds Jewry: The First Hundred Years* (Leeds: Jewish Historical Society of England (Leeds branch), 1992); BJHS, *Birmingham Jewry*, Vol. 1: *1749–1914* (Oldbury: Birmingham Jewish History Research Group, 1980) and Vol. 2; Ben Braber, *Jews in Glasgow, 1879–1939* (Ilford: Vallentine Mitchell & Co Ltd, 2007).
71  An exception is Endelman's *Broadening Jewish History*.

72  David Englander, *A Documentary History of Jewish Immigrants in Britain, 1840–1920* (Leicester: Leicester University Press, 1994), 63–4.
73  Laidlaw, 'Jews in the British Isles: Birthplaces'; Petra Laidlaw 'Jews in the British Isles in 1851: Marriage and Childbearing', *Jewish Journal of Sociology* 57, nos 1 and 2 (2015): 7–43.
74  This book uses the terms 'industrial' and 'commercial' interchangeably, in recognition of the fact that the selected towns had diverse economies, which were not all based in manufacturing. It also consistently uses the term 'British' rather than 'Anglo', since there were growing Jewish communities in Scottish, Irish and Welsh towns.
75  This can be searched for individuals at www.jgsgb.org.uk or via the UK Data Service at https://discover.ukdataservice.ac.uk/catalogue/?sn=7668. On the collection of the data, see Laidlaw, 'Jews in the British Isles: Birthplaces', 30–1.
76  Laidlaw, 'Jews in the British Isles: Birthplaces', 30.
77  Ibid., 33. The AJDB gives a population of around 850 in Liverpool in 1851 compared with earlier estimates of 1,300 to 2,500. Ongoing work by Phil Sapiro indicates that there may have been significantly more Jews in Liverpool in 1851 than are enumerated in the AJDB, although it is not yet clear how many of these were long-term residents (Phil Sapiro, personal communication, November 2019).
78  On the different local character of some of these cities, see Briggs, *Victorian Cities*, *passim*. It was cheaper to take a boat to America from England than from Dutch or German ports by the 1880s, hence the popularity of transmigration across the narrow point of northern England (Feldman, *Englishmen and Jews*, 154). Some of the Jews settling in Glasgow had arrived at the Scottish port of Leith.
79  Briggs, *Victorian Cities*, 86.
80  Ibid., 32, 112–28, and 88–138, *passim*.
81  Ibid., 36.
82  Gerry Kearns, Paul Laxton and Joy Campbell, 'Duncan and the Cholera Test: Public Health in Mid-Nineteenth-Century Liverpool', *Transactions of the Historic Society of Lancashire and Cheshire*, 143 (1993): 87–115; A. T. McCabe, 'The Standard of Living on Merseyside, 1850–1875', in *Victorian Lancashire*, ed. S. Peter Bell (Newton Abbot: David & Charles, 1974), 127–49.
83  Briggs, *Victorian Cities*, 34, 60.
84  There were around 100 Jews in Leeds at mid-century; by the end of the 1870s, this had grown to 2,250 (Feldman, *Englishmen and Jews*, 121). Finestein, 'Jews in Hull', 33–5. On Sheffield, see K. Lunn, 'Historical Introduction', in Barry A. Kosmin, Marzy Bauer and Nigel Grizzard, *Steel City Jews: A Study of Ethnicity and Social Mobility in the Jewish Population of the City of Sheffield, South Yorkshire* (London: Research Unit Board of Deputies of British Jews, 1976): 1–6.
85  Williams, *Making of Manchester Jewry*, 327.

## 2. Households and family structures

1. Anderson, *Family Structure*.
2. Reay, 'Kinship and the Neighbourhood'; Tadmor, 'Early Modern Kinship'.
3. The census listings at www.ancestry.com were used for this purpose, later supplemented by those at www.findmypast.com, which offers better tools for searching on specific addresses. If a household could not be identified in the census they were omitted from the detailed analysis, although they were included in the basic counts. A number of the household listings for Hull were not connected to the correct digital image of the census form at www.ancestry.com, which again precluded some positive links. The transcribed listings for Glasgow were not linked to the digitized forms, with the same effect. Further work was done for Manchester, Liverpool and Birmingham using CD Rom sets supplied by S&N Genealogy.
4. Laidlaw, 'Jews in the British Isles: Birthplaces', 35–6.
5. It should be borne in mind that the Jewish population of Liverpool as captured in the AJDB is lower than was expected from other estimates. See Chapter 1, and Laidlaw, 'Jews in the British Isles: Birthplaces'.
6. Males comprise 50.7 per cent of the AJDB as a whole compared with 48.8 per cent in the British Isles (Laidlaw, 'Jews in the British Isles: Birthplaces', 34).
7. Laidlaw has suggested that the latter may have been a factor in explaining the unexpectedly small size of the Jewish community in Liverpool in 1851 (Petra Laidlaw, personal communication, July 2019).
8. Laidlaw, 'Jews in the British Isles: Marriage and Childbearing', 16–19.
9. Many of these men were 'pushed' by a lack of economic opportunities at home. There were also significant 'pull' factors from the British manufacturing and port towns.
10. Though note Tadmor's ideas about the expansiveness of the term 'family', which could include co-resident non-kin (N. Tadmor, *Family and Friends in Eighteenth-Century England: Household, Kinship and Patronage* (Cambridge: Cambridge University Press, 2001). For further discussion on this topic, see Tadmor, 'Early Modern Kinship'.
11. Laslett, 'Introduction', 48.
12. Laidlaw suggests, based on long birth intervals between children, that completed family sizes are commonly understated in the AJDB, partly because much of migrant women's childbearing could take place before arriving in Britain. She offers a correction in her article 'Jews in the British Isles: Marriage and Childbearing', 7–43 (see discussion on 31–2).
13. For example, see Silvia Sovič, 'European Family History: Moving Beyond Stereotypes of "East" and "West"', *Cultural and Social History* 5, no. 2 (2008): 141–63 (151).

14 See Laslett, 'Introduction', 26–32. The amendments follow the United Nations classification of households, which can be found at https://unstats.un.org/Unsd/demographic/sconcerns/fam/fammethods.htm.
15 All households on Verdon Street and Moreton Street in Manchester, Paradise Street and a section of Mount Pleasant in Liverpool, and Pershore Street and Edgbaston Street in Birmingham were reconstructed from the census returns for the purpose of this comparison.
16 For example, Laslett, 'Introduction', Table 1.15, 85, showing that 78 per cent of households in Ealing in 1599 were nuclear in form; 73 per cent of households in Anderson's Preston were nuclear (*Family Structure*, 44).
17 Cited in Laidlaw, 'Jews in the British Isles: Marriage and Childbearing', 26.
18 Ibid.
19 An extended family in Laslett's classification could also mean two or more related persons, none of whom are a family nucleus.
20 Laslett, 'Introduction', 61; W. A. Armstrong, 'A Note on the Household Structure of Mid-C19th York in Comparative Perspective', in *Household and Family*, ed. Peter Laslett (Cambridge: Cambridge University Press, 1972), 205–14 (213). Enumeration areas from Leeds, Birmingham, Hull and Manchester were included in this sample. Michael Anderson, 'Household Structure and the Industrial Revolution: Mid Nineteenth-Century Preston in Comparative Perspective', in *Household and Family*, ed. Peter Laslett (Cambridge: Cambridge University Press, 1972), 215–35 (220). Anderson compared the industrial town of Preston to a non-industrial sample and found a similar incidence of extended families there.
21 The most common experience across all of the sampled towns was to have one, two or three children in the home. There were many individual exceptions: in all of the towns except Manchester and Hull a quarter to a third of families with children had seven or more, and the Liverpool community held a particularly high number of very large households: seventeen had ten or more children, as did nine cases in Birmingham. There was only a slight correlation between number of children and the age of the household head (a rough proxy for life-cycle stage) in Manchester and Birmingham, and a weak negative relationship in Liverpool. There is also some small evidence that heads in more skilled or leisured professions had more children, but again, the relationship is not particularly strong. Completed family sizes in the AJDB as a whole comprised 5.9 to 6.3 children (which is similar to the British population in general), and around 80 per cent of couples recorded as married or cohabiting had three or more children. See Laidlaw, 'Jews in the British Isles: Marriage and Childbearing', 20, 22.
22 Anderson, 'Household Structure', 220.
23 Where adult life expectancy is low, there will be fewer grandparents available to co-reside or offer help; ditto grown siblings. The length of intergenerational gaps

and ages at child-bearing will also affect whether younger adults are able to offer help to their parents.

24  Lynch has noted that the strongest family bonds were between parents and children, and between siblings, which would explain the prevalence of nieces and nephews (Katherine A. Lynch, 'Kinship in Britain and Beyond From the Early Modern to the Present: Postscript', *Continuity and Change* 25, no. 1 (2010): 185–90 (187)). Anderson, *Family Structure*, 44. This pattern of lone children living with grandparents was also found in Anderson's rural sample from 1851 ('Household Structure', 224).

25  Anderson, *Family Structure*, e.g. on 56.

26  Anderson, 'Household Structure', 227–30.

27  Laidlaw, 'Jews in the British Isles: Marriage', 25.

28  Tadmor, 'Early Modern Kinship', 26–7.

29  Susannah Ottaway, *The Decline of Life: Old Age in Eighteenth-Century England* (Cambridge: Cambridge University Press, 2004), 141–72 and esp. 150–5; Pat Thane, *Old Age in English History: Past Experiences, Present Issues* (Oxford: Oxford University Press, 2000), 119–46.

30  Steven Ruggles, 'Multigenerational Families in Nineteenth-Century America', *Continuity and Change* 18, no. 1 (2003): 139–65.

31  Richard Wall has noted that the widowed and elderly in England were also less likely to live with children ('Economic Collaboration of Family Members within and beyond Households in English Society, 1600–2000', *Continuity and Change* 25, no. 1 (2010): 83–108).

32  The complete AJDB 'reconstitutes' families who were separated on census night, but who can be linked by other internal evidence. These missing partners are therefore unlikely to have been simply staying elsewhere, and a note would also have been made if they had been found in subsequent censuses.

33  Williams, *Making of Manchester Jewry*, 164.

34  Although Abraham was the only one of the brothers who seems to have married, this is the closest to the traditional 'frèreche' (consisting of two or more married, co-residing brothers) household that we have in our sample. See Laslett, 'Introduction', 30.

35  Few of the over-sixty-fives lived apart from relatives in Preston, and only 37 per cent were living with a spouse. Eighty per cent of those who had a child alive were living with them in 1851 (Anderson, 'Household Structure', 224–5). In rural Kent, 45–56 per cent of elderly men and women co-resided with kin in 1851 and also in 1881, and almost three-quarters of widow/ers lived with children or other kin. Twenty-eight to 37 per cent lived alone with a spouse. About 80 per cent of men over the age of sixty-five were employed, however (Reay, 'Kinship and the Neighbourhood', 96).

36  The proportion of over-sixties was smaller in several of the Jewish provincial populations than the AJDB as a whole: 7.6 per cent of all adults in Liverpool, 7.6 per cent in Manchester and 8.1 per cent in Birmingham compared with 10.5 in the full dataset. The average age of all adults was similar though, ranging between 34 and 37 (Manchester was several years younger than the other two towns, or than the whole dataset).

37  The two largest occupational categories according to the scheme used in the AJDB were miscellaneous (which is where many of the potentially higher-status occupations are classed) and clothing, footwear and textiles. Most were categorized as semi-skilled rather than skilled or professional, however. In Liverpool, five of the elderly were classed as leisured, two of whom were also household heads. See Chapter 4 for more on occupations.

38  Anderson, *Family Structure*, 38.

39  The figure for Sheffield was 5.9 per cent.

40  By the time that *Household and Family* was published in 1972, Laslett had corrected this oversight, finding that lodgers made up 3.4 per cent of the population from the sixteenth to the nineteenth century, and that they were present in 18 per cent of domestic groups, occurring more frequently than extended kin (Peter Laslett, 'Mean Household Size in England since the C16th', in *Household and Family*, ed. Peter Laslett (Cambridge: Cambridge University Press, 1972), 125–58 (134)). Boarders (who paid for extras like food) are more likely to be seen as part of the household since they share domestic spaces, but the terminology is fluid and the two terms are often used interchangeably.

41  Modell and Hareven see this emphasis on pseudo-family changing over time, towards a greater service-based exchange which facilitated independence (John Modell and Tamara K. Hareven, 'Urbanization and the Malleable Household: An Examination of Boarding and Lodging in American Families', *Journal of Marriage and the Family* 35, no. 3 (1973): 467–79).

42  Modell and Hareven, 'Urbanization'. See also Mark Peel, 'On the Margins: Lodgers and Boarders in Boston, 1860–1900', *Journal of American History* 72, no. 4 (1986): 813–34.

43  Jeff Meek, 'Boarding and Lodging Practices in Early Twentieth-Century Scotland', *Continuity and Change* 31, no. 1 (2016): 79–100.

44  Endelman, *Jews of Georgian England*, 177.

45  Meek, 'Boarding and Lodging Practices', 83–4, showing that 25 per cent of Jewish households contained lodgers. In Anderson's Preston sample the proportion was 23 per cent of households, and in both York and Nottingham it was 22 per cent (Anderson, 'Household Structure', 220; Armstrong, 'A Note', 220). See Anderson for some of the other reasons that people took up lodging.

46  In both Liverpool and Birmingham, heads with lodgers were around three years younger on average than those without: approximately thirty-nine years compared

with forty-two or forty-three. In Manchester, there was almost no difference between the two categories. The number of children in the family was also slightly lower than the average, suggesting that the family was not yet complete (in Birmingham 2.9 for households with lodgers and 4.6 for those without; Liverpool 4.7 and 5.2; Manchester 3.5 and 4.2).

47 The only exception was again Glasgow where 40 per cent were married (but numbers of lodgers were very small).
48 Pooley and Turnbull, *Migration and Mobility*, 193–4.
49 Williams, *Making of Manchester Jewry*, 319–24. The first Sephardi synagogue in Manchester is now the city's Jewish Museum.
50 Lipman, *History of the Jews*, 4.
51 This was true in Vaughan's study of Jews in nineteenth-century Manchester too: more than 70 per cent of households with co-residents had common national origins, while only 42 per cent shared an occupation. Both were more common among Jews than non-Jews (Laura Vaughan, 'The Unplanned "Ghetto": Immigrant Work Patterns in 19th Century Manchester', paper given at the 10th conference of the International Planning History Society, University of Westminster, July 2002, London, http://discovery.ucl.ac.uk/662/). In all three of the towns studied here, household heads with lodgers were more than three times more likely to share nationality with their lodgers than occupation.
52 Two of the seven Jewish female lodging house keepers in Manchester were widowed and another was single. Several of the others were described as married (or were imputed to be so from other evidence), but had no partner at home on census night. Furthermore, in two out of three cases where both halves of the couple were present, it was the woman who was described as the lodging house keeper. See, for example, Leonore Davidoff, 'The Separation of Home and Work? Landladies and Lodgers in Nineteenth and Twentieth Century England', in *Fit Work for Women*, ed. Sandra Burman (London and New York: Routledge, 1979), 64–97.
53 Petra Laidlaw, 'Jews in the British Isles in 1851: Occupations', *Jewish Journal of Sociology* 56, nos. 1 and 2 (2013): 114–57 (125).
54 In Preston, 21 per cent of lodgers shared a house with more than six other lodgers and 11 per cent with twelve or more. Anderson, *Family Structure*, 47.
55 Endelman, *Jews of Georgian England*, 86–117.
56 It is worth noting in passing that in Liverpool a high proportion of the households extended by non-kin only can be identified as belonging to the community elite, with their names appearing frequently in synagogue and charity records. This is because large household size in this town often correlated with an extensive domestic staff – although they also tended to have above-average numbers of children. In several of the other towns, and particularly Birmingham, Hull and Leeds, large households containing many non-family members were housing

lodgers, which is generally a proxy for poorer socio-economic status. This was also reflected in the generally unskilled status of the household heads.

57 In York, 29 per cent of households had servants in 1851, and 10 per cent in Preston, although the latter was an exclusively working-class sample (Anderson, 'Household Structure', 220). Armstrong suggests that between 5 and 15 per cent of households in parts of Leeds, Birmingham, Manchester and Liverpool contained servants, with a further 0.5 to 3 per cent including trade assistants (Armstrong, 'A Note', 205–14). A detailed whole-street analysis showed that Jews living on Verdon Street in Manchester's Red Bank (around a third of households) were notably more likely to contain servants than their non-Jewish neighbours, extremely few of whom employed one at all. All of the Jewish servants here were domestics rather than business employees. Jewish households on this street were also much more likely than non-Jews to contain lodgers (80 per cent, often consisting of whole families).

58 'Salis Schwabe, 1800–53', *Dictionary of National Biography*. Endelman notes this tendency for German migrants, especially those from urban areas (where Jews experienced considerable discrimination), to be 'indifferent or hostile' to Judaism, and to use their move to Britain as a way to reshape their identity. Unitarianism was a relatively popular alternative in the manufacturing cities like Manchester as it represented the norm in the socially elite social circles they wished to emulate, as well as being broad-minded and anti-Trinitarian. It is possible, therefore, that the Germanness of the Schwabes' cook was more important than her Jewishness (Endelman, *Broadening Jewish History*, 145–67). Almost 200 Jewish households in the dataset employed a cook, but only three (one in Liverpool and two in Manchester) have been identified as Jewish.

59 According to Laidlaw only 4.3 per cent of the Jews in the AJDB were in domestic service compared with 13.8 per cent in the British population. Laidlaw, 'Jews in the British Isles: Occupations', 120.

60 BJHS, *Birmingham Jewry*, Vol. 2, 37.

61 Keith A. Cowlard, 'The Identification of Social (Class) Areas and Their Place in C19th Urban Development', *Transactions of the Institute of British Geographers* 4, no. 2 (1979): 239–57 (241) makes this suggestion about the symbolic status of servant keeping in this period (having a lodger had the opposite effect). It could thus be a way of demonstrating knowledge of British norms and aspirations.

62 Clive A. Lawton, 'Judaism', in *Ethical Issues in Six Religious Traditions*, ed. Peggy Morgan and Clive Lawton (Edinburgh: Edinburgh University Press, 2007), 168–215 (170).

63 Scott, *Social Network Analysis*, 35.

64 Anderson, *Family Structure*, quotation on 101.

## 3. Residence patterns and neighbourhoods

1. Scott, *Social Network Analysis*, 32.
2. For details of the skill classification see Laidlaw, 'Jews in the British Isles: Occupations', 114–57.
3. Permission to reproduce the maps was kindly given by David Rumsey Collections Online (www.davidrumsey.com). The maps were originally printed in *The Illustrated Atlas, and Modern History of the World Geographical, Political, Commercial & Statistical*, ed. R. Montgomery Martin, Esq. (London and New York: J & F Tallis, 1851).
4. See R. S. Holmes, 'Identifying Nineteenth-Century Properties', *Area* 6, no. 4 (1974): 273–7 for these and similar problems. Some of the potential imprecision can be overcome by linking census households to rate books, but it is likely that many of the Jewish households were not ratepayers.
5. The only comparably detailed studies have been based on the 1881 census and data from Manchester, Leeds and London only. See Laura Vaughan and Alan Penn, 'Jewish Immigrant Settlement Patterns in Manchester and Leeds, 1881', *Urban Studies* 43, no. 3 (2006): 653–71.
6. It is a commonplace of urban studies that minority groups tend to cluster in particular parts of town: perfect assimilation is equated with uniform dispersal across the town, but this is rarely found. Segregation is thus identified if there is any deviation from this pattern, with greater deviation representing greater segregation. See, for example, M. A. Poole and F. W Boal, 'Religious Residential Segregation in Belfast in Mid-1969: A Multi-Level Analysis', in *Social Patterns in Cities* 5 (1973): 1–40 (22). There are several ways to quantify such deviation, but the small size of the Jewish populations at this time do not lend themselves to this sort of approach.
7. Colin G. Pooley, 'The Residential Segregation of Migrant Communities in Mid-Victorian Liverpool', *Transactions of the Institute of British Geographers* 2, no. 3 (1977): 364–82 (366).
8. Kidd describes Chorlton as a working-class suburb with better sanitary facilities than the city centre; Alan J. Kidd, *Manchester*, 2nd edn (Keele: Keele University Press, 1996), 47.
9. BJHS, *Birmingham Jewry*, Vol. 1, 10.
10. Ibid., 64.
11. It is worth remembering that there is a degree of imprecision in the location of individual houses, and this could particularly affect the impression of clustering on long roads.
12. For example, see Richard Lawton and Colin G. Pooley, 'The Social Geography of Nineteenth-Century Merseyside: A Research Project', *Historical Methods Newsletter* 7, no. 4 (1974): 276–84.

13 Pooley, 'Residential Segregation', 370. Over 90,000 Irish entered Liverpool in the first three months of 1846 and nearly 30,000 in the year from July 1847 (*A History of the County of Lancaster*, Vol. 4: *Liverpool: Trade, Population and Geographical Growth*, originally published by Victoria County History, London, 1911, https://www.british-history.ac.uk/vch/lancs/vol4/pp37-38).

14 https://matt-houghton.squarespace.com/the-yatessamuel-family (this is the site associated with the history of the Jewish Deane Street Cemetery).

15 It should be remembered that there is some doubt over the size of the Liverpool Jewish community as captured in the AJDB. On the expansion of suburbs like Everton, see *History of the County of Lancaster*, https://www.british-history.ac.uk/vch/lancs/vol4/pp1-4 and McCabe, 'The Standard of Living'.

16 Vaughan found that Jewish institutions in London's East End at the end of the nineteenth century were usually on streets with a high density of Jews, although they tended to be a street or two off the most integrated (most used) roads. Schools were more integrated into the Jewish parts of town than the synagogues. Vaughan, 'Study of the Spatial Characteristics', 57.

17 See *History of the County of Lancaster*, https://www.british-history.ac.uk/vch/lancs/vol4/pp43-52. Liverpool Jewry had had a recognized meeting place since about 1750.

18 Vaughan, 'Unplanned "Ghetto"', 3; Williams, *Making of Manchester Jewry*, 125.

19 See Williams, *Making of Manchester Jewry*, 125–6 on the creation of this 'inner suburb' which came about with greater wealth from retail in the 1840s.

20 Vaughan and Penn, 'Jewish Immigrant Settlement Patterns', *passim*. The authors suggest that Jewish areas of settlement were not the most integrated parts of town when it came to easy movement into central facilities, although they may have been close enough to access them when necessary.

21 Williams, *Making of Manchester Jewry*, 268.

22 Vaughan and Penn, 'Jewish Immigrant Settlement Patterns', 656. Jews made up 2.3 per cent of the population of Manchester at this time. By way of contrast, the immigrant Leylands area of north Leeds housed 80 per cent of the Jewish population of that town (intensive Jewish immigration had only started in Leeds in the 1880s).

23 Williams, *Making of Manchester Jewry*, 201, 270–1.

24 Ibid., 72–4, see also 85–6 for examples.

25 Ibid., 253, 323.

26 Ibid., 310–17. There were also more fundamental differences of opinion with the OHC at the heart of this new congregation.

27 Ibid., 204. The Manchester Hebrew Philanthropic and Loan Society used its committee room for its meetings.

28 Margoliouth, *History of the Jews*, Vol. 3, 105; BJHS, *Birmingham Jewry*, Vol. 1, 10.

29  Birmingham Jewish Local History Study Group, 'A Portrait of Birmingham Jewry'.
30  'Birmingham Hebrew Congregation', Birmingham Archives and Heritage Online Catalogue, http://calmview.birmingham.gov.uk/calmview/Record.aspx?src=CalmView.Catalog&id=JA&pos=1.
31  BJHS, *Birmingham Jewry*, Vol. 1, 5.
32  Ibid., 12.
33  'Report on the State of the Public Health in the Borough of Birmingham by a Committee of Physicians and Surgeons', in *Sanitary Inquiry: Local Reports on the Sanitary Condition of the Labouring Population of England, in Consequence of an Inquiry Directed to Be Made by the Poor Law Commissioners. Presented to Both Houses of Parliament, by Command of Her Majesty, July, 1842*, https://archive.org/stream/b21366202/b21366202_djvu.txt.
34  See Vaughan and Penn, 'Jewish Immigrant Settlement Patterns'.
35  Pooley, 'Residential Segregation', 370–2. He calls the Scottish and Welsh pattern an 'ethnic community' model, where cultural preferences outweigh economic opportunities to live elsewhere.
36  Pooley, 'Residential Segregation', 369.
37  For example, Williams notes that Jews tended to avoid the 'German' Greenheys area of Manchester, suggesting that they did not see themselves in terms of their 'foreignness' (*Making of Manchester Jewry*, 85–6).
38  In Pooley's terms a 'voluntarily cohesive' ethnic community ('Residential Segregation', 367).
39  Vaughan and Penn, 'Jewish Immigrant Settlement Patterns', 664.
40  This figure was reached by recording all of the households on these streets in the census and cross-matching with the AJDB to identify Jews. Vaughan and Penn found a similar density of 14 per cent Jewish households in Manchester outside Red Bank in the 1880s (with some clusters where it was higher) (see 'Jewish Immigrant Settlement Patterns').
41  In most case this relates to the status of the household head. Lodgers are also included, but only where they shared the same skill status (or where they were the single lodger).
42  Non-Jewish households with Jewish lodgers of different skill statuses were omitted.
43  See Laidlaw, 'Jews in the British Isles: Occupations', 127–9.
44  In Liverpool, 19.4 per cent of lodgers were unskilled compared with just under 7 per cent of household heads, while for semi-skilled manual workers the proportions were 25.8 and 14.6 per cent. The balance was much more even among semi-skilled non-manual workers, but there were no lodgers at all in the managerial, leisured and professional categories.
45  Vaughan and Penn, 'Jewish Immigrant Settlement Patterns'; Williams, *Making of Manchester Jewry*, 274. The authors of the 'Report on the State of the Public

Health of Birmingham' in 1842 made a similar point for the inner-city residence of master manufacturers.
46 Williams calls cap making in particular the 'boom industry' of the late 1840s and 1850s (*Making of Manchester Jewry*, 179).
47 This suggests that Vaughan ('The Unplanned "Ghetto"') is not entirely correct in dating a shift from hawking and selling to occupations characteristic of the industrial proletariat from the period 1853 to 1881. In fact, it seems that the occupational profile was already more mixed in 1851 than she allows.
48 Laidlaw suggests that Liverpool Jewry may have gone through a phase of international out-migration in the years before 1851, which could explain both its lower than expected size at mid-century, and the relative paucity of heads from overseas (Petra Laidlaw, personal communication, July 2019).
49 Pooley, 'Residential Segregation', 371. Liverpool Jews had a higher rate of servant keeping than either of the other two towns: 64 per cent of households.
50 Williams, *Making of Manchester Jewry*, passim.
51 This was a family named Levy, who worked in the clockmaking industry. See http://www.birminghamconservationtrust.org/our-projects/bct-finished/back-to-backs.
52 Poole and Boal, 'Religious Residential Segregation'.
53 For example, see Colin Pooley, 'Residential Mobility in the Victorian City', *Transactions of the Institute of British Geographers* 4, no. 2 (1979): 258–77. Pooley singled out the Mount Pleasant and Princes Park areas of Liverpool as places with particularly high persistence rates ('Residential Segregation', 265). The older, inner residential districts like Scotland and Great George wards had very high population turnover as people established themselves and moved on, to be replaced with new immigrants.
54 Vaughan and Penn, 'Jewish Immigrant Settlement Patterns'.
55 Pooley, 'Residential Segregation', 374–5.
56 Ibid., 375, 377.
57 Ibid., 377–8. See also Busteed, *The Irish in Manchester*; Belchem, *Irish, Catholic and Scouse*; and for a more critical interpretation, Hickman, *Religion, Class and Identity*.
58 Vaughan and Penn's study of Manchester and Leeds also suggested that Jewish migrants were much more likely than non-Jewish migrants to marry people from the same national background as themselves ('Jewish Immigrant Settlement Patterns', 668).
59 Endelman, *Broadening Jewish History*, 95–114.
60 The Manchester OHC organized overflow services for poor Jews as early as 1853 (Williams, *Making of Manchester Jewry*, 232).
61 Anderson, *Family Structure*, 56–62; Reay, 'Kinship and the Neighbourhood'; Wrightson and Levine, *Poverty and Piety*. See also Di Cooper and Moira Donald, 'Households and "Hidden" Kin in Early C19th England: Four Case Studies in Suburban Exeter, 1821–1861', *Continuity and Change* 10, no. 2 (1995): 257–78.
62 Lynch, *Individuals, Families and Communities*, 61.

63  Scott, *Social Network Analysis*, 13.
64  Households headed by Jews or containing Jewish lodgers.
65  Reay, 'Kinship and the Neighbourhood', 93; Wrightson and Levine, *Poverty and Piety*, 87, and see also 187–97 for further discussion.
66  Anderson, *Family Structure*, 57–9, using a sample of households with extra life history information. Quotation on 61.
67  'Moses Samuel', *Dictionary of National Biography*.
68  Elizabeth is not listed as one of Louis and Henrietta's offspring in the AJDB but they are named as her parents in her own entry. Kate Yates's daughter Clara was to marry Elizabeth's brother Edwin Louis in 1855. One of Edwin Louis's brothers, Samuel Montagu, was to become Baron Swaythling (see his entry in the *Dictionary of National Biography*).
69  Williams, *Making of Manchester Jewry*, 138.
70  Ibid., 350–1.
71  BJHS, *Birmingham Jewry*, Vol. 1, 73–4.
72  Williams asserts that in Manchester pawnbrokers were men 'of solid substance who commanded respect within and beyond the community'. Pawn tickets were a form of currency (Williams, *Making of Manchester Jewry*, 118).
73  The distances are approximate given the lack of precision over exact locations on the street.
74  'Centrality' is one of the key measures of a social network, referring to the importance of a single node within the network (Borgatti et al., 'Network Analysis', 901).
75  Women are often instrumental in maintaining the social contacts between families and households (Scott, *Social Network Analysis*, 79).
76  Wrightson and Levine find that neighbours and friends were important in daily networks (*Poverty and Piety*, 99–103).
77  The list of other towns range from coastal resorts and ports, smaller market towns and other northern communities like Birkenhead, Preston, Newcastle-upon-Tyne and Salford. A handful of others had connections overseas, from Ireland to Jamaica.
78  Williams, *Making of Manchester Jewry*, 201, 270–1.
79  Ibid., 86, 271.
80  This was Joseph Braham (see ibid., 121).
81  Vaughan, 'Study of Spatial Characteristics', abstract.

## 4. Occupations, poverty and wealth

1  For the most recent treatment, see Laidlaw, 'Jews in the British Isles: Occupations'.
2  See, for example, the two volumes of the Birmingham Jewish History Society's *Birmingham Jewry*, which is very detailed, but does not make much comparison with wider patterns in the city.

3   See https://www.campop.geog.cam.ac.uk/research/occupations/datasets/coding. This ESRC-funded project was led by Leigh Shaw-Taylor, Amy Erickson and Tony Wrigley.
4   In Laidlaw's words, 'The AJDB system is a four-way taxonomy, classifying by *product* (eg clothing, jewellery, commercial finance … ), by *activity* (eg "manufacturing", "selling", "providing a service"); by *position in labour market* (eg "in training", "self-employed", "employer"); and by *skill level* (eg "skilled manual", "professional")' ('Jews in the British Isles: Occupations', 177).
5   These can be downloaded from the project website at https://www.campop.geog.cam.ac.uk/research/occupations, or from the UK Data Archive at https://www.data-archive.ac.uk.
6   These individuals were placed in the primary sector under the Booth–Armstrong taxonomy on which Laidlaw's scheme is based. However, most would be attributed to other classes according to Wrigley, because they were actually engaged in dealing or manufacture of agricultural products (primarily animals). Two were also certified kosher animal slaughterers, one in Birmingham and one in Salford, Lancashire.
7   According to Endelman, most of the German and Polish immigrants who arrived between 1700 and 1830 were unskilled and fell into hawking and peddling, which also had the benefit of not requiring much English (*Jews of Georgian England*, 179). Later waves of Eastern European Jews were often skilled artisans (Endelman, *Jews of Britain*, 91). Kidd reminds us that we should not overstate the impact of manufacturing in the occupational structure of Manchester more generally, either, although cotton was the 'driving force' of the local economy (*Manchester*, 23–30, quotation on 36).
8   Laidlaw, 'Jews in the British Isles: Occupations'. Forty-four per cent of the AJDB were self-employed or sole traders based on their census returns (130). According to Williams, shopkeepers became particularly important within the Jewish workforce in Manchester from the early 1840s onwards (*Making of Manchester Jewry*, 111).
9   Early habituation to factory discipline is thought to be an important part of securing a job in this sector. See Katrina Honeyman, *Child Workers in England, 1780–1820: Parish Apprentices and the Making of the Early Industrial Labour Force* (Aldershot: Ashgate, 2007).
10  These are the largest specific categories within the Wrigley/Booth–Armstrong scheme. Others may have been described as general clothiers, workers in shoe trades, or traders and so on.
11  Twenty-seven per cent in Birmingham and 23 per cent in Liverpool.
12  Laidlaw, 'Jews in the British Isles: Occupations', 124–5. The cap-making sector was quite small, so Jews were proportionally quite significant.
13  Williams, *Making of Manchester Jewry*, 67, 121.
14  Ibid., 67.
15  There were 158 glaziers in the AJDB in total, with the largest single group in Birmingham (twenty-four). There were a further twenty-three in Aldgate,

London (another fourteen were based in Spitalfields and five in Whitechapel), and ten to twelve each in a number of other provincial towns including Hull, Dudley, Liverpool, Manchester, Merthyr Tydfil and North Shields. According to Laidlaw, it was particularly an occupation of young immigrants, while Mills noted the high number of glaziers who were poor Poles (Laidlaw, 'Jews in the British Isles: Occupations', 125; Mills, *British Jews*, 262).

16  See BJHS, *Birmingham Jewry*, Vol. 1, 81–96 on jewellers, smiths and watchmakers in the town. Most Jewish jewellers were probably 'jobbing' ones, requiring small amounts of capital and working for factors (83).

17  Gunmaking, for instance, was a closed shop to outsiders in Birmingham (BJHS, *Birmingham Jewry*, Vol. 1, 8).

18  Laidlaw, 'Jews in the British Isles: Occupations', quotation on 121.

19  Sellers of tobacco products were more prominent in Manchester (ten) than in the other two towns (four each). According to Williams, the Jewish trade in tobacco, cigars and snuff was started by David Goodman in 1840 (*Making of Manchester Jewry*, 121). Laidlaw characterizes cigar retail as a 'starter' occupation of young immigrants, unlike the sale of tobacco, which was one the older generation had tended to settle in for longer periods ('Jews in the British Isles: Occupations', 125).

20  Sixty-three, seventy-nine and thirty-seven people respectively sold products in this category in Manchester, Birmingham and Liverpool. This was 54.3, 51.0 and 34.9 per cent of those in dealing and retail compared with 33.8, 8.2 and 14.3 per cent in the town as a whole. Quotation is from Laidlaw, 'Jews in the British Isles: Occupations', 121.

21  See BJHS, *Birmingham Jewry*, Vol. 1, 42–52 on pawnbrokers. There were apparently at least sixteen Jewish pawnbrokers in the town in 1852. Most probably they dealt with small pledges and some made money on the side by lending cash, buying or selling.

22  Williams, *Making of Manchester Jewry*, passim.

23  Ibid., 62–4.

24  In Birmingham in the late 1860s, almost all of the fathers of children listed in the Hebrew School's log book were hawkers (BJHS, *Birmingham Jewry*, Vol. 1., 54).

25  Margoliouth, *History of the Jews*, Vol. 3, 105.

26  Williams, *Making of Manchester Jewry*, 64.

27  Vaughan and Penn, 'Jewish Immigrant Settlement Patterns', 659.

28  Ibid., 661–2.

29  Only one other person in the three towns was listed under an institutional address: a patient in the general hospital at Summer Lane in Birmingham – his occupation was given as traveller.

30  Almost 30 per cent of children aged ten to fourteen alone were employed in England and Wales according to the 1851 census, and this is almost certainly a

significant under-representation of girls in particular. See Peter Kirby, *Child Labour in Britain, 1750–1870* (Basingstoke: Palgrave Macmillan, 2003), 11.

31  It is impossible to isolate children in the occupational dataset, which is divided at age twenty. Comparable figures, therefore, have to focus on individuals coded as scholars relative to the whole population. It is, of course, highly likely that the vast majority of these were children. We can take a more fine-grained approach for the Jewish populations, which reveals that 25 to 30 per cent of all Jewish children (sixteen and under) were scholars. On the growth of Jewish education, see Endelman, *Jews of Georgian Britain*, 187 and 228–30.

32  Kirby, *Child Labour*, 9–13.

33  A. Kershen, *Uniting the Tailors: Trade Unionism amongst the Tailors of London and Leeds, 1870–1939* (Ilford: Frank Cass & Co, 1995), 15, cited by Vaughan and Penn, 'Jewish Immigrant Settlement Patterns', 659.

34  In the 1860s, there were several complaints of children being taken out of the Jews School in Manchester for work (Williams, *Making of Manchester Jewry*, 274).

35  Fifty-six married women had an occupational descriptor. One Manchester widow was labelled as a tailor in her own right, supporting Laidlaw's supposition that widows often continued with their late husband's trade (Laidlaw, 'Jews in the British Isles: Occupations', 135).

36  Laidlaw, 'Jews in the British Isles: Occupations', 135–8.

37  Williams, *Making of Manchester Jewry*, 274.

38  A notable exception to this assumption is foreign-born rabbis, who, despite their training and status in the community, were frequently mentioned in communal records as being in need of charity. This is because they were often new immigrants with little or nothing saved from their meagre salaries, sometimes in transit to America.

39  BJHS, *Birmingham Jewry*, Vol. 2, 36–7. On Hyam, see Williams, *Making of Manchester Jewry*, 85.

40  In 1857, Pirani emigrated to Australia with his family where he set up another Pantechnetheca in Ballarat (BJHS, *Birmingham Jewry*, Vol. 2, 37).

41  Laidlaw, 'Jews in the British Isles: Occupations', 131. Three per cent of people in the AJDB as a whole were classed as independently wealthy, and 7 per cent as managerial, entrepreneurial or professional (that is, 'the elite').

42  Williams, *Making of Manchester Jewry*, 122–3. Several earlier practitioners in medicine and dentistry were more of the quack variety. Also see Rubinstein (*History of the Jews*, 66) on the lack of Jewish engagement with the professions and intelligentsia, partly because of barriers to participation until full emancipation, and – again – partly from disinclination.

43  There was only one named religious professional (a *shochet*, or ritual slaughterer, in Manchester), although others were classified under teachers.

44  See Williams, *Making of Manchester Jewry*, 81–4 on the arrival of foreign- and London-based merchant families in Manchester from the 1830s.

45  Birmingham Jewish Local History Study Group, 'A Portrait of Birmingham Jewry in 1851'. Rate books show that eleven Jews owned houses and other property in the town in 1851.
46  BJHS, *Birmingham Jewry*, Vol. 1, 116–18. Phillips was to be an important figure in both the Jewish and wider communities in Birmingham for the rest of his life. Among other accomplishments, he oversaw the reunion of the two Birmingham congregations.
47  Williams, *Making of Manchester Jewry*, 85.
48  Ibid., 83 and 85–6.
49  BJHS, *Birmingham Jewry*, Vol. 1, 119–21.
50  Laidlaw, 'Jews in the British Isles: Occupations', 145–7.
51  Slop-selling had been largely taken over by the Irish, though Mayhew still commented on it as a profession of elderly poor Jews in London in the 1850s (Williams, *Making of Manchester Jewry*, 115; Endelman *Jews of Georgian England*, 182).
52  Vaughan and Penn downgraded tailoring to the partly skilled category in their occupational classification of urban Jews in 1881, unless individuals were noted to be masters, cutters or employers of others (Vaughan and Penn, 'Jewish Immigrant Settlement Patterns', 659). Also see Williams, *Making of Manchester Jewry*, 67–71.
53  Laidlaw, 'Jews in the British Isles: Occupations', 127–9. Laidlaw notes that it is hard to be exact about skill status based on the census descriptions of what people were doing, and that some jobs changed in nature over time. However, it is a useful and consistently applied indicative measure of skill.
54  Laidlaw, 'Jews in the British Isles: Occupations', 128.
55  This may be one reason for the low population figure for Jewish Liverpool in 1851 (Petra Laidlaw, personal communication, July 2019).
56  See Briggs, *Victorian Cities*, 12–14.
57  In 1843, Duncan had published a pamphlet on the condition of Liverpool's courts and slums which had shocked readers by showing that almost half of the working classes lived in cellars, and that sewerage in the poorer areas was almost completely lacking (W. H. Duncan, 'On the Sanitary State of Liverpool', in *Sanitary Inquiry: Local Reports on the Sanitary Condition of the Labouring Population of England, in Consequence of an Inquiry Directed to Be Made by the Poor Law Commissioners. Presented to Both Houses of Parliament, by Command of Her Majesty, July, 1842*, https://archive.org/stream/b21366202/b21366202_djvu.txt.) See McCabe, 'Standard of Living', 134–42 for specific details on the context and improvements made in Liverpool, and the *History of the County of Lancaster* entry at https://www.british-history.ac.uk/vch/lancs/vol4/pp38-41.
58  W. S. Trench, *Report on the Health of Liverpool During the Year 1864* (Liverpool: Henry Greenwood, 1865); *History of the County of Lancaster*, https://www.british-history.ac.uk/vch/lancs/vol4/pp38-41.

59  McCabe, 'Standard of Living', 137–42.
60  Briggs, *Victorian Cities*, 89.
61  Charles Mott, 'Report on the State of the Residence of the Labouring Classes in the Manufacturing Districts of Lancashire, Cheshire, Derbyshire and Staffordshire', in *Sanitary Inquiry: Local Reports on the Sanitary Condition of the Labouring Population of England, in Consequence of an Inquiry Directed to Be Made by the Poor Law Commissioners. Presented to Both Houses of Parliament, by Command of Her Majesty, July, 1842*, https://archive.org/stream/b21366202/b21366202_djvu.txt. Mott cites a report from the Manchester Statistical Society which found that the minimum weekly rent for a room or a cellar was one shilling.
62  Briggs, *Victorian Cities*, 110.
63  Williams, *Making of Manchester Jewry*, 176, 273.
64  'Report on the State of the Public Health of Birmingham'. See Briggs, *Victorian Cities*, 186–7 on the distinctive condition of work in Birmingham.
65  Briggs, *Victorian Cities*, 215–24.
66  'Report on the State of the Public Health of Birmingham'. BJHS, *Birmingham Jewry*, Vol. 1, 12.
67  'Report on the State of the Public Health of Birmingham'. Imprecision over exactly where individual houses lay on the street means that it is difficult to be specific about whether this was where the Jewish family lived.
68  This had changed by 1881, when Vaughan and Penn found that many more of the Jewish households in Manchester and Leeds shared their homes than non-Jews (Vaughan and Penn, 'Jewish Immigrant Settlement Patterns', 659).
69  These were St Andrew and Russell Streets. Trench, *Report*, 35.
70  The 1851 census enumerators denoted shared housing with a short line separating households at the same address. People returned as lodgers were grouped with the main family. Single lodgers were occasionally marked as separate households, which can confuse the situation, although that rarely seems to have been the case in the returns used here.
71  The correlations were −0.329 for Liverpool, 0.034 for Birmingham and −0.230 for Manchester.
72  These were Lace Street, North Street and Oriel Street (W. H. Duncan, 'On the Sanitary State of the Labouring Classes in the Town of Liverpool', in *Sanitary Inquiry: Local Reports*).
73  'Report on the State of the Public Health of Birmingham'. Smithfield Passage, Inkleys, Lady Well Walk, Dean Street – and Pershore Street, which we have seen was a common address for Jews at mid-century – were all named as roads that contained lodging houses used by prostitutes.
74  McCabe, 'Standard of Living', 131.

75 The borough engineer for Liverpool noted in 1862 that court houses were often not numbered (James Newlands, *Report to the Health Committee of the Borough of Liverpool on the Sewerage, Paving, Cleansing and Other Works, Under the Sanitary Act from 1856 to 1862 Inclusive* (Liverpool: Henry Greenwood, 1863), 26).
76 Duncan, *On the Sanitary State of Liverpool*.
77 'Report on the State of the Public Health of Birmingham'. The charge of ignorance and extravagance was often a misunderstanding of the home conditions of the labouring poor, who frequently lacked good storage and cooking facilities.
78 BAC [Birmingham Archive and Collections] MS1678-1, Minutes of the Birmingham Hebrew Philanthropic Society, Report of Sub-Committee, 8 January 1861.
79 Ibid.
80 MLIA [Manchester Libraries, Information and Archives] Research Papers of Bill Williams, GB127.M790/2/2, 5th Annual Report of the Manchester Jewish Board of Guardians (MJBG), Medical Report (1871/2). The previous year the annual report had recorded the deaths of ten children under one year from whooping cough (3rd Annual Report of the MJBG, Medical Officer's Report, 1869/70).
81 4th Annual Report of the MJBG, 1870/1; 9th Annual Report of the MJBG, Medical Officer's Report, 1875/6.
82 8th Annual Report of the MJBG, 1874/5; Minutes of the MJBG, 6 July 1870. The Medical Officer also noted that the increased inspection of lodging houses had brought about some improvement in levels of crowding.
83 LROLS [Liverpool Record Office and Local Studies] 296 OHC 18/7, Medical Report given by S. Lewis M.D. to the Congregation, 1874. This family paid 3s. 6d. per week in rent.
84 Minutes of the MJBG, 23 June 1872.
85 See Williams, *Making of Manchester Jewry*, 275, 293 on increasing poverty in the 1860s and early 1870s. One of the reasons he offers was the 'fluctuating fortunes' of the workshop-based trades favoured by Jews, plus the lack of 'mechanical knowledge' of the new arrivals.
86 LROLS 296 OHC 34-2, Vouchers and Petitions for Poor Relief, Liverpool OHC. This man could not be traced in the AJDB.
87 Vouchers and Petitions for Poor Relief, Liverpool OHC. By way of comparison, a hawker working in Birmingham in the 1860s earned about six to nine shillings per week; Patsy Davis, 'Green Ribbons: The Irish in Birmingham in the 1860s: A Study of Housing, Work and Policing' (MA diss., University of Birmingham, 2003), 116.
88 Vouchers and Petitions for Poor Relief, Liverpool OHC. Trench's 1856 *Report* lists rents for single rooms in Liverpool from three to five shillings per week (28). According to McCabe, however, 3s. 6d., which was the going rate for new housing built in the 1850s, was one fifth of a labourer's income, or more than was reasonably

affordable (36). Rents in Birmingham's courts were also two to four shillings per week, although this was likely for a whole house ('Report on the State of the Public Health of Birmingham').

89 Vouchers and Petitions for Poor Relief, Liverpool OHC.
90 Lara Marks, *Model Mothers: Jewish Mothers and Maternity Provision in East London, 1870-1939* (Oxford: Clarendon Press, 1994).
91 The congregations in Liverpool and Manchester both had access to a *mikvah* (ritual bath); in Birmingham they used the 'extensive' public baths instead ('Statistical Accounts of all the Congregations of the British Empire', 1845, https://www.jewishgen.org/jcr-uk/Newman_papers/Provincial_Jewry_Victorian/statistical_accounts_I_page_01.htm). The *mikvah* was used by Jewish women to purify themselves after menstruation and childbirth, by people who had been in contact with the dead, and for spiritual purification. The records of the Hebrew school committees also show that they were used for bathing the school children. There was growing provision of public wash houses for personal and clothes washing in this period generally, which were clearly used by Jews, although they did not meet the specific requirements of a *mikvah*. Trench, *Report*, 57.
92 5th Annual Report of the MJBG, 1871/2. The Manchester board undertook to pay for any cleansing and whitewashing ordered by the Medical Officer of Health in the autumn of 1871 where people could not afford to pay the cost themselves. Their children had to be regular attenders at the school, however (Minutes of the MJBG, 6 September 1871).
93 MJBG, Report of the Visiting Committee, 5 September 1883.
94 See Jan de Vries, *The Industrious Revolution: Consumer Behavior and the Household Economy c.1650 to the Present* (Cambridge: Cambridge University Press, 2008).
95 Williams, *Making of Manchester Jewry*, passim; BJHS, *Birmingham Jewry*, Vols 1 and 2.
96 Williams cites both residential and occupational clustering to suggest that by the 1850s Manchester saw the start of a real Jewish working class (*Making of Manchester Jewry*, 179-80).

## 5. Philanthropy, religion and community from 1840 to 1865

1 Williams, *Making of Manchester Jewry*; Black, *Social Politics*.
2 Lipman, *Social History*, 6-7.
3 On the relationship between the state and voluntary welfare sectors, see Geoffrey Finlayson, *Citizen, State, and Social Welfare in Britain, 1830-1990* (Oxford: Clarendon Press, 1994). On the charitable landscape in the early industrial period, see David Owen, *English Philanthropy, 1660-1960* (Cambridge, MA: Belknap Press of Harvard University Press, 1964), 97-133 and 134-62.

4   For example, the statutory Poor Laws had restrictions based on 'settlement', which had to be earned by employment, ratepaying, marriage or birth. See A. Brundage, *The English Poor Laws, 1700–1930* (Basingstoke: Palgrave Macmillan, 2002), 9–10 and 102–4.
5   Endelman, *Jews of Britain*, 86–7.
6   *Jewish Chronicle*, 10 June 1881.
7   Ibid. On Samson, see Williams, *Making of Manchester Jewry*, 336. Another article in the *Jewish Chronicle* on 4 February 1848 emphasized the 'philanthropy of the *soul*' (original emphasis) set out in texts like Deuteronomy, and compared it favourably with the contemporary British emphasis on poor houses and relieving officers.
8   Mills, *British Jews*, 257.
9   The discussion that follows is indebted to several sources: Lawton, 'Judaism', 168–215; Alan Avery-Peck, 'Charity in Judaism', in *The Encyclopedia of Judaism*, 3 vols, ed. Jacob Neusner, Alan J. Avery-Peck and William Scott Green (Brill: New York, 1999), Vol. 1: 50–63; Demetrios J. Constantelos, 'Charity', in *Encyclopedia of Religion*, 2nd edn, ed. Lindsay Jones, Vol. 3 (Detroit: Macmillan Reference USA, 2005): 1553–1556, available at Gale Ebooks, https://link-gale-com.oxfordbrookes.idm.oclc.org/apps/doc/CX3424500543/GVRL?u=brookes_itw&sid=GVRL&xid=fa4abc8c]. Donors were also meant to learn and feel humbled by the act of giving, while recipients could feel that they were enabling the donor to participate in God's work (see https://www.chabad.org/library/article_cdo/aid/45916/jewish/The-Myth-of-Charity.htm).
10  These were specifically referenced in an article on Jewish charity in the *Jewish Chronicle*, 17 March 1876.
11  *Jewish Chronicle*, 3 November 1854.
12  See also Deuteronomy 15: 7–11, which stresses the attitude of the donor in the gift relationship: he or she should give ungrudgingly and without unworthy thoughts.
13  Maria Heim, 'Almsgiving', in *Encyclopedia of Religion*, 2nd. edn, ed. Lindsay Jones, Vol. 1 (Detroit: Macmillan Reference USA, 2005), 266–8, available at Gale eBooks, http://link.galegroup.com/apps/doc/CX3424500120/GVRL?u=brookes_itw&sid=GVRL&xid=57a89b10; Lawton, 'Judaism', 181–2, 193. According to Mills, the Great Synagogue in Duke's Place, London, collected £800 at the Jewish New Year and Day of Atonement combined, while the Sephardi Bevis Marks received £500 (Mills, *British Jews*, 286–7).
14  See Brian Pullan, 'Catholics, Protestants and the Poor in Early-Modern Europe', *Journal of Interdisciplinary History* 35, no. 3 (2005): 441–56; Ciarán McCabe, *Begging, Charity and Religion in Pre-Famine Ireland* (Liverpool: Liverpool University Press, 2018), *passim*.
15  Deuteronomy makes much of the need to relieve strangers without oppressing them, for example at 25:35 and 10:19. However, it is also found in Matthew 25:35.
16  *Jewish Chronicle*, 3 November 1854.

17  See Gertrude Himmelfarb, *Poverty and Compassion: The Moral Imagination of the Late Victorians* (New York: Vintage Books, 1992), 12. Even prior to this, Englander points out the shift to ideas about the dependent and non-dependent poor rather than the undeserving and deserving (David Englander, *Poverty and Poor Law Reform in Nineteenth-Century Britain, 1834–1914: From Chadwick to Booth* (Longman: London and New York, 1998), 1–13).
18  For example, see Brundage, *English Poor Laws*, 61–9 on the ethos of the New Poor Law, and 84–7 on the challenges presented by industrial unemployment. Local practices often remained more sympathetic to the able-bodied and to relief given in the home rather than in a workhouse.
19  Finlayson, *Citizen, State, and Social Welfare*, 24–31, 33–5.
20  This is an important part of Black's argument for London Jewry (Black, *Social Politics*).
21  Williams, *Making of Manchester Jewry*, 52.
22  Ibid., 142–4.
23  Ibid., 268.
24  The synagogues usually had a designated overseer of charity among its officers (Lipman, *Social History*, 42–3). This could be a way of getting kudos within the community while working up to the more senior offices.
25  Endelman, *Jews of Georgian England*, 166–8.
26  Ibid., 168.
27  Lipman, *Social History*, 6–7, also 52–66 on Jewish welfare in London.
28  Endelman, *Jews of Georgian England*, 231–7.
29  Steven King, *Poverty and Welfare in England, 1700–1850: A Regional Perspective* (Manchester: Manchester University Press, 2000), 194–5 on the north-west in particular; see also 238.
30  Williams, *Making of Manchester Jewry*, 52.
31  Bas van Bavel and Auke Rijpma, 'How Important Were Formalized Charity and Social Spending before the Rise of the Welfare State? A Long-Run Analysis of Selected Western European Cases, 1400–1850', *Economic History Review* 69, no. 1 (2016): 159–87. England saw a high point of 2.4 per cent of GDP in 1818, but with an abrupt fall from 1834.
32  Minutes of the Liverpool OHC, 28 March 1841.
33  Minutes of the Birmingham OHC, 3 August 1853. They also received £8 from their charity box. Over £500 was spent on salaries.
34  Williams, *Making of Manchester Jewry*, 171.
35  van Bavel and Rijpma, 'How Important', 175. Numbers of recipients of the Jewish charity are estimates because of lack of precision over names. A column recording length of residence in the town was, unfortunately, rarely filled in. The population estimate is based on the known population sizes for the town in 1851 and 1896 (see https://www.jewishgen.org/jcr-uk/Liverpool.htm).

36  LROLS, 296 OHC 34/3, Register of Poor Relief Payments, 1861–9.
37  Jews could also marry before a magistrate and then have the marriage solemnized in a synagogue, but as one writer in the *JC* stated, in the context of the practice forced on the early members of the Manchester Reform community, this was 'disgraceful' (see Williams, *Making of Manchester Jewry*, 225).
38  LROLS 296 OHC 2-2, Minutes of the Liverpool OHC, 30 October 1836. Naming ceremonies were often held for girls.
39  Minutes of the Liverpool OHC, 6 November 1837.
40  Minutes of the Liverpool OHC, 31 December 1836. These burial costs were those charged for 'non-free' members and rose for older children and adults. 'Free' members (who paid a higher membership fee) were not charged for the use of the ground (Minutes, 28 January 1838).
41  Minutes of the Liverpool OHC, 8 August 1838. The committee also agreed to bury Mrs Rebecca Hart at their own expense since she had been the widow of a Free Member, and had not left any property to defray her funeral costs (Minutes, 16 January 1839).
42  Minutes of the Liverpool OHC, 8 March 1840.
43  Ibid., 12 April 1840. Williams, *Making of Manchester Jewry*, 146. MLIA M139/6/1/1, Manchester Hebrew Congregation Passover Relief Book from 1865. Seventy-nine per cent in total received cash in the 1860s, with the average payment being 3s. Manchester population figures are from Williams, *Making of Manchester Jewry*, Appendix B, 336.
44  Manchester Hebrew Congregation Passover Relief Book.
45  See notes on the congregation at http://calmview.birmingham.gov.uk/CalmView/Record.aspx?src=CalmView.Catalog&id=JA, citing council minutes from the 1850s. An example pro forma for the Liverpool fund can be found at LROLS, 296 OHC 2-3-1, General Minute Book of the OHC.
46  Minutes of the Birmingham OHC, 28 February 1847.
47  For example, Minutes of the Birmingham OHC, 11 November 1855, reporting a meeting of the special relief fund.
48  Finlayson, *Citizen, State, and Social Welfare*, 105 on the departures from state ideology on relief in the 1860s; also Owen, *English Philanthropy*, 462.
49  Subcommittee report, Birmingham Philanthropic Society, 8 January 1861.
50  This was the wording used by the Poor Law Commission of 1837 (see Englander, *Poverty and Poor Law Reform*, 119). Recent arrivals would have no such formal claim until they had earned it via residence, ratepaying or employment.
51  Englander, *Poverty and Poor Law Reform*, 33. In most communities the lowest class of people associated with the synagogue were *orchim*, or strangers, below the 'free' and yearly renters of seats (Lipman, *Social History*, 41–2).
52  Williams, *Making of Manchester Jewry*, 142.

53 Ibid., 151, 157–8. Direction of the board alternated between the two congregations, resulting in swinging priorities from year to year, and the set-up was ill equipped to deal with sudden emergencies. In Birmingham, too, the Chief Rabbi had helped to negotiate a 75:25 split between the resources donated by the two synagogues, and the representation they got on the various charity committees (Minutes of the Birmingham OHC, 6 February 1853). This was rapidly rejected by the OHC, who instituted a Board of Relief for the casual poor instead (Minutes, 21 February, 28 April 1853).

54 Williams, *Making of Manchester Jewry*, 171.

55 Ibid., 175.

56 *Jewish Chronicle*, 4 April 1862.

57 Williams, *Making of Manchester Jewry*, 156–7.

58 The authorities in Hamburg, Hull, Liverpool, Birmingham and London were all advised of the new policy. Jewish lodging house keepers were also warned against sheltering unemployed youths under threat of exclusion from the festival relief funds themselves. Expenditure on poor relief reached £305 in 1852/3. Williams, *Making of Manchester Jewry*, 201, 218.

59 Ibid., 232.

60 Ibid., 146.

61 Ibid., 144.

62 Minutes of the Liverpool OHC, 20 February 1838.

63 Ibid., 18 May 1838, 8 November 1840.

64 LROLS 296/34/4, Payments to the casual and resident poor, 1861–9.

65 BJHS, *Birmingham Jewry*, Vol. 1, 54–72.

66 Minutes of the Birmingham Philanthropic Society, 4 May 1837.

67 LROLS, 296 OHC 61-3-3, Minutes of the Liverpool Hebrew Mendicity Society, 10 December 1845, 7 July 1846.

68 Minutes of the Liverpool OHC, 7 November 1852.

69 Ibid., 11 January 1837. £30 12s. 0d. was spent on the resident poor and £142 16s. 6d. on casuals out of a total of £1226 19s. 9d. The half-yearly accounts for 1864 show £24 13s. 8d. being expended on casual poor and £89 16s. 6d. on residents (296 OHC 451/1, Balance Sheets for Half-Yearly Accounts, Liverpool OHC, 1864).

70 Minutes of the Birmingham OHC, 8 February 1849.

71 Minutes of the Liverpool OHC, 17 June 1849. The individual concerned had died in the lunatic asylum at Lancaster, which was closer to Manchester than Liverpool. The Chief Rabbi directed both congregations to split the costs of interment, and they subsequently came to an agreement over where responsibility lay for poor Jews who died between the two towns (Minutes of the Liverpool OHC, 23 June 1849, 14 January 1850).

72 It is not clear from the way that Williams collated these data whether any of the applications 'entertained' (his term) were refused. This would nuance the patterns shown here.

73  See Donna Andrew, *Philanthropy and Police: London Charity in the Eighteenth Century* (Princeton: Princeton University Press, 1989).
74  Mills, *British Jews*, 275–86.
75  See McCabe, *Begging, Charity and Religion* for a similar point about the 'transnational discourse of social improvement' in this period (applied, in his case, to the treatment of mendicity) (quotation on 182).
76  See Kokosalakis, *Ethnic Identity*, 48–51.
77  The Liverpool Society spent £80 on applicants in 1836; the one in Manchester laid out £49 in doles of two to five shillings per week to ten pensioners in 1847 (LROLS 296 OHC 61/5/1/3, Records of the Liverpool Hebrew Philanthropic Society, Accounts 1836; Williams, *Making of Manchester Jewry*, 146). By 1816, the Liverpool Society had eighty-six regular subscribers giving up to £100 annually, reaching £150 by 1820 (Kokosalakis, *Ethnic Identity*, 50). On the later difficulties, see minutes of the Birmingham Philanthropic Society, 2 June 1850, though in 1855 it was able to offer the congregation a loan of £40 (Minutes, 30 September 1855). See BJHS, *Birmingham Jewry*, Vol. 2, 93–101 on the Society generally.
78  BJHS, *Birmingham Jewry*, Vol. 2, 95.
79  Williams, *Making of Manchester Jewry*, 52.
80  *Jewish Chronicle*, 24 December 1841.
81  Minutes of the Birmingham Philanthropic Society, 25 April 1869.
82  Records of the Liverpool Hebrew Philanthropic Society, Report for 1851/2.
83  She also received 'perquisites' for keeping the congregational baths and committee rooms (Records of the Liverpool Philanthropic Society, Petitions). Mrs Benedict died early in 1851, but her duties overseeing the baths were passed on to her daughter Frances, who was still listed with that occupation in the census of 1871 (Minutes of the Liverpool OHC, 30 March 1851; AJDB).
84  Records of the Liverpool Philanthropic Society, Petitions.
85  See Peter Jones and Steven King, 'From Petition to Pauper Letter: The Development of an Epistolary Form', in *Obligation, Entitlement and Dispute under the English Poor Laws*, ed. Peter Jones and Steve King (Newcastle upon Tyne: Cambridge Scholars Publishing, 2015), 53–77 and references.
86  The Liverpool OHC received two offers of medical attendance in two months in the spring of 1838 for example; in May 1852, they thanked 'Behrend Esq MRCS' for 'the skilful and continued attention afforded by him gratuitously to the sick poor of our community'. He was made a Free Member of the congregation in recognition of his efforts (Minutes of the Liverpool OHC, 4 March, 15 April 1838, 23 May 1852).
87  For example, see minutes of the Birmingham Philanthropic Society, 2 April 1843, 7 February 1844, 4 November 1849.
88  Williams, *Making of Manchester Jewry*, 155. Kokosalakis, *Ethnic Identity*, 89. On female-led charity, see F. K. Prochaska, *Women and Philanthropy in Nineteenth-Century England* (Oxford: Clarendon Press, 1980).

89  The Old Testament promotes the elderly as particularly worthy of respect and assistance, for example, Leviticus 19:32: 'You shall rise up before the grey head, and honour the face of the elderly, and you shall fear your God; I am the Lord.' Lawton, 'Judaism', 184. Also, see Black, *Social Politics*, 172–7.

90  See LROLS 296 HPS/2, 'Laws of the Liverpool Hebrew Provident Society' (Liverpool: Yates & Hess, 1878). The size of the pension list was variable and could be determined by the committee.

91  Kokosalakis, *Ethnic Identity*, 89.

92  Minutes of the Birmingham Philanthropic Society, 30 October 1860. The new scheme was launched at the same time as the Society's loan fund. Numbers of pensioners were to grow as the fund became more established. BJHS, *Birmingham Jewry*, Vol. 2, 96.

93  Vaughan, 'Study of the Spatial Characteristics', 11, footnote 12. A child being relieved by the Birmingham Philanthropic Society in August 1864 seemed to have been living with the person who applied for relief on her behalf: one Harris Bolcher 'having had a child left with him to support' (Minutes of the Birmingham Philanthropic Society, 28 August 1864).

94  Black, *Social Politics*, 184–9.

95  Marks, *Model Mothers*.

96  Lawton, 'Judaism', 185–6. Lawton notes that the community is less able to replace the care of a lost mother; hence this category is not listed among those especially deserving of aid. One example which did come to the attention of the Birmingham Hebrew Philanthropic Society in January 1843 was the case of Michael Abrahams and his five orphaned children, recent arrivals from America. They were relieved with £7 10s. (Minutes of the Birmingham Philanthropic Society, 29 January 1843). Cases are very rarely recorded as going to the Poor Law authorities either.

97  Mrs Michael was not deemed eligible for a new grant because she had been relieved the previous December, but the charity chose to eke her money out in instalments until she could be assisted again (Minutes of the Birmingham Philanthropic Society, 2 and 9[?] April 1843). Mrs Robinson received ten shillings (ibid., 26 July 1843). This volume is mislabelled as the Hebrew Benevolent Board and Clothing Society in the archive catalogue. There is no sign of Lazarus or his wife in the AJDB under that name.

98  MLIA M790 2/6/1, Williams papers, 'Voluntary Agencies', notes on the OHC Select Committee, 1848–9.

99  Records of the Liverpool Philanthropic Society, group petition dated 18 February 1838; Minutes of the Birmingham Philanthropic Society, 10 December 1839; Minutes of the Liverpool OHC, 20 February 1838.

100  Records of the Liverpool Philanthropic Society, Annual Report, 1851/2.

101  Minutes of the Birmingham OHC, 19 June 1854.
102  In January 1858, one ex-member of the Birmingham Philanthropic Society had his relief raised from a guinea to five pounds after it was realized that his previous standing had not been taken into account when his case was first judged (Minutes of the Birmingham Philanthropic Society, 3 January 1858).
103  See Minutes of the Birmingham Philanthropic Society, 21 July 1841, for a statement about not assisting insolvency cases. On 10 October 1852, they minuted their agreement to aid a Mr Harris of Bath Passage with three guineas when he was threatened with distraint by his landlord for arrears of rent. There were other similar cases.
104  Minutes of the Birmingham Philanthropic Society, 14 August 1870.
105  Ibid., 13 October 1829, 6 February 1870.
106  See, for example, minutes of the Birmingham OHC, 26 April 1853 on the minimum residency (and financial contributions) necessary to be elected a Free Member of the congregation.
107  Kokosalakis, *Ethnic Identity*, 87–8; Williams, *Making of Manchester Jewry*, 144–6; an approach from Birmingham was noted in the minutes of the Liverpool Mendicity Society, 7 December 1846.
108  For example, see M. J. D. Roberts, 'Reshaping the Gift Relationship: The London Mendicity Society and the Suppression of Begging in England 1818–1869', *International Review of Social History* 36 (1991): 201–31; McCabe, *Begging, Charity and Religion*, 146–84.
109  LROLS 296 OHC 61/3/3, Preliminary Meeting of a Society for the Suppression of Mendicity and the More Effectual Relief of Deserving Casual Poor, 1845; LROLS 296 OHC 61/3/4, Report of the Board of Management Presented at 1st AGM of the Mendicity Society, 7 March 1847; Minutes of the Hebrew Mendicity Society, 29 December 1845, 5 January 1846. The Society hoped to end private almsgiving, and the burden on the synagogues, which was apparently so onerous that it put people off taking on committee offices. The Society estimated in 1847 that about 1,000 casuals had been assisted every year by Jewish authorities in the town prior to the foundation of their charity (Report, 1847).
110  Minutes of the Liverpool Hebrew Mendicity Society, 10 December 1845. The two congregations were co-operating more fully in the 1840s and 1850s, and in June 1851, the OHC called a special meeting at the request of the Chief Rabbi to consider an amalgamation of the two congregations in the town (Minutes of the Liverpool OHC, 1 June 1851).
111  McCabe, *Begging, Charity and Religion*, 146–84, esp. 159.
112  Minutes of the Liverpool Mendicity Society, 1 March, 7 March 1846. Applicants in this situation could apply for temporary relief from the Secretary of up to 5s. 6d.
113  Ibid., 4 May, 4 June 1846.

114 Ibid., 2 July, 4 August, 4 September, 8 October 1846.
115 Ibid., 8 October 1846.
116 Liverpool Hebrew Mendicity Society, Report of the Board of Management, 1847.
117 Ibid.
118 Ibid. Only 112 of the 900 relieved in 1847 had a trade.
119 Kokosalakis, *Ethnic Identity*, 88.
120 Williams, *Making of Manchester Jewry*, 145. He links this to the emancipation movement, which stressed the respectability and trustworthiness of British Jews.
121 Kokosalakis, *Ethnic Identity*, 88.
122 Minutes of the Hebrew Philanthropic Society, 20[?] April 1849, 1 September, 25 September 1850.
123 Finlayson, *Citizen, State, and Social Welfare*, 19–45.
124 Lawton, 'Judaism', 180. According to the Talmud 'No labour, however humble, is dishonouring' (quoted on 180).
125 Minutes of the Free Loan Committee of the Hebrew Mendicity Society, 22 February 1863.
126 Ibid., 8 December 1861.
127 Ibid.
128 Ibid., 5 February 1865.
129 Ibid.
130 Minutes of the Birmingham Philanthropic Society, 26 September 1858. Where reasons were given they were to support business endeavours, including some by women.
131 Birmingham Philanthropic Society Loan Annual Report, 1863. The terms regarding securities were tightened up in 1862 (see Minutes, 8 June 1862).
132 Minutes of the Birmingham Philanthropic Society, 21 October 1860.
133 Ibid., 18 October 1868, 25 April, 4 July 1869.
134 See M. G. Jones, *The Charity School Movement: A Study of Eighteenth-Century Puritanism in Action* (London: Cass, 1964).
135 For example, Black, *Social Politics*, 104–32; Williams, *Making of Manchester Jewry*, 89–90; Lipman, *History of the Jews*, 28–31. Education is also valued highly in Judaism because of the importance of reflection on religious texts and because it provides the means by which both boys and girls know how to keep the customs at home, in synagogue and in public (Lawton, 'Judaism', 168–9).
136 MJBG 6th Annual Report, 1871/2.
137 Endelman, *Jews of Georgian England*, 228–30 on earlier efforts in London; see also Williams, *Making of Manchester Jewry*, 89–98, 181–2, 204–8; BJHS, *Birmingham Jewry*, Vol. 2, 129–37; also Mills, *British Jews*, 292–3 and 296–8. A summary of the

Jewish schools in Britain, Ireland and the colonies can be found in Chief Rabbi's Statistical Accounts of all the Congregations of the British Empire.
138  Hickman, *Religion, Class and Identity*, 121–57.
139  This was accompanied by plans to provide more subjects for the better-off children, which could justify charging higher fees (OHC's School Committee, Minutes of the Birmingham OHC, 3 December 1853).
140  Ibid., 20 November 1853.
141  Williams, *Making of Manchester Jewry*, 204.
142  Ibid., 205. Birmingham's congregation founded a Benevolent Book and Clothing Society in 1854 (also referred to as the Birmingham Hebrew Educational Benevolent Society) to provide the necessaries for school attendance, and to organize apprenticeships for boys who had completed their studies (see BAC MS 1678-3). Manchester had a Ladies Clothing Society (est. 1853) which gave out clothing, soup and food to poor children, and from the late 1870s, a Manchester Jews School Soup Kitchen dispensed thousands of free and subsidized dinners over the winter (Ruth Cohen, 'The Problem of Jewish Poverty Relief in Victorian Manchester with Specific Reference to the Jewish Board of Guardians' (MA diss., University of Manchester, 1986), 15). Liverpool's Educational Institution also had a fund for clothing and feeding poor children (Kokosalakis, *Ethnic Identity*, 88).
143  The Birmingham Book and Clothing Society also paid for the training of pupil-teachers. See Annual Reports of the Birmingham Hebrew Educational Benevolent Society, 1865 and 1866.
144  Minutes of the Liverpool OHC, 24 March 1850.
145  Chief Rabbi's Statistical Accounts.
146  *Jewish Chronicle*, 24 December 1841.
147  Ibid.
148  For example, a Cracow Benevolent Society was set up in Manchester in 1869 (Rainer Liedtke, 'The Uses of Benevolence: Charity among Jewish Immigrants in Manchester, 1905–1930', *Jewish Culture and History* 1, no. 1 (1998): 54–71 (56). See also Williams, *Making of Manchester Jewry*, 271–3.
149  On 8 September 1871, an article in the *Jewish Chronicle* noted that '[n]o town of similar size in the kingdom has a larger number of foreign Jews direct from foreign climes'.
150  *Jewish Chronicle*, 12 March 1858.
151  Finlayson, *Citizen, State, and Social Welfare*, 63–6; Anderson, *Family Structure*, 62–4.
152  Minutes of the Birmingham OHC, 20 April 1848. Services for the dead and dying were noted by Mills, who described them as part of a Jew's 'incumbent duty' (*British Jews*, 33–48).
153  Avery-Peck, 'Charity in Judaism', 61.

## 6. Consolidation, reflection and discrimination: Jewish charity from 1865 to 1880

1. Freedman, *Leeds Jewry*; Kenneth E. Collins, *Glasgow Jewry: A Guide to the History and Community of the Jews in Glasgow* (Glasgow: Scottish Jewish Archives Committee, 1993).
2. *Jewish Chronicle*, 6 August 1869.
3. For fuller details, see Karel Williams, *From Pauperism to Poverty* (London: Routledge & Kegan Paul, 1981).
4. Goschen's circular was followed up two years later by a minute issued by the Poor Law Board along the same lines. See Williams, *From Pauperism to Poverty*, 96–107; Elizabeth Hurren, '"World Without Welfare": Pauper Perspectives on Medical Care under the Late-Victorian Poor Law 1870–1900', in *Obligation, Entitlement and Dispute under the English Poor Laws*, ed. Peter Jones and Steve King (Newcastle upon Tyne: Cambridge Scholars Publishing, 2015), 292–320. The reform was welcomed in many of the larger towns. On this and the later context in Manchester, see Alan J. Kidd, 'Outcast Manchester: Voluntary Charity, Poor Relief and the Casual Poor, 1860–1905', in *City, Class and Culture: Studies of Cultural Production and Social Policy in Victorian Manchester*, ed. A. J. Kidd and K. W. Roberts (Manchester: Manchester University Press, 1985), 48–73.
5. Jane Lewis, *The Voluntary Sector, the State and Social Work in Britain: The Charity Organisation Society/Family Welfare Association Since 1869* (Aldershot: Edward Elgar, 1995), 9. Also see Owen, *English Philanthropy*, 215–46.
6. Finlayson notes that there was in fact considerable overlap of aims between the voluntary and statutory sectors (*Citizen, State, and Social Welfare*, 81, and 80–100 generally on the state's actions to promote voluntary self-help organizations like savings banks and friendly societies).
7. See, for example, Lewis, *The Voluntary Sector*.
8. Finlayson, *Citizen, State, and Social Welfare*, 77.
9. Lewis, *Voluntary Sector*, 33.
10. Williams, *Making of Manchester Jewry*, 157.
11. Lipman, *Social History*, 55; Cesarani, *Jewish Chronicle*, 24.
12. See Margaret Simey, *Charity Rediscovered: A Study of Philanthropic Effort in Nineteenth-Century Liverpool* (Liverpool: Liverpool University Press, 1992); Owen, *English Philanthropy*, 443–68. The Central Relief Society took over the work of the District Provident Society, the Strangers' Friend Society and the Charitable Society. On equivalents in Manchester, see Michael E. Rose, 'Culture, Philanthropy and the Manchester Middle Classes', in *City, Class and Culture: Studies of Cultural Production and Social Policy in Victorian Manchester*, ed. A. J. Kidd and K. W. Roberts (Manchester: Manchester University Press, 1985), 103–117.

13  See Black, *Social Politics*, 71–103, and Owen, *English Philanthropy*, 420–8. A Jewish Board of Guardians had been mooted as early as 1844 in a pamphlet by Henry Faudel (Cesarani, *Jewish Chronicle*, 24).
14  Endelman, *Jews of Britain*, 88.
15  Cesarani, *Jewish Chronicle*, 33–5. Michael Henry, who edited the paper in the 1860s, was also influenced, in his own way, by the ethos of the COS: in Cesarani's words, 'his Jewishness impinged on his general outlook in ways that provoked self-examination and forced him to explain, as well as justify, how he was not quite a "typical Victorian Englishman"' (50–1).
16  *Jewish Chronicle*, 5 September 1856.
17  Ibid., 9 March 1860.
18  Lipman, *Social History*, 56.
19  Minutes of the Birmingham Hebrew Philanthropic Society, 30 August 1864.
20  Both Williams and Kokosalakis make this point about the need for a new direction in welfare in Manchester and Liverpool (Williams, *Making of Manchester Jewry*, 294; Kokosalakis, *Ethnic Identity*, 90).
21  Endelman, *Jews of Britain*, 88; Freedman, *Leeds Jewry*, 9; Finestein, 'Jews in Hull', 55.
22  MJBG 9th Annual Report, 1875/6.
23  On the Manchester Benevolent Fund and Landeshut, see Williams, *Making of Manchester Jewry*, 281–2 and on Manchester Reform, 240–67. Landeshut left to become the secretary of the London Jewish Board of Guardians in the summer of 1869 (289).
24  MLIA M139/6/1/1, Manchester Hebrew Congregation Benevolent Fund. A column in the register was set aside for the name of the person who had visited and initially this was usually filled in. Later, it was repurposed to note the number of people in the family and the need for a visit was instead sometimes recorded separately.
25  Williams, *Making of Manchester Jewry*, 281–2. Isaac Franklin, later MO to the Manchester Jewish Board of Guardians, gave his time gratis.
26  Ibid., 281–2.
27  Minutes of the Birmingham Hebrew Philanthropic Society, 31 October 1870.
28  Williams, *Making of Manchester Jewry*, 278–9. The Benefit Society had about sixty members by the mid-1860s. On 13 July 1877, the *Jewish Chronicle* reported on a meeting of the Hull Hebrew Mutual Friendly Benefit Society. See Black, *Social Politics*, 194–221 on Jewish friendly societies and self-help generally, and 197 on the Birmingham Society, which was founded in 1853.
29  The two Liverpool congregations together disbursed £227 14s. 6d. from May 1873 to April 1874, for example (LROLS, OHC 296/34/7, Liverpool Old and New Hebrew Congregation Poor Fund Account, 1873–4).
30  Kokosalakis, *Ethnic Identity*, 91. The joint fund dispensed over £300 in the year from April 1868 to April 1869 on tickets for groceries, meat, bread, cash and emigration.

31  Williams notes that this was probably symptomatic of a more general bitterness between the congregations (*Making of Manchester Jewry*, 282).
32  Cohen, 'Problem of Jewish Poverty Relief', 40; the grant was later raised to £250 when the OHC passed over responsibility for Passover relief. By the early 1880s, the OHC claimed that it was now 'composed of working men and small shopkeepers'. On the other hand, as representatives of the other congregations pointed out, it alone retained the income from the Shechita (ritual slaughter) board (Minutes of the MJBG, 14 November 1882).
33  BAC MS1678-4, Laws of the Birmingham Hebrew Board of Guardians, 1870.
34  MLIA, Williams Papers, M790/2/2 *Laws of the Board of Guardians for the Relief of the Jewish Poor of Manchester* (Manchester, 1867).
35  LROLS, BOG 5/1/1, 2nd Annual Report of the Liverpool Jewish Board of Guardians (LJBG) 1877/8.
36  MJBG 2nd Annual Report, 1868/9. Three years later, they reported a reduction in street begging since the foundation of the Board (5th Annual Report of the MJBG, 1871/2).
37  These concerns were to loom larger in later decades with the rise of more professional, female visiting officers. There is a wealth of information on the latter in MLIA, Bill Williams Papers, M790/2/16, 'Jewish Women and Philanthropy'.
38  For example, MJBG 7th Annual Report, 1873/4.
39  *Jewish Chronicle*, 23 May 1873.
40  Lewis, *The Voluntary Sector*, esp. 46, 52–4, 61.
41  *Jewish Chronicle*, 3 December 1875.
42  MJBG 10th Annual Report, 1876/77.
43  *Jewish Chronicle*, 3 December 1875.
44  Ibid., 23 May 1873.
45  Minutes of the Birmingham Hebrew Philanthropic Society Loan Fund, 9 September 1860, 10 February 1852.
46  This was the COS theory. In fact, many visitors felt either unequipped to carry it through, or were moved by compassion to act beyond the official remit. See Lewis, *Voluntary Sector*.
47  The latter issue was noted when the Liverpool Board was first mooted – see a report in the *Jewish Chronicle*, 3 December 1875. The Manchester OHC asked the Board to take over the Passover relief fund in 1872 so that applicants could be more fully investigated (MJBG 6th Annual Report, 1872/3).
48  The Reform congregation granted £20 in 1874 but the South Manchester synagogue sent their regrets that they could not contribute. The Portuguese synagogue gave £3 (in April 1874, they did not make a grant but made up the same sum in private contributions from members). Minutes of the MJBG, 4 March, 15 April, 7 April 1874. The Reform synagogue could not contribute in 1876 because of

the 'low condition' of their charity fund (Minutes of the MJGB, 6 April 1876). The first president, vice-president and one of the honorary secretaries were all members of the Reform synagogue, and there were eight other Reformers in the first membership of twenty-one (Williams, *Making of Manchester Jewry*, 284). On 6 December 1782, a meeting of all the Manchester congregations was reported (with the exception of the Spanish and Portuguese), at which several grants were promised, but by the summer of 1878 congregational support was again an issue (see minutes of meetings 5 June, 3 July, 7 August 1878, for example).

49 Kokosalakis, *Ethnic Identity*, 92; BAC, MS 1678-3, Minutes of the Hebrew Benevolent Book and Clothing Society, 1854-75, 11 March 1866.
50 For example, see BAC MS1678-4, Laws of the Birmingham Hebrew Board of Guardians. There, the Board met twice-weekly. The second Annual Report of the Manchester Board noted the use of a paid investigating officer, and also that it made enquiry into as many casual cases as possible, too (1868/9).
51 See MJBG 4th Annual Report, 1870/1, Medical Officer's Report.
52 The founding 'Laws of the Birmingham Hebrew Board of Guardians' specifically stated that the organization would act as security for Jewish workmen for sums up to £5; see Minutes of the MJBG, 19 May 1873 on their industrial fund which loaned sums up to £20, and Black, *Social Politics*, 80-1.
53 MJBG 1st Annual Report, 1867/8.
54 LJBG 2nd Annual Report, 1877/8.
55 Ibid.
56 Cohen, 'Problem of Jewish Poverty Relief', Appendix N.
57 Minutes of the MJBG, 2 February 1876; see Minutes 7 May 1873 for the first proposal for a loan scheme, which it was hoped would relieve the deserving and remove the need for casual relief. The new loan fund committee met for the first time on 25 June 1873 having raised £960.
58 Williams, *Making of Manchester Jewry*, 293, 296.
59 For an overview of this thinking, see Michael Rose, 'The Disappearing Pauper: Victorian Attitudes to the Relief of the Poor', in *In Search of Victorian Values: Aspects of Nineteenth-Century Thought and Society*, ed. Eric M. Sigsworth (Manchester: Manchester University Press, 1988), 56-72.
60 LJBG 2nd Annual Report, 1877/8; Minutes of the MJBG, 2 February 1876.
61 LJBG 4th Annual Report, 1879/80. This first success story was marred by the fact that the boy's father did not adequately maintain him, so the Board had to step in using funds provided by a member. The boy did, however, successfully complete the first year of his apprenticeship. See also Minutes of the LJBG, 10 March 1880.
62 LJBG 6th Annual Report, 1881/2. The Manchester Jewish Guardians found that some of the proposed placements were unsuitable, citing a desire to focus only on industrial employment (MJBG 8th Annual Report, 1874/5).

63 MJBG 10th Annual Report, 1876/7.
64 Cesarani, *Jewish Chronicle*, 23–4. The earlier Jewish paper, *The Voice of Jacob*, also occasionally printed letters setting out the desirability of Jewish employers preferentially employing Jews – something they said was not being done often enough (for example, see correspondence published 27 October 1843).
65 LJBG 2nd Annual Report, 1877/8; 3rd Annual Report, 1878/9. This necessitated a cut in the average amount given to each applicant.
66 LJBG 3rd Annual Report, 1878/9.
67 Cohen, 'Problem of Jewish Poverty Relief', Appendix J; 2nd Annual Report of the MJGB, 1868–9.
68 LJBG 2nd Annual Report, 1877/8.
69 Ibid.
70 LJBG 3rd Annual Report, 1878/9, 6th Annual Report, 1881/2. An income of around £400 was consistently being challenged by expenditure of closer to £600.
71 Aubrey Newman, 'Birmingham – Introductory Data' (extract from Newman, *Provincial Jewry*), at https://www.jewishgen.org/jcr-uk/Community/Birmingham/articles/Birmingham-vic.htm.
72 Laws of the Birmingham Hebrew Board of Guardians.
73 MJBG 1st Annual Report, 1869/70.
74 LJBG 2nd Annual Report, 1877/8.
75 MJBG 9th Annual Report, 1875/6.
76 MJBG 3rd Annual Report, 1869–70. Longer-term residents tended to be relieved more times: in 1868/9, the Board assisted twenty residents of three months 124 times in total, and thirty-two of six months 378 times. In 1869/70, this had risen to thirty-six and forty-seven cases aided 160 and 416 times. See MJBG 7th Annual Report, 1873/4 on people only applying when in great need.
77 MJBG 7th Annual Report, 1873/4.
78 Minutes of the LJBG, 9 June 1880, 10 August 1881. In July 1880, the Liverpool Board reported a 'want of system' between themselves and the Foreign Aid Society when it came to assisting emigration, while another case brought negotiation with the German Society. Some degree of mutual discussion was subsequently achieved (Minutes of the LJBG, 14 July, 22 September, 13 October 1880).
79 MJBG 3rd Annual Report, 1869/70.
80 LJBG, 5th Annual Report, 1880/1.
81 In March 1882, the Manchester Board was given credit by the Manchester and Salford Fund for Persecuted Russian Jews to help them in their attempts to assist refugees (Minutes of the MJBG, 1 March 1882). By the mid-1880s, they were referring Russian refugees to the Mansion House and other similar funds (for example, Minutes of the MJBG, 7 October 1885).
82 Black, *Social Politics*, 84–7, 158–67.

83　The Manchester Board of Guardians noted that this situation was particularly common during the winter of 1870/1, when economic conditions were poor, and when transport had been disrupted by war. The numbers had necessitated 'less stringent' treatment than usual. MJBG 4th Annual Report, 1870/1. These were the circumstances under which the Board's MO reported finding many deserted women using the facility to apply for medical relief as a way of getting themselves noticed.

84　Black, *Social Politics*, 85–6.

85　This latter point is also made by Williams, *Making of Manchester Jewry*, 288. The Manchester Board thanked the local Guardians of the Poor in 1870 for their pursuit of deserting husbands via legal means (MJBG, 3rd Annual Report, 1869/70).

86　Minutes of the MJBG, 5 October 1879, 7 January 1880. The Poor Law had also tightened up its treatment of deserted wives by this time as part of a move to get women off outdoor relief (Englander, *Poverty and Poor Law Reform*, 18), and they were seen as a problematic group for the COS too (alongside children and the elderly), since their economic condition was often chronic rather than improvable. The best response was to direct them to other charities or to family aid (Lewis, *Voluntary Sector*, 48).

87　Minutes of the MJBG, 7 July 1880; Minutes of the LJBG, 1 June 1880. Quotation from LJBG 2nd Annual Report, 1877/8.

88　MJBG 11th Annual Report, 1877/8.

89　*Jewish Chronicle*, 23 May 1873.

90　Ibid.

91　*Jewish Chronicle*, 5 April 1878.

92　Minutes of the Birmingham Philanthropic Society, 25 April 1869, 15 June 1879.

93　Report of the Joint Committee of the Board of Guardians and Philanthropic and Educational Societies. This was noted in the minutes of the Birmingham Philanthropic Society, 24 July 1881.

94　The Manchester Board sent individuals to the sea baths at Southport (for example, see Minutes of the MJBG, 7 June 1871) and to the spa town of Buxton (Minutes, 2 August 1871). In 1873, the Annual Report identified this as a policy of early intervention, especially for working-age adults: the MOs in both Liverpool and Manchester recorded their frustration that Jewish parents would not allow their children to be taken to hospitals as they were too far away (MJBG 6th Annual Report, 1872/3, 2nd Annual Report, 1868/9, LJBG 3rd Annual Report, 1878/9. See also Minutes of the MJBG, 6 November 1878, 6 April 1881).

95　Minutes of the MJBG, 1 August 1883. As in London, these materials were to be translated into the languages spoken locally; another sign of the changing character of the Jewish population by the 1880s.

96 For example, see LJBG 3rd Annual Report, 1878/9 noting outbreaks of scarlatina and whooping cough. The Manchester MO reported a virulent form of scarlatina in the Jewish area in November 1875, which had caused some deaths among the children. A smallpox epidemic was reported in August 1876 and measles in February 1870 when there had been two deaths in a month. Overcrowding and poor sanitary conditions were cited in the cases of both scarlatina and measles (Minutes of the MJBG, 3 November 1875, 2 August 1876, 4 February 1870).

97 MJBG 2nd Annual Report, 1868/9, 4th Annual Report, 1870/1.

98 Institutional meals, it must be admitted, did not contain much meat – 'diet number three' offered in workhouses, for example, featured a meat dinner only once a week (Englander, *Poverty and Poor Law Reform*, 39). However, there would also have been concerns about the mixing of acceptable and non-acceptable foods, and the lack of supervision by the Jewish authorities.

99 The Liverpool OHC minuted that a list of sick Jews in hospitals and poor houses had been read out to them in July 1838, but this was rare. On that occasion they ordered the treasurer to distribute appropriate sums to help them, but to indicate that no more financial aid would be forthcoming (Minutes of the Liverpool OHC, 2 July 1838).

100 Minutes of the MJBG, 30 June 1867. See *Jewish Chronicle,* 15 January and 5 February 1869 for coverage of these negotiations.

101 For example, Minutes of the MJBG, 5 August 1868, noting 'the inefficiency of Hospital accommodation for the Jewish poor'. The boards all subscribed annually to the town hospitals, as had several of the Jewish charities before them. See BJHS, *Birmingham Jewry,* Vol. 1, 22 on discussions with the general hospital; Black, *Social Politics,* 161 on the Jewish wards at the London hospital from 1842.

102 See Act of Parliament 31&32 Vict., C. CVVII, and coverage in the *Jewish Chronicle,* 5 February 1869. The Certified Schools Act of 1862 also allowed for religious education of non-Anglicans in the workhouse (Cohen, 'Problem of Jewish Poverty Relief', 38). In Manchester, these terms led to the congregation of all Jews on indoor parish relief in one workhouse, at Bridge Street, for convenience. It subsequently became standard practice to thank the town's Guardians of the Poor in the Jewish Board of Guardians' annual reports because of their support in accommodating Jewish paupers.

103 Lipman, *History of the Jews*, 34. In Liverpool, 'pluralist religious provision' had been organized to accommodate the Famine Irish in the 1840s, though ultimately Catholics set up their own institutions. In the 1850s, too, Catholics were pushing for religious provision in workhouses in the town (Belchem, *Irish, Catholic and Scouse*, 70–1, 77–8).

104 Minutes of the MJBG, 6 November 1878.

105 In 1879, there were twenty-eight children at the Jews Hospital and Orphan Asylum in Lower Norwood paid for under the terms of the Pauper's Removal Act (of a total of 195 children). Black, *Social Politics*, 184. For one such case, see LJBG 5th Annual Report, 1881/2.
106 MJBG 9th Annual Report, 1875/6. They also noted a fall in outdoor relief generally and a rise in that given indoors; the result of the changing wider priorities in poor relief.
107 Minutes of the MJBG, 20 February, 1 March, 28 June 1871; MJBG 4th Annual Report, 1870/1. See also discussions in the *Jewish Chronicle* on terms allowed for Jewish workmen to substitute a half day on Friday for Sunday closing (*Jewish Chronicle*, 15 February, 5 April, 7 June 1878). Following an unprecedented summons of a Jewish travelling glazier taken up for working without a licence under the Hawkers Act, the Manchester Board agreed to provide licences for anyone who could not afford one (the man's case was dismissed after the Board's honorary solicitor intervened, provided that he take out a licence. MJBG 8th Annual Report, 1874/5). In the subsequent annual report the Board noted with some satisfaction that amendments had been secured to Mr Cross's Factory Act to the benefit of Jewish employees (MJBG 11th Annual Report, 1877/8).
108 BAC JA/1/6/1/1, Minutes of the Birmingham Hebrew School, School Committee, 10 March, 28 April 1870.
109 Cited in Finlayson, *Citizen, State, and Social Welfare*, 1.
110 Williams, *Making of Manchester Jewry*, 154–5, 201; Mordechai Rozin, *The Rich and the Poor: Jewish Philanthropy and Social Control in Nineteenth-Century London* (Brighton: Sussex Academic Press, 1999), Preface.
111 LJBG 5th Annual Report 1881/2.
112 Williams, *Making of Manchester Jewry*, 286.
113 See Prochaska, *Women and Philanthropy*, 103 for a metropolitan example of a Jewish mother who rejected the advice of a non-Jewish home-visiting charity on the basis that Jews were 'not like the *goyem* [non-Jews]': they did not drink and already knew how to bring up their children.
114 For some examples, see Krausz, *Leeds Jewry*, 10–15. The Leeds Jewish Workers' Burial and Trading Society had its own butcher. Black, *Social Politics*, ix, makes a similar point about the growth of subcultures within British Jewry.
115 For example, see Prochaska, *Women and Philanthropy*, 42.
116 Laidlaw, 'Jews in the British Isles: Occupations', 142–5; Endelman, *Jews of Georgian Britain*, 185–6.
117 The Irish were apparently more concerned with the risk of being removed under the settlement laws (Englander, *Poverty and Poor Law Reform*, 44).
118 Himmelfarb, *Poverty and Compassion*, 139, citing government reports from the late 1880s.

## 7. A community of British Jews?

1. Cited by Vaughan, 'Study of the Spatial Characteristics', 35.
2. We know very little about the mobility of Jewish households between the census (see Laidlaw, 'Jews in the British Isles: Birthplaces', 48–9), but since moves within the city were often short-range this would not necessarily detract from a sense of community. Briggs also reminds us that urban neighbourhoods, even in large towns in Manchester and Liverpool, did not necessarily lead to 'anonymity' for individuals and families (Briggs, *Victorian Cities*, 110).
3. BJHS, *Birmingham Jewry*, Vol. 1., 109. See note 32, below, on his roles in the town.
4. For similar discussions within a Protestant framework, see S. J. D. Green, *Religion in the Age of Decline: Organisation and Experience in Industrial Yorkshire, c. 1870–1920* (Cambridge: Cambridge University Press, 1996); E. R. Wickham, *Church and People in an Industrial City* (London: Lutterworth Press, 1957).
5. Endelman, *Jews of Georgian England*, 272–6.
6. This can be seen in letters and articles in the *Jewish Chronicle*, which frequently talk about British characteristics, and not uncommonly sign off with descriptors like 'a British Jew'.
7. Rubinstein, *History of the Jews*, 54–6.
8. The London Jewish Board of Guardians was careful never to state how many Jews were sent to the workhouse because it implied that they were unable to look after all of their own poor. See Black, *Social Politics*, 79.
9. Bill Williams, 'The Anti-Semitism of Tolerance: Middle-Class Manchester and the Jews, 1870–1900', in *City, Class and Culture: Studies of Cultural Production and Social Policy in Victorian Manchester*, ed. A. J. Kidd and K. W. Roberts (Manchester: Manchester University Press, 1985), 74–102.
10. See Williams, *Making of Manchester Jewry*, 294.
11. Boys entering the high school section of the Birmingham Hebrew School had to be certified by the headmaster as to their 'neatness in person and respectability of habits' (Minutes of the Birmingham Hebrew Benevolent Book and Clothing Society, 1854–75. The aims of the Society were recorded at the first meeting).
12. Endelman, *Broadening Jewish History*, 95–114.
13. Endelman, 'Communal Solidarity', 503–4. He calls this type of religious practice a 'latitudinarian "Anglican" Judaism'.
14. Some of the philosemitism was based on a belief that redemption could only come when Jews were scattered to the four ends of the earth (Rubinstein, *History of the Jews*, 44).
15. Endelman, *Broadening Jewish History*, 95–114. See also M. L. Rozenblit, 'European Jewry, 1800–1933', in *The Cambridge Guide to Jewish History, Religion and Culture*, ed. Judith R Baskin and Kenneth Seeskin (Cambridge: Cambridge University Press,

2010), 169–79. When Birmingham's David Barnett took up his seat on the town corporation, he was allowed to take a modified oath that did not contain the words 'on the true faith of a Christian'. BJHS, *Birmingham Jewry*, Vol. 1, 106.
16  *Jewish Chronicle*, 21 March 1879. There were apparently fifteen of these synagogues with at least 2,000 people associated with them. See also Williams, 'Anti-Semitism of Tolerance' on the changes of the 1870s.
17  See Cheyette, *Constructions of 'the Jew'*.
18  Feldman has made this point for British Jewry (*Englishmen and Jews*, 5).
19  Another criticism is that such labels down-weight the more cultural aspects of adaptive behaviour. On this and other related problems, see, for example, Kokosalakis, *Ethnic Identity*, 9.
20  Some of these remained attached to their faith thanks solely to the strong local community of Jews in the town. Others rejected their religion or converted altogether, like the Unitarian Salis Schwabe. See Williams, *Making of Manchester Jewry*, 82–3, 196–7; also Endelman, *Broadening Jewish History*, 95–114 and 145–67.
21  David Cesarani, 'The Dynamics of Diaspora: The Transformation of British Jewish Identity', *Jewish Culture and History* 4, no. 1 (2001): 53–64.
22  Kokosalakis, *Ethnic Identity*, 47.
23  *Jewish Chronicle*, 20 October 1876; *Voice of Jacob*, 16 September 1841.
24  The community in Hull declined in take part in the election process, though this was probably for financial reasons (Finestein, 'Jews in Hull', 59).
25  Minutes of the Liverpool OHC, 6 May 1851. On the increasing desire for independence in Manchester see Williams, *Making of Manchester Jewry*, 209–17.
26  Schiller-Szinessy eventually took up the leadership of the new Manchester (Reform) Congregation of British Jews, having also established a brief and controversial relationship with the congregation in Hull (Williams, *Making of Manchester Jewry*, 182–93, 211–18 and more generally, 191–267).
27  *Jewish Chronicle*, 17 May, 24 May, 7 June 1872.
28  In Manchester, both the OHC and the Reform congregation built costly new synagogues in 1853, the former designed to make more of a statement than the latter, which was intended to blend in with its surroundings. The lord mayors of Manchester and Salford attended the gala to mark the opening of the OHC's new building. Both buildings cost around £5,500 (Williams, *Making of Manchester Jewry*, 255–6). In Birmingham, the new Singers Hill synagogue was erected in 1851, while Liverpool's OHC moved to its site on Princes Street in 1874 (BJHS, *Birmingham Jewry*, Vol. 1, 10; Kokosalakis, *Ethnic identity*, 73).
29  Minutes of the Hebrew Benevolent Book and Clothing Society, 15 February 1863.
30  Minutes of the Liverpool OHC, 26 June 1838. Prayers are still said for the Royal Family in British Sabbath morning synagogue services and the practice dates back at least to the 1650s.

31 *Laws of the Board of Guardians for the Relief of the Jewish Poor of Manchester*.
32 Examples include Birmingham's David Barnett, who was an overseer of the poor and lent his influence to the election campaigns of local MPs; Liverpool's Charles Mosley was the town's first Jewish lord mayor as well as a major player in the Jewish charities; Augustus Sichell and Abraham Bauer in Manchester were among the founders of the Anti-Corn Law League. See BJHS, *Birmingham Jewry*, Vol. 1, 25 and 106–9; Kokosalakis, *Ethnic Identity*, 89; Williams, *Making of Manchester Jewry*, 86. On citizenship of entitlement and of contribution, see Finlayson, *Citizen, State, and Social Welfare*.
33 Cesarani, 'Dynamics of Diaspora'.
34 *Voice of Jacob*, 16 September 1841.
35 Black, *Social Politics*, 44–50.
36 Ibid., 67–70. The congregation in Liverpool was apparently the only one to ignore the writ of excommunication, perhaps because their secretary and second reader, David Woolf Marks, had become the minister of the new synagogue. See Williams, *Making of Manchester Jewry*, 103–5.
37 Laidlaw, 'Jews in the British Isles: Marriage', 16–19.
38 Kokosalakis (*Ethnic Identity*, 128–39) makes this point for Liverpool in the 1870s. The newcomers set up their own *chevroth*, friendly societies and charities – and ultimately, their own burial ground and *mikvah* too. There were at least fifteen *chevroth* in Manchester by 1876 (David Englander, 'Anglicized not Anglican: Jews and Judaism in Victorian Britain', in *Religion in Victorian Britain, Vol 1: Traditions*, ed. Gerald Parsons (Manchester: Manchester University Press, 1988), 245–6). In Glasgow, too, the Jewish authorities fought the establishment of small congregations in private houses; this was a common form of worship in Scotland outside the two largest cities, because of the paucity of synagogues (Levy, *Origins of Glasgow Jewry*, 45).
39 Finestein, 'Jews in Hull', 63.
40 *Jewish Chronicle*, 7 June 1878.
41 LJBG 2nd Annual Report, 1877/8.
42 Prior to the opening of the first Jewish cemetery in Glasgow, in 1831, bodies were taken to Edinburgh for burial, such was the importance of the proper ritual (Levy, *Origins of Glasgow Jewry*, 23).
43 See Gilbert, *Religion and Society*, 24, 70–5.
44 Minutes of the MJBG, 1 July 1874. In other cases, applicants were denied relief if they had married 'out'. Marrying out was probably more common than outright conversion and did not necessarily bring exclusion from the faith. The four Rothschild daughters who married non-Jews were not ostracized (perhaps partly because in a matrilineal religion their children would still be Jewish); the men of the same generation all married 'in' (Endelman, 'Community Solidarity', 509, 513).

The most high profile was of course the marriage between Hannah Rothschild and the future prime minister, the Earl of Rosebery in 1878. Laidlaw estimates that no more than 4 per cent of all Jewish couples registered their marriages outside a synagogue (Laidlaw, 'Jews in the British Isles: Marriage', 14–16).

45　This is explored in several of the Jewish books of guidance, including the *Gemarah* and the *Mishnah*.

46　The case was turned over to the Chief Rabbi to adjudicate and both men involved were suspended for a period (Minutes of the Birmingham OHC, 28 October 1852). It hinged on the fact that the slaughterer had apparently 'used a notched knife to perform the act, which is forbidden (Minutes 10 and 17 October 1852). The Chief Rabbi could order *shochets* to undergo examination to check their credentials; in fact an article in the *Jewish Chronicle* in 1872 noted that the ritual slaughterers had greater certification than preachers (7 June 1872).

47　Finestein, 'Jews in Hull', 44.

48　Minutes of the MJBG, 4 July, 1 August 1877; MJBG 4th Annual Report, 1870/1.

49　Birmingham Jewish Local History Study Group, 'A Portrait of Birmingham Jewry'.

50　Leeds did have its own *shochet*, who also provided the meat for the community in Hull and was sent to Birmingham while their own officials were suspended (he was called back to his own duties almost immediately – see minutes of the Birmingham OHC, 28 October 1852). Finestein, 'Jews in Hull', 43.

51　Finestein, 'Jews in Hull', 49. The minutes of the Birmingham OHC make occasional reference to negotiations with co-religionists in the other two towns over their rights and entitlements.

52　Mills, *British Jews*, *passim*, quotation on 174. It should be noted that Mills was concerned with what he called 'observant' Jews.

53　Ibid., 45.

54　For example, Williams, *Making of Manchester Jewry*, 86–8.

55　Endelman, *Broadening Jewish History*, 155; *Jewish Chronicle*, 8 April 1859.

56　Mills, *British Jews*, 239.

57　'Statistical Accounts of all the Congregations'. These alternatives would not have fulfilled the strict requirements of the ritual bath. According to Mills, converts to Judaism often had to go to Holland to be immersed in a *mikvah* (*British Jews*, 253).

58　Notes to 'Statistical Accounts of all the [Jewish] Congregations of the British Empire', https://www.jewishgen.org/jcr-uk/Newman_papers/Provincial_Jewry_Victorian/statistical_accounts_I_intro.htm.

59　Williams, *Making of Manchester Jewry*, 203–4.

60　Kokosalakis, *Ethnic Identity*, 55–6 (quotation on 56).

61　Endelman, *Jews of Georgian England*, 4.

62　Williams characterizes the Reform movement in Manchester as being largely a German import, but one that also gave the community 'a religious safety-net for the future – a means of retaining the loyalty of assimilated families whose subsequent distaste for traditional Judaism might otherwise have entailed their departure from the faith' (*Making of Manchester Jewry*, 262).

63  Endelman, *Broadening Jewish History*, 30–3.
64  *Jewish Chronicle*, 3 December 1875.
65  For example, a third or more of all non-Jewish heads on Moreton Street and Edgbaston Street in Birmingham were Irish by birth. Mayhew's vivid descriptions of London Jews in *London Labour and the London Poor* of 1851 made moves in this direction, but on the whole the underclass he identifies is that of the costermongers generally, and his Jewish portraits, while colourfully 'othered', were essentially benign. See Gertrude Himmelfarb, *The Idea of Poverty England in the Early Industrial Age* (London: Faber, 1984), 333–4 (though see Williams, *From Pauperism to Poverty*, 237–77 for qualifications).
66  Mills, *British Jews*, 347–8.
67  Lipman, *Social History*, 102; Rubinstein, *History of the Jews*, 103.

# Select bibliography

## Archival primary sources

### Newspapers

*The Jewish Chronicle* (available at https://www.thejc.com/archive).
*The Voice of Jacob* (available at https://www.thejc.com/archive).

### Birmingham Archives and Collections, Library of Birmingham

JA/1/A/1/, Minutes of the Birmingham Hebrew Congregation.
JA/1/6/1/1, Minutes of the Birmingham Hebrew School Committee.
MS 1678/1, Minutes of the Birmingham Hebrew Philanthropic Society.
MS 1678/3, Records of the Hebrew Benevolent Book and Clothing Society.
MS 1678/4, Laws of the Birmingham Hebrew Board of Guardians, 1870.

### Liverpool Record Office and Local Studies

296 OHC 2/2, Minutes of the Liverpool Old Hebrew Congregation.
296 OHC 18/7, Medical Report given by S. Lewis, M. D., to the Liverpool Old Hebrew Congregation.
296 OHC 34/2, Vouchers and Petitions for Poor Relief, Liverpool Old Hebrew Congregation.
296 OHC 34/3, Register of Poor Relief Payments, 1861–9, Liverpool Old Hebrew Congregation.
296 OHC 34/7, Liverpool Old and New Hebrew Congregation Poor Fund Account, 1873–4.
296 OHC 34/4, Payments to the Casual and Resident Poor, Liverpool Old Hebrew Congregation, 1861–9.
296 OHC 61/3/2-4, Records of the Liverpool Hebrew Mendicity Society.
296 OHC 61/5/1/1, Records of the Liverpool Hebrew Philanthropic Society.
296 OHC 451/1, Balance Sheets for Half-Yearly Accounts, 1864, Liverpool Old Hebrew Congregation.
296 HPS/2, *Laws of the Liverpool Hebrew Provident Society*. Liverpool: Yates & Hess, 1878.
BOG 5/1/1, Annual Reports of the Liverpool Jewish Board of Guardians.

## Manchester Libraries, Information and Archives, Manchester Central Library

GB127.M139/6/1/1, Manchester Hebrew Congregation Benevolent Fund, Treasurer's Account Book and Passover Relief Fund.

GB127.M790/2/2, Bill Williams Papers, Papers of Manchester Board of Guardians of the Jewish Poor.

GB127.M790 2/6/1, Bill Williams Papers, Voluntary Agencies.

GB127.M790/2/16, Bill Williams Papers, Jewish Women and Philanthropy.

## Printed primary sources

Chief Rabbi's Statistical Accounts of all the Congregations of the British Empire, 1845. Available at https://www.jewishgen.org/jcr-uk/Newman_papers/Provincial_Jewry_Victorian/statistical_accounts_I_page_01.htm.

Duncan, W. H. 'On the Sanitary State of Liverpool'. In *Sanitary Inquiry: Local Reports on the Sanitary Condition of the Labouring Population of England, in Consequence of an Inquiry Directed to Be Made by the Poor Law Commissioners. Presented to Both Houses of Parliament, by Command of Her Majesty, July, 1842*. London, 1842. Available at https://archive.org/stream/b21366202/b21366202_djvu.txt.

Margoliouth, Rev. Moses. *The History of the Jews in Great Britain*, 3 vols. London: Richard Bentley, 1851.

Mills, John. *The British Jews*. London: Houlston & Stoneman, 1853.

Mott, Charles. 'Report on the State of the Residence of the Labouring Classes in the Manufacturing Districts of Lancashire, Cheshire, Derbyshire and Staffordshire'. In *Sanitary Inquiry: Local Reports on the Sanitary Condition of the Labouring Population of England, in Consequence of an Inquiry Directed to Be Made by the Poor Law Commissioners. Presented to Both Houses of Parliament, by Command of Her Majesty, July, 1842*. London, 1842. Available at https://archive.org/stream/b21366202/b21366202_djvu.txt.

Newlands, James. *Report to the Health Committee of the Borough of Liverpool on the Sewerage, Paving, Cleansing and Other Works, Under the Sanitary Act from 1856 to 1862, Inclusive*. Liverpool: Henry Greenwood, 1863.

'Report on the State of the Public Health in the Borough of Birmingham by a Committee of Physicians and Surgeons'. In *Sanitary Inquiry: Local Reports on the Sanitary Condition of the Labouring Population of England, in Consequence of an Inquiry Directed to Be Made by the Poor Law Commissioners. Presented to Both Houses of Parliament, by Command of Her Majesty, July, 1842*. London, 1842. Available at: https://archive.org/stream/b21366202/b21366202_djvu.txt.

Trench, W. S. *Report on the Health of Liverpool During the Year 1864*. Liverpool: Henry Greenwood, 1865.

Trench, W. S. 'On the Sanitary State of the Labouring Classes in the Town of Liverpool'. In *Sanitary Inquiry: Local Reports on the Sanitary Condition of the Labouring Population of England, in Consequence of an Inquiry Directed to Be Made by the Poor Law Commissioners. Presented to Both Houses of Parliament, by Command of Her Majesty, July, 1842*. London, 1842. Available at https://archive.org/stream/b21366202/b21366202_djvu.txt.

## Secondary sources

Anderson, Benedict. *Imagined Communities*. London and New York: Verso, 2006.
Anderson, Michael. *Family Structure in Nineteenth-Century Lancashire*. Cambridge: Cambridge University Press. 1971.
Anderson, Michael. 'Household Structure and the Industrial Revolution: Mid-Nineteenth-Century Preston in Comparative Perspective'. In *Household and Family in Past Time*, edited by Peter Laslett with Richard Wall, 215–35. Cambridge: Cambridge University Press, 1972.
Armstrong, W. A. 'A Note on the Household Structure of Mid-Nineteenth-Century York in Comparative Perspective'. In *Household and Family in Past Times*, edited by Peter Laslett with Richard Wall, 205–14. Cambridge: Cambridge University Press, 1972.
Avery-Peck, Alan. 'Charity in Judaism'. In *The Encylopedia of Judaism*, 3 vols, edited by Jacob Neusner, Alan J. Avery-Peck and William Scott Green, Vol. 1, 50–63. New York: Brill, 1999.
Belchem, John. *Irish, Catholic and Scouse: The History of the Liverpool Irish, 1800–1939*. Liverpool: Liverpool University Press, 2007.
Birmingham Jewish History Society. *Birmingham Jewry*, Vol. 1: *1749–1914*. Oldbury: Birmingham Jewish History Research Group, 1980.
Birmingham Jewish History Society. *Birmingham Jewry*, Vol. 2: *More Aspects, 1740–1930*. Oldbury: Birmingham Jewish History Research Group, 1984.
Birmingham Jewish Local History Study Group. 'A Portrait of Birmingham Jewry in 1851'. Available at https://www.jewishgen.org/jcr-uk/Community/Birmingham/articles/birmingham-vic2.htm.
Black, Eugene. C. *The Social Politics of Anglo-Jewry, 1880–1920*. Oxford: Basil Blackwell, 1988.
Borgatti, Stephen P., Ajay Mehra, Daniel J. Brass and Giuseppe Labianca. 'Network Analysis in the Social Sciences'. *Science* 323, no. 5916 (1990): 892–5.
Braber, Ben. *Jews in Glasgow, 1879–1939*. Ilford: Vallentine Mitchell & Co. Ltd, 2007.
Briggs, Asa. *Victorian Cities*. Harmondsworth: Penguin, 1968.
Brown, Callum. *The Death of Christian Britain: Understanding Secularisation 1800–2000*. London and New York: Routledge, 2001.

Busteed, Mervyn. *The Irish in Manchester c. 1750–1921: Resistance, Adaptation and Identity*. Manchester: Manchester University Press, 2016.

Calhoun, C. J. 'Community: Toward a Variable Conceptualization for Comparative Research'. *Social History* 5, no. 1 (1980): 105–29.

Cesarani, David. 'The Dynamics of Diaspora: The Transformation of British Jewish Identity'. *Jewish Culture and History* 4, no. 1 (2001): 53–64.

Cesarani, David. *The Jewish Chronicle and Anglo-Jewry, 1841–1991*. Cambridge: Cambridge University Press, 1994.

Colley, Linda. *Britons: Forging a Nation, 1703–1837*. New Haven and London: Yale University Press, 1992.

Collins, Kenneth E. *Glasgow Jewry: A Guide to the History and Community of the Jews in Glasgow*. Glasgow: Scottish Jewish Archives Committee, 1993.

Connell, J. 'Social Networks in Urban Society'. In *Social Patterns in Cities*, Institute of British Geographers Special Publication no. 5. London: Institute of British Geographers, 1973: 41–52.

Constantelos, Demetrios J. 'Charity'. In *Encyclopedia of Religion*, 2nd edn, edited by Lindsay Jones, Vol. 3, 1553–1556. Detroit: Macmillan Reference USA, 2005. Available at Gale eBooks, https://link-gale-com.oxfordbrookes.idm.oclc.org/apps/doc/CX3424500543/GVRL?u=brookes_itw&sid=GVRL&xid=fa4abc8c.

Endelman, Todd. *Broadening Jewish History: Towards a Social History of Ordinary Jews*. Oxford and Portland, Oregon: Littman Library of Jewish Civilization, 2011.

Endelman, Todd. 'Communal Solidarity among the Jewish Elite of Victorian London'. *Victorian Studies* 28, no. 3 (1985): 491–526.

Endelman, Todd. 'English Jewish History'. *Modern Judaism* 11 (1991): 91–109.

Endelman, Todd. 'Jews, Aliens and Other Outsiders in British History'. *Historical Journal* 37, no. 4 (1994): 959–69.

Endelman, Todd. *The Jews of Britain, 1656 to 2000*. Berkeley and London: University of California Press, 2002.

Endelman, Todd. *The Jews of Georgian England, 1741–1830: Tradition and Change in a Liberal Society*. Philadelphia: Jewish Publication Society of America, 1979.

Englander, David. 'Anglicized not Anglican: Jews and Judaism in Victorian Britain'. In *Religion in Victorian Britain*, Vol. 1: *Traditions*, edited by Gerald Parsons, 235–73. Manchester: Manchester University Press, 1998.

Englander, David. *A Documentary History of Jewish Immigrants in Britain, 1840–1920*. Leicester: Leicester University Press, 1994.

Englander, David. *Poverty and Poor Law Reform in Nineteenth-Century Britain, 1834–1914: From Chadwick to Booth*. London and New York: Longman, 1998.

Feldman, David. *Englishmen and Jews: Social Relations and Political Culture, 1840–1914*. New Haven and London: Yale University Press, 1994.

Field, C. D. 'Counting Religion in England and Wales: The Long Eighteenth Century, c.1680–c.1840'. *Journal of Ecclesiastical History* 63, no. 4 (2012): 693–720.

Finestein, Israel. 'The Jews in Hull between 1766 and 1880'. *Jewish Historical Studies* 35 (1996–8): 33–91.

Finlayson, Geoffrey. *Citizen, State, and Social Welfare in Britain, 1830–1990*. Oxford: Clarendon Press, 1994.

Freedman, M. *Leeds Jewry: The First Hundred Years*. Leeds: Jewish Historical Society of England, 1992.

Gartner, Lloyd P. *The Jewish Immigrant in England, 1870–1914*. London: Allen & Unwin, 1960.

Gilbert, A. D. *Religion and Society in Industrial England: Church, Chapel and Social Change, 1740–1914*. London and New York: Longman, 1976.

Green, S. J. D. *Religion in the Age of Decline: Organisation and Experience in Industrial Yorkshire, c. 1870–1920*. Cambridge: Cambridge University Press, 1996.

Hareven, Tamara, 'The History of the Family and the Complexity of Social Change', *American Historical Review* 96, no. 1 (1991): 95–124.

Heim, Maria. 'Almsgiving'. In *Encyclopedia of Religion*, 2nd edn, edited by Lindsay Jones, Vol. 1, 266–8. Detroit: Macmillan Reference USA, 2005. Available at Gale eBooks, http://link.galegroup.com/apps/doc/CX3424500120/GVRL?u=brookes_itw&sid=GVRL&xid=57a89b10.

Hickman, Mary. *Religion, Class and Identity: The State, the Catholic Church and the Education of the Irish in Britain*. Aldershot: Avebury, 1995.

Himmelfarb, Gertrude. *Poverty and Compassion: The Moral Imagination of the Late Victorians*. New York: Vintage Books, 1992.

*A History of the County of Lancaster*, Vol. 4: *Liverpool: Trade, Population and Geographical Growth* (originally published by Victoria County History, London, 1911). Available at https://www.british-history.ac.uk/vch/lancs/.

Kearns, Gerry, Paul Laxton and Joy Campbell. 'Duncan and the Cholera Test: Public Health in Mid-Nineteenth-Century Liverpool'. *Transactions of the Historic Society of Lancashire and Cheshire* 143 (1993): 87–115.

Kidd, Alan J. *Manchester*, 2nd edn. Keele: Keele University Press, 1996.

Kidd, Alan J. 'Outcast Manchester: Voluntary Charity, Poor Relief and the Casual Poor, 1860–1905'. In *City, Class and Culture: Studies of Cultural Production and Social Policy in Victorian Manchester*, edited by A. J. Kidd and K. W. Roberts, 48–73. Manchester: Manchester University Press, 1985.

King, Steven. 'Migrants on the Margin? Mobility, Integration and Occupations in the West Riding, 1650–1820'. *Journal of Historical Geography* 23, no. 3 (1997): 284–303.

King, Steven, and Geoff Timmins. *Making Sense of the Industrial Revolution*. Manchester: Manchester University Press, 2001.

Kokosalakis, N. *Ethnic Identity and Religion: Tradition and Change in Liverpool Jewry*. Washington: University Press of America, 1982.

Laidlaw, Petra. 'Jews in the British Isles in 1851: Birthplaces, Residence and Migrations'. *Jewish Journal of Sociology* 53 (2011): 29–56.

Laidlaw, Petra. 'Jews in the British Isles in 1851: Marriage and Childbearing'. *Jewish Journal of Sociology* 57, nos 1 and 2 (2015): 7–43.

Laidlaw, Petra. 'Jews in the British Isles in 1851: Occupations'. *Jewish Journal of Sociology* 56, nos 1 and 2 (2013): 114–57.

Laslett, Peter. 'Introduction'. In *Household and Family in Past Time*, edited by Peter Laslett with Richard Wall, 1–89. Cambridge: Cambridge University Press, 1972.

Laslett, Peter. 'Mean Household Size in England Since the Sixteenth Century'. In *Household and Family in Past Time*, edited by Peter Laslett with Richard Wall, 125–58. Cambridge: Cambridge University Press, 1972.

Lawton, Clive A. 'Judaism'. In *Ethical Issues in Six Religious Traditions*, edited by Peggy Morgan and Clive Lawton, 168–215. Edinburgh: Edinburgh University Press, 2007.

Lawton, Richard, and Colin G. Pooley. 'The Social Geography of Nineteenth-Century Merseyside: A Research Project'. *Historical Methods Newsletter* 7, no. 4 (1974): 276–84.

Levy, A. *The Origins of Glasgow Jewry, 1812–1895*. Glasgow: A. J. Macfarlane Ltd, 1949.

Lewis, Jane. *The Voluntary Sector, the State and Social Work in Britain: The Charity Organisation Society/Family Welfare Association Since 1869*. Aldershot: Edward Elgar, 1995.

Liedtke, Rainer. 'The Uses of Benevolence: Charity among Jewish Immigrants in Manchester, 1905–1930'. *Jewish Culture and History* 1, no. 1 (1998): 54–71.

Lipman, Vivian D. *A History of the Jews in Britain since 1858*. Leicester: Leicester University Press, 1990.

Lipman, Vivian D. *Social History of the Jews in England, 1850–1950*. London: Watts & Co., 1954.

Lunn, K. 'Historical Introduction'. In *Steel City Jews: A Study of Ethnicity and Social Mobility in the Jewish Population of the City of Sheffield, South Yorkshire*, by Barry A. Kosmin, Marzy Bauer and Nigel Grizzard, 1–6. London: Research Unit Board of Deputies of British Jews, 1976.

Lynch, Katherine. *Individuals, Families and Communities in Europe, 1200–1800: The Urban Foundation of Western Society*. Cambridge: Cambridge University Press, 2003.

McCabe, A. T. 'The Standard of Living on Merseyside, 1850–1875'. In *Victorian Lancashire*, edited by S. Peter Bell, 127–49. Newton Abbot: David & Charles, 1974.

Meek, Jeff. 'Boarding and Lodging Practices in Early Twentieth-Century Scotland'. *Continuity and Change* 31, no. 1 (2016): 79–100.

Modell, John, and Tamara Hareven. 'Urbanization and the Malleable Household: An Examination of Boarding and Lodging in American Families'. *Journal of Marriage and the Family* 35, no. 3 (1973): 467–79.

Newman, Aubrey. 'Birmingham: Introductory Data'. In *Provincial Jewry in Victorian Britain*, edited by Aubrey Newman. Available at https://www.jewishgen.org/jcr-uk/Community/Birmingham/articles/birmingham-vic.htm.

Newman, Aubrey. *Provincial Jewry in Victorian Britain*. London: Jewish Historical Society of England, 1975.

Owen, David. *English Philanthropy, 1660–1960*. Cambridge, MA: Belknap Press of Harvard University, 1964.

Parsons, Gerald. 'A Question of Meaning: Religion and Working-Class Life'. In *Religion in Victorian Britain*, Vol. 2: *Controversies*, edited by Gerald Parsons, 63–87. Manchester and New York: Manchester University Press, 1988.

Peel, Mark. 'On the Margins: Lodgers and Boarders in Boston, 1860–1900'. *Journal of American History* 72, no. 4 (1986): 813–34.

Pooley, Colin G. 'The Residential Segregation of Migrant Communities in Mid-Victorian Liverpool'. *Transactions of the Institute of British Geographers* 2, no. 3 (1977): 364–82.

Pooley, Colin G. 'Residential Mobility in the Victorian City'. *Transactions of the Institute of British Geographers* 4, no. 2 (1979): 258–77.

Pooley, Colin, and Jean Turnbull. *Migration and Mobility in Britain since the Eighteenth Century*. London and New York: Routledge, 1998.

Reay, Barry. 'Kinship and the Neighbourhood in Nineteenth-Century Rural England: The Myth of the Autonomous Nuclear Family'. *Journal of Family History* 21, no. 1 (1996): 87–104.

Roberts, M. J. D. 'Reshaping the Gift Relationship: The London Mendicity Society and the Suppression of Begging in England, 1818–1869'. *International Review of Social History* 36 (1991): 201–31.

Rose, Michael. 'The Disappearing Pauper: Victorian Attitudes to the Relief of the Poor'. In *In Search of Victorian Values: Aspects of Nineteenth-Century Thought and Society*, edited by Eric M. Sigsworth, 56–72. Manchester: Manchester University Press, 1988.

Roth, Cecil. *A History of the Jews in England*, 3rd edn. Oxford: Clarendon Press, 1964.

Rozenblit, M. L. 'European Jewry, 1800–1933'. In *The Cambridge Guide to Jewish History, Religion and Culture*, edited by Judith R. Baskin and Kenneth Seeskin, 169–207. Cambridge: Cambridge University Press, 2010.

Rozin, Mordechai. *The Rich and the Poor: Jewish Philanthropy and Social Control in Nineteenth-Century London*. Brighton: Sussex Academic Press, 1999.

Rubinstein, W. D. *A History of the Jews in the English-Speaking World: Great Britain*. Basingstoke: Macmillan, 1996.

Ruggles, Steven. 'Multigenerational Families in Nineteenth-Century America'. *Continuity and Change* 18, no. 1 (2003): 139–65.

Scott, John. *Social Network Analysis: A Handbook*, 2nd edn. London: Sage Publications, 2000.

Simey, Margaret. *Charity Rediscovered: A Study of Philanthropic Effort in Nineteenth-Century Liverpool*. Liverpool: Liverpool University Press, 1992.

Smelser, Neil J. *Social Change in the Industrial Revolution: An Application of Theory to the British Cotton Industry*. Aldershot: Gregg Revivals, 1959.

Swift, Roger, and Sheridan Gilley, eds. *The Irish in Britain: The Local Dimension*. Dublin: Four Courts Press, 1999.

Tadmor, Naomi. 'Early Modern Kinship in the Long Run: Reflections on Continuity and Change'. *Continuity and Change* 25, no. 1 (2010): 15–48.

Tönnies, Ferdinand. *Community and Association*, translated by Charles P. Loomis. London: Routledge and Kegan Paul, 1955.

Vaughan, Laura. 'A Study of the Spatial Characteristics of the Jews in London, 1695 & 1895'. MSc diss., University College London, London, 1994.

Vaughan, Laura. 'The Unplanned "Ghetto": Immigrant Work Patterns in Nineteenth-Century Manchester'. Paper given at the 10th conference of the International Planning History Society, University of Westminster, London, July 2002. Available at http://discovery.ucl.ac.uk/662/.

Vaughan, Laura, and Alan Penn. 'Jewish Immigrant Settlement Patterns in Manchester and Leeds, 1881'. *Urban Studies* 43, no. 3 (2006): 653–71.

Williams, B. 'The Anti-Semitism of Tolerance: Middle-Class Manchester and the Jews, 1870–1900'. In *City, Class and Culture. Studies of Cultural Production and Social Policy in Victorian Manchester*, edited by A. J. Kidd and K. W. Roberts, 74–102. Manchester: Manchester University Press, 1985.

Williams, B. *The Making of Manchester Jewry, 1740–1875*. Manchester: Manchester University Press, 1976.

# Index

Acculturation (*see also* assimilation) 9, 11, 42, 173-7, 178, 181-2
adaptation 5, 12, 14, 21, 34, 40, 84, 86, 104, 161, 170, 175, 182, 184
Adler, Nathan Marcus (*see also* Chief Rabbi) 8, 173, 174, 176
Anglo Jewish Database (AJDB) 13, 14, 16, 31, 32, 40, 69, 71, 76, 195 n.32, 196 n.36.
　completed family sizes 193 n.12, 194 n.21
　enriched 16, 22, 35
　households 26, 31
　immigrants 23, 24, 29
　Jewish population size 184, 192 n.77, 193 n.5, 200 n.15
　lodgers 35, 40
　occupations 38, 82, 83, 86, 96, 97, 196 n.37, 198 n.59, 204 n.8, n.15
　sex ratios 193 n.6, 242
America, as destination for emigrants 114, 121, 141, 155, 192 n.78
Anti-semitism *see* discrimination, persecution
apprenticeship 92, 97, 135, 150, 151-2, 164, 219 n.142
assimilation (*see also* acculturation) 9, 12, 66, 67, 135, 174-7, 181-3, 188 n.36, 199 n.6

beggars (*see also* Mendicity Societies *under* Hull, Jews *and* Liverpool, Jews) 113, 120, 130-1, 147
Beth Din 8
Birmingham 15, 48, 121, 188 n.31, 193 n.3, 198 n.57
　housing conditions 65, 99-100, 101-2
　Irish 101, 232 n.65
　occupations 82-4, 90, 91
　public health 55-6, 99
Birmingham, Jews 6-7, 15, 22-3, 33, 71, 105, 179-80, 188 n.35

charity 130, 132, 146, 149; Benevolent Book and Clothing Society (Birmingham Hebrew Educational Benevolent Society) 135, 150, 176, 219 n.142; Hebrew National School (*see also* Benevolent Book and Clothing Society) 55, 75, 134, 135, 160, 176; Hebrew Philanthropic Society 135, 137, 144, 146, 149, 157, 216 n.96; Jewish Board of Guardians 145, 147, 150, 153, 158; synagogue 55, 116, 118, 119, 121, 122
congregational schism (1852) 191 n.65, 207 n.46
Edgbaston Street 65, 74, 76, 194 n.15, 198 n.57, 232 n.65
elite 74-5, 94-6, 97, 136
evidence of social networks 55, 75-6, 97, 136-7, 138, 171, 180
households 25, 27-8, 30, 31, 33, 43, 194 n.21, 197-8 n.56; connected to other households 70, 72, 73, 74-5, 75-6; head born overseas 63, 65, 66; skill status of head 60, 63-4, 66
housing conditions 65, 66, 99-101, 101-2
*kashrut* 179-80, 204 n.6, 231 n.49
lodgers 35, 36-7, 40, 196-7 n.46, 197-8 n.56
migration 23, 65
occupations 40, 64, 81, 82-4, 85-9, 91, 93, 94-6, 97, 104
Pershore Street 55, 58, 65, 194 n.15, 198 n.57, 208 n.73, 232 n.65
population characteristics 23-4, 196 n.36; sex ratios 23-4
population size 15, 22, 23, 197 n.56
religious practice 119, 138, 188 n.35
residence patterns 45, 46, 48, 49-50, 54-6, 60, 63, 64, 65, 66, 75-6, 169-70
servants 41

synagogue, Severn Street 55; Singers Hill (est 1856) 45, 46, 48, 49–50, 54–6, 60, 63, 64, 65, 66, 75–6, 169–70
Board of Deputies of British Jews 8–9, 68, 121, 161
Bradford, Jews 181
Brighton, Jewish charity 135
Bristol, Jews 22, 77, 135
Britishness, and Jews 4, 9, 14, 17, 114, 134, 165, 172, 173–8, 182, 183
burial grounds, Jewish 54, 64, 96, 147, 230 n.38
burials, Jewish 7, 118, 122, 146, 179

Canterbury, Jews 76
Cardiff, Jewish charity 135
Catholics 11, 112, 134, 159, 165, 176, 187 n.28, 188 n.31, 226 n.103
Census (1851) and methodology (*see also* AJDB) 14, 15, 22, 34–5, 46, 92, 100, 193 n.3, 201 n.40
Census of Worship (1851) 6–7, 14, 188 n.31, n.35
charity (*see also individual named towns*)
  Charity Organisation Society (COS) 142–3, 144, 145, 147, 148, 149, 158, 221 n.15, 225 n.86
  Jewish 7, 16, 17, 29, 32, 94, 104, 109–39, 141–65, 171; aims of 17, 109, 121, 134–5, 136; apprenticeship 150, 151–2, 164, 219 n.142; to casual poor 119–22, 130–2, 135, 147–8, 152–3; condition of recipients 88, 98, 101–3, 126, 127–9, 131, 146, 156–7, 159–6; for deserted families 128, 148, 155–6, 159, 171, 225 n.83; 'deservingness' 117, 118–19, 125, 129–30, 131, 137, 143, 148, 156, 161, 163; expenditure 115, 116, 117, 122, 123–4, 134, 152, 153, 214 n.58, 224 n.70; financial constraints 120, 122, 123, 136, 146–7, 149–50, 152–3, 154–5, 171; home visiting 97, 102, 104, 125, 129, 133, 143, 144, 145, 147, 148, 150, 162; industrial funds 146, 149, 150, 151, 157, 223 n.52; informal 113, 137, 138, 165; Jewish Boards of Guardians 143–65; loans 75, 124, 130, 132–3, 138, 144, 145, 146, 150–1, 152, 162; London 115, 124, 144, 152, 159–60, 227 n.105; medical relief 102, 104, 125, 126–7, 145, 150, 152, 155, 158, 159; numbers relieved 116–17, 118, 120, 121, 122–4, 126, 127, 131, 132–3, 146, 150, 151, 152, 153–4; philosophy 42, 110, 111–14, 124, 127, 129, 131, 132, 135, 135–6, 148–9, 161, 171; planning and consolidation 17, 141, 143–4, 145, 146, 147, 149, 157–3, 164; relief in goods 115, 117, 118, 119, 125, 126, 131, 133, 134–5, 145, 150, 152, 159–60; schools 54, 55, 75, 130, 133–5, 150, 160–1, 163, 164, 174, 176, 178, 179, 181, 210 n.91, 218–19 n.137, n.142; self-help (*see also* loans *under* charity, Jewish) 114, 119, 124, 132, 134, 142, 146, 149, 154, 161, 164–5, 178; social networks 2, 7, 16, 76, 78, 105, 109, 115, 118–19, 129, 134, 136–7, 163, 164, 171, 172, 183; to support Jewish observance 113, 116, 117–18, 122, 138, 146, 150, 152, 163, 179; synagogue 115–24, 131, 145, 146–7, 159, 170
  wider ideas 110, 119, 124, 132, 133, 135–7, 141–3, 144, 147, 161, 162, 165
Cheltenham, Jewish charity 135
*chevroth* 68, 90, 135, 137, 146, 165, 178, 230 n.38
Chief Rabbi (*see also* Adler, Nathan Marcus)
  office of 8, 12, 68, 184, 189 n.44
  Statistical Accounts of all the Congregations of the British Empire 8, 135, 181, 218–19 n.137
children, in employment 91–2, 206 n.31
Christianity 7, 9, 41, 112, 134, 164, 173, 174, 181, 182–3, 185 n.7, 228 n.4, 228–9 n.15
  church attendance 6–7, 67, 190 n.57
community
  definitions 1–6
  'imagined' (transpatial) 2, 3, 9, 13, 34, 79, 119, 136, 137, 155, 162, 163, 169, 170

Jewish, perceptions from outside 5, 56, 114, 121, 124, 132, 163, 174, 176, 179–80, 187 n.25
congregational schisms 8, 12, 52, 115, 120, 122–3, 177, 191 n.65, 200 n.26, 207 n.46
conversion, to Christianity 7, 96, 174, 181, 229 n.20, 230 n. 44
conversionists 110, 181

Derby, Jews 122
discrimination against Jews (prejudice) 21, 56, 57, 68, 84, 86, 160, 161, 172, 190 n.62, 198 n.58, 205 n.17

Edinburgh, Jewish cemetery 230 n.42
education *see* schools
Education Act (1870) 130, 160, 174, 179
emancipation, Jewish 8, 11, 12, 132, 141, 162, 173, 174, 177, 206 n.42, 218 n.120
emigration (*see also* America, transmigrants) 144, 145, 148, 152, 155
employment *see* occupations

Falmouth, Jews 77, 135
family *see* households
friendly societies (*see also* self-help) 7, 132, 220 n.6, 221 n.28, 230 n.38

German Jews 8, 37, 41, 175, 182, 198 n.58, 201 n.37, 204 n.7, 231 n.62
Germany 15, 35, 155, 178, 186 n.19, 192 n.78
Glasgow 12, 15, 36, 135, 141, 176
  congregational schism 120, 191 n.65
  Hebrew Philanthropic Society 125
  Jews in 15, 22–3, 24, 25, 27–8, 30, 180, 183–4, 230 n.38, n.42
  lodgers 25, 35, 36, 37, 43, 197 n.47
glaziers/glazing 39, 62, 85, 86, 89, 93, 97, 116, 118, 134, 146, 151, 204 n.15

hawkers/hawking 7, 23, 38, 39, 40, 64, 85, 87–8, 91, 92, 97, 116, 134, 151, 152, 171, 202 n.47, 204 n.7, 209 n.84, 227 n.107
Hebrew (language) 8, 111, 134, 173
hospitals, Jewish patients 7, 121, 122, 126, 152, 158, 159, 160, 179, 205 n.29, 225 n.94, 226 n.99, n.101
households (*see also* lodgers, servants, AJDB)
  and industrialization 2–3, 21–2, 42–3, 172, 174, 189 n.56
  Jewish 21–44; children in 26–7, 29, 31–2, 36, 42, 65, 102, 118, 127, 128, 146, 194 n.21, 196–7 n.46, n.56; classification 21–2, 24–9, 194 n.14, n.19; elderly 32, 32–4, 36, 40, 42, 127, 195 n.35; 'extended'/composite 22, 25, 26–34; fluidity of 22, 26, 29, 34, 42, 73, 74; Jewish distinctiveness 22, 24, 26, 29, 31–2, 34, 36, 40, 41, 79, 169; kin links between 68–77, 170; 'nuclear' 26–8, 34, 73; size 24–5, 197 n.56; spatial locations of 45–79, 169–70; structure 22–4, 169
housing conditions
  among Jews 65 66, 95, 98–104, 158, 170
  rents 22, 53, 57, 103, 125, 130, 152, 208 n.61, 209 n.83, n.88, 217 n.103
Hull, Jews 12, 14, 15, 138, 178, 180, 193 n.3, 194 n.21, 197–8 n.56, 214 n.58, 221 n.28, 229 n.24, n.26
  congregational schism 120, 191 n.65
  Hebrew Mendicity Society 130
  Hebrew Philanthropic Society (1848) 125, 135
  households 24, 25, 26, 27–8, 39, 72
  Jewish Board of Guardians 145
  kosher butchers 180, 231 n.50
  lodgers 36, 37, 39
  servants 41

illegitimacy, Jewish 31–2
immigrants, Jewish (*see also* Irish, Jews, born overseas)
  charity 110, 132, 136, 139, 144–5, 150, 153, 155–6
  integration 35, 40, 44, 84, 156–7, 172, 173
  occupations 85, 86, 204 n.7, 205 n.15, n.19
  lodgers 35, 40
  poverty 17, 115, 134, 148, 155, 156, 163, 164, 171, 206 n.38

in seven industrial towns 14–15, 22, 23, 37, 38, 48, 64–5, 109, 138, 141, 180, 182; Birmingham 48, 55; Glasgow 15, 183; Leeds 15, 183, 200 n.22; Liverpool 51, 202 n.53; Manchester 53, 54, 65, 78
immigration, Jewish 4, 17, 26, 53, 66, 68, 83, 114, 134, 141, 153, 163, 165, 171, 172, 174, 175, 177–8, 178, 180, 182–4
   in the 1880s 5, 12, 16, 22, 161, 187 n.25, 200 n.22
industrial economy (*see also* housing conditions, industrialization, *individual towns*) 135, 142
   in case study towns 15, 144, 83–93, 105
   Jewish participation in 81, 83–93, 93–5, 96–8, 104–5, 164, 170
   occupations 3, 93–5, 96–8, 81–93, 104, 202 n.47, 223 n.62
industrialization (*see also* housing conditions, industrial economy, occupations) 1, 105
   and community/households 3, 6, 21, 42, 190 n.56
   impact on Jews 1, 4, 22, 169, 172, 174, 183
   and religion 6
Irish 81, 134, 165, 184, 207 n.51, 226 n.103, 227 n.117
   Catholics 5, 134, 187 n.28
   immigrants 5, 15, 50, 187 n.28
   in Liverpool 5–6, 15, 50, 51, 56–7, 65, 67, 100
Italians 165, 184, 188 n.28

Jewish Boards of Guardians (*see also individual towns*) 17, 144–65, 171, 174
*Jewish Chronicle* 9, 68, 111, 112, 138, 141, 143, 144, 148, 152, 157, 161, 174, 176, 177, 181, 187 n.28, 190 n.48, 221 n.28, 222 n.47, 227 n.107, 228 n.6, 231 n.46
Jewish festivals, observance 6, 35, 131, 135, 159, 179
   Day of Atonement (Yom Kippur) 6, 18, 112, 118, 188 n.34
   New Year (Rosh Hashanah) 6, 18, 118

Passover 118, 179
Jews (*see also* AJDB)
   born overseas 23–4, 29, 35, 40, 42, 43, 48, 51, 56, 58, 61, 62, 63, 64–5, 66, 69, 77–8, 100, 157, 162, 178, 181, 202 n.48, 206 n.38, 206 n.44
   British-born 5, 24, 42, 45, 65, 68, 97, 177, 178
   as Britons 4, 9, 14, 17, 114, 134, 165, 172, 173–8, 182, 183
   employers of non-Jews 22, 24, 41–2, 74
   interactions with non-Jews 12, 26, 40, 42, 54, 57, 76, 79, 92, 127–8, 131, 137, 155, 159, 164, 173, 180, 181, 184, 186 n.18, 227 n.113, 230 n.44
   living with non-Jews 14, 16, 21, 22, 24, 35, 39–40, 40–1, 42, 100
   as 'others' 4–5, 8, 68, 174, 175, 232 n.65
Judaism
   belief 7–8, 111–13, 122, 178–80, 189 n.39
   observance 7, 8, 9, 35, 39, 67–8, 78, 87, 96, 97, 110, 117–19, 124, 126, 135, 136, 159–60, 174, 178–82, 189 n.39; burial 7, 118, 122, 147, 179, 230 n.42; circumcision 7, 117, 124, 179; marriage 56, 69, 179, 180, 189 n.37, 213 n.37, 230–1 n.44; Sabbath 6, 7, 8, 35, 87, 126, 131, 135, 159, 160, 178, 180, 181, 189 n.39; *shivah* (mourning) 113, 138, 150, 152, 179

*kashrut* (dietary laws) 7–8, 39, 103, 181, 189 n.40
kosher
   butchers 54, 180
   food 7–8, 39, 103, 181, 189 n.40
   slaughterers (shechita) 180, 204 n.6, n.43, 222 n.32, 231 n.50

Lancashire Cotton Famine 102, 114, 142, 144, 145
Leeds, Jews 15, 180
   in the 1880s 62, 77, 141, 184, 199 n.5, 200 n.22, 202 n.58
   characteristics 15, 22–3, 24, 192 n.84
   charity 135, 145
   households 24–5, 30, 169, 197 n.56, 208 n.68

immigrants 23, 35, 180, 183
kosher meat 180, 227 n.114, 231 n.50
lodging 36, 37, 39, 40, 32
Liverpool 6, 14–15, 58, 138, 188 n.31, 198 n.57, 202 n.53, 228 n.2
　charity 143, 155, 162, 224 n.78
　housing conditions 100, 101, 209–10 n.88
　immigration 56–7, 67
　Irish 5–6, 56–7, 65, 67, 68, 101, 226 n.103
　occupations 82, 84, 86, 88, 89, 90, 91
　port 14, 42, 120, 121, 130, 138, 141, 155
　public health 15, 98–9, 100, 207 n.57
Liverpool, Jews 13, 14, 15, 43, 71, 76, 77, 91, 93, 105, 176, 177, 180, 181, 182, 183, 230 n.32, 230 n.36, n.38
　charity 118, 125, 127, 135, 148, 224 n.78, 225 n.94, 226 n.99; Board of Relief 121; Hebrew Mendicity Society 121, 130, 143; Hebrew Philanthropic Society 45, 51, 103, 125, 126, 129–33; Hebrew Provident Society 127, 130, 154; Jewish Board of Guardians 102, 143, 145, 147, 148, 149, 150, 151, 152, 153, 155, 156, 163, 164, 179, 183; Hebrew School 135, 219 n.42; synagogue 116, 117, 118, 121, 122, 147
　congregational schism (1839) 147, 191 n.65, 217 n.110
　elite 66, 94–6, 138, 175, 197–8 n.56
　evidence of social networks 54, 77, 136–7, 180
　households 24–5, 26, 27–8, 29, 30, 31, 33, 45–6, 74, 77, 194 n.21; connected to other households 70, 72–3, 75, 77; head born overseas 61, 64–5, 66, 202 n.48; lodgers 35–7, 39, 43, 196–7 n.46, 201 n.44; servants 41, 198 n.58, 200 n.49; skill status of head 58, 60–1, 63, 66
　housing conditions 100–3
　immigrants 23, 35, 56
　*kashrut* 54, 179, 180
　Mount Pleasant 55, 96, 194 n.15, n.15, 198 n.57, 202 n.53
　occupations 61, 81, 82, 84, 86–9, 91, 93–7, 103, 196 n.37, 204–5 n.15

Paradise Street 58, 96, 194 n.15, 198 n.57
population characteristics 23, 169 n.36; sex ratios 23–24
population size 14, 22–3, 95, 116, 184, 192 n.77, 200 n.15, 202 n.48, 207 n.55
religious practice 210 n.91
residence patterns 45–6, 47–8, 50–2, 54, 55, 58, 61, 64–5, 66, 75, 96, 100, 169–70
synagogue, Hardman Street (New Hebrew Congregation) 52; Hope Place (New Hebrew Congregation from 1857) 52; Princes Road (Old Hebrew Congregation from 1874) 48, 229 n.28; Seel Street (Old Hebrew Congregation) 46, 52, 77
transmigrants 23, 114, 120, 121, 155
lodgers 22, 24, 26, 29, 34, 34–41, 42, 43, 47, 58, 59, 60–4, 67, 79, 100, 101, 169, 197–8 n.56, 198 n.57, 208 n.70
　marital status 37, 40, 43, 197 n.47
　skill status 58–64
　in non-Jewish households 39–41
　overseas birth 35, 37–9
　sex ratios 36
lodging and social networks 35, 38, 43, 169
lodging-house keepers (as an occupation) 40, 89, 103, 139, 197 n. 52, 214 n.58
lodging houses 100, 208 n.73, 209 n.82
　Jewish 25, 38, 39, 40, 41, 88, 89, 103, 169, 197 n.52, 214 n.58
London
　Jews 8, 9, 11, 13, 14, 15, 22, 26, 31, 35, 38, 50, 73, 74, 76, 77, 79, 111, 128, 160, 170, 175, 177, 181, 184, 189 n.47, 190 n.50, n.62, 200 n.16, 206 n.44, 232 n.65
　Jewish welfare 109, 113, 115, 124, 128, 143, 152, 158, 159–60, 165, 211 n.13; Jewish Board of Guardians 143, 144, 148, 151, 155, 156, 157, 171, 228 n.8
　occupations 83, 85, 86, 89, 95, 96

Manchester 6, 14–15, 138, 188 n.31, 198 n.57, n.58, 228 n.2
　charity 120, 137, 220 n.12
　housing conditions 99, 208 n.61

occupations 81–2, 83–4, 89, 90, 91, 204 n.7
politics 145, 162
public health 99, 158
Manchester, Jews 12, 14, 15, 78, 105, 173–4, 176, 177, 178, 181, 184, 193 n.3, 200 n.22, 209 n.85, 210 n.96, 230 n.32
   charity 96–7, 109, 110, 114, 127, 130, 135, 146, 219 n.142, n.148; Hebrew Benevolent Fund 145, 150, 221 n.23; Hebrew National School 54, 134–5, 164, 206 n.34, 210 n.92, 219 n.142; Hebrew Philanthropic Society 125, 128, 133, 200 n.27, 215 n.77; Jewish Board of Guardians 54, 73, 103, 104, 110, 111, 134, 145, 147–56, 158–61163, 164, 174, 179, 180, 223 n.62, 224 n.81, 225 n.94, 226 n.96, n.102, 227 n.107; United Board of Relief 120, 143
   congregational schism (1844) 52, 120–1, 147, 164, 191 n.65, 221 n.31
   elite 50, 53–3, 94, 95, 96–7, 105
   evidence of social networks 38, 54, 57–8, 66–7, 77–8, 180
   households 22–3, 25, 26, 27–8, 33, 76, 77, 194 n.21, 196 n.36, 201 n.40; connected to other households 70, 71–2, 73, 74, 76; head born overseas 62, 65, 78; skill status of head 59, 62–3, 66
   lodgers 35–6, 37–9, 32, 196–7 n.46; servants 41, 65, 198 n.57, n.58; skill status of head 59, 62–3, 66;
   housing conditions 54, 66, 100–1, 102, 104, 158, 208 n.68
   immigrants 23, 71, 77, 114, 134, 156, 174, 175, 180, 181, 206 n.44
   *kashrut* 54, 158, 160, 180, 206 n.43
   Moreton Street 194 n.15
   occupations 33, 62–3, 63, 81–2, 83–4, 85–9, 91–6, 118, 203 n.72, 204 n.8, n.15, 205 n.19, 209 n.85
   population characteristics 15, 23, 33, 196 n.36, 199 n.5; sex ratios 23–24
   population size 15, 22, 184
   religious practice 78, 158, 160, 178–9, 180, 181, 210 n.91, 230 n.38
   residence patterns 45, 46, 48–9, 50, 52–4, 55, 59, 62–3, 66, 71–2, 83, 169–70, 201 n.37, n.40
   synagogue, Cheetham Hill Road (united congregations, from 1858) 54, 229 n.28; Halliwell Street (Old Hebrew Congregation) 52, 53; Reform (est. 1858) 54, 73, 120, 145, 147, 149, 213 n.37, 222–3 n.48, 229 n.26, n.28, 231–2 n.62; South Manchester (est. 1872) 54, 222 n.48; Spanish and Portuguese Jews, Cheetham Hill Road (est. 1873–4) 54, 149, 186 n.18, 222–3 n.48
   Verdon Street 37, 38, 52, 58, 62, 65, 146, 194 n.15, 198 n.57
mapping, methodology 46–7, 68–9, 208 n.67
marriage, Jewish 13, 24, 26, 30, 35, 56, 69, 179, 180, 189 n.37, 213 n.37
   to non-Jews 230–1 n.44
Merthyr Tydfil, Jews 40, 204–5 n.15
migration 4, 5, 13–15, 21, 23, 32, 33, 35, 42, 43, 46, 50, 54, 56, 66, 67, 69, 71, 74, 76–7, 78, 95, 99, 101, 112, 116, 120–2, 135, 150, 153–4, 163, 165, 169, 170, 172, 186 n.18
   chain 3, 37, 69, 90
   transmigration 14, 23, 117, 121, 130, 138, 164, 171, 192 n.78, 206 n.38
*mikvah* (pl. *mikveh*) 181, 210 n.91, 230 n.38, 231 n.57

Newcastle, Jews 6, 40, 77, 135, 203 n.77

occupations (*see also individual towns and occupations*)
   classification 81, 82, 83, 90, 94–5, 197, 196 n.37, 204 n.4, n.6, n.10
   Jews 31, 33, 38–40, 42, 61, 62, 64, 81–93, 93–5, 96, 97, 103, 105, 116, 118, 131, 134, 135, 146, 151, 170; children 91–2; no occupation 83, 90–3; women 41–2, 91–3, 197 n.52, 206 n.35

pawnbrokers 74, 85, 87, 89, 94, 203 n.72
peddlers *see* hawkers/hawking
Penzance, Jews 77
persecution 4, 112, 114, 115, 155, 175, 186 n.19

Plymouth, Jews 22, 76, 77, 135
Poland (as place of origin of Jews) 5, 15, 35, 38, 39, 45, 73, 114, 186 n.19, 187 n.19
Poles, Jewish, occupations 204 n.7, 205 n.15
Poor Law 3, 31, 94, 110, 113, 115–17, 119, 120, 121, 122, 126, 136, 141–3, 148–9, 155, 156, 158, 162, 163, 164, 172, 211 n.4, 212 n.18, 213 n.50, 220 n.4, 225 n.86
  Jews under the care of 32, 91, 110, 117, 158, 216 n.96
  provision for Jews 29, 122, 141, 159–60, 226 n.98
poor relief, Jewish *see* charity
Portsea, Jewish charity 137
Portsmouth, Jews 22, 76
poverty (*see also* charity, housing conditions)
  deservingness 17, 111, 112, 113–16, 124, 129, 139, 131, 132, 137, 142, 143, 148, 156, 161, 163, 171, 216 n.96, 223 n.57
  and pauperism 114, 138, 141, 148, 151
prejudice *see* discrimination
public health *see individual towns*

Reform 9, 177, 182
  Manchester 54, 73, 120, 145, 147, 149, 213 n.37, 222–3 n.48, 229 n.26, n.28, 231 n.62
religion (general) (*see also* Jew, Judaism, kashrut, marriage, *mikvah*, synagogue) 1, 8, 14, 112, 137, 160, 169, 178, 179
  and community 2, 3, 8, 44, 51, 57, 66, 67, 109, 178, 183, 185 n.7, 226 n.103
  and industrialization 3, 6, 171–2, 174
  and social networks 10, 21, 78–9, 137, 178, 190 n.57
residential arrangements (*see also* Birmingham, Liverpool, Manchester)
  Jews 45–79
  cultural explanations 67–77
  economic explanations 57–67
Russia (as place of origin of Jews) 4, 5, 35, 114, 155, 178, 187-7 n.19, 224 n.81

sabbath (*see also* Judaism, observance)
  observance 6–7, 180, 181
  protection for Jewish workmen 8–9, 160, 173, 178–9, 227 n.107
scholars 31, 32, 36, 46, 91–2, 206 n.31
schools, Jewish 54, 55, 56, 75, 79, 92, 97, 104, 130, 133–5, 141, 150, 160–1, 163, 164, 174, 176, 178, 179, 181, 210 n.91, 218–19 n.137, n.142
secularization 6, 9, 172, 181–2
self-help 114, 119, 124, 132, 134, 142, 146, 149, 154, 161, 164–5, 178
Sephardi Jews 4, 115, 177, 186 n.18, 211 n.13
  in Manchester 38, 54
servants 22, 24, 25, 26, 29, 34, 36, 41–2, 59, 65, 78, 79, 90, 101, 198 n.57, 202 n.49
  Jewish 34, 41–2, 89, 198 n.57
  non-Jewish 41–2, 90, 96
Sheffield 6, 15, 188 n.31
  Jews 12, 15, 74; characteristics 24; households 22–3, 24–5, 26, 27–8, 29, 30, 34; immigrants 23; lodging 36, 37; kosher food 180
*shivah* (mourning) *see* Judaism, observance
social networks (*see also* Birmingham, charity, Liverpool, lodging, Manchester) 10–11, 21, 23, 31, 35, 42, 43–4, 45, 57, 76, 203 n.74
  benefits of 10–11, 23, 43–4, 57, 77–9, 115, 128, 136–7, 170, 171, 172, 182
  Jewish 9, 21, 42, 43–4, 77–9, 97, 115, 128, 136–7, 170, 171, 182
  and occupations 11, 97, 103, 104–5
  and religion 10, 21, 78–9, 137, 178, 190 n.57
synagogue *see also individual towns* 115, 170, 176, 200 n.16, 229 n.28
  attendance 6–7, 67, 119, 135, 137, 159, 178, 181, 188 n.34, n.35, 202 n.60

tailors 64, 85–6, 89, 90, 91, 92, 93–4, 97, 103, 116, 118, 134, 135, 151, 160, 206 n.35, 207 n.52

*Voice of Jacob* 176, 177, 190 n.48, 224 n.64

widowers 33, 37, 128, 195 n.35

widows 33, 92–3, 112, 127–8, 195 n.31, n.35, 197 n.52 206 n.35, 213 n.41
Wolverhampton, Jews 180
women 32, 128, 195 n.35
    Jewish 24, 42, 83, 91, 94, 124, 174, 178, 193 n.12, 206 n.35, 210 n.91; charity donors 45, 96–7, 127, 222 n.37; charity recipients 124, 127, 156, 218 n.130, 225 n.83, n.86, 227 n.113; occupations *see individual occupations*

workhouses *see* Poor Law

www.ingramcontent.com/pod-product-compliance
Lightning Source LLC
Chambersburg PA
CBHW072139290426
44111CB00012B/1918